Connecting People with Jobs: The Labour Market, Activation Policies and Disadvantaged Workers in Slovenia

OECD
BETTER POLICIES FOR BETTER LIVES

Please cite this publication as:
OECD (2016), *Connecting People with Jobs: The Labour Market, Activation Policies and Disadvantaged Workers in Slovenia*, OECD Publishing, Paris.
http://dx.doi.org/10.1787/9789264265349-en

ISBN 978-92-64-26533-2 (print)
ISBN 978-92-64-26534-9 (PDF)

Photo credits: Cover © Sergio77/Shutterstock.com

Corrigenda to OECD publications may be found on line at: *www.oecd.org/about/publishing/corrigenda.htm*.

Foreword

Giving people better opportunities to participate in the labour market improves well-being and strengthens economic growth. Better activation policies help countries to cope with rapid population ageing by mobilising potential labour resources more fully. Many OECD countries achieved record employment levels prior to the global financial crisis, but in all countries employment rates differ markedly across population groups. High unemployment and the weak labour market attachment of some groups in society reflect a range of barriers to working or moving up the jobs ladder. And in many countries the crisis has accentuated long-standing structural problems that are causing these disadvantages. It is a major challenge for policy makers in the coming years to address these problems and make OECD labour markets and, thus, OECD economies more inclusive.

Therefore, the OECD Employment, Labour and Social Affairs Committee is carrying out a new set of reviews of activation policies to encourage greater labour market participation of all groups in society with a special focus on the most disadvantaged, who face the greatest barriers and disincentives to finding work. This includes a series of country studies, *Connecting People with Jobs*, which provide an assessment of how well activation policies help all groups to move into productive and rewarding jobs and a number of policy recommendations that could improve the situation.

This report on Slovenia is the second country study published in this series. It has a special focus on activation policies to improve labour market outcomes for four groups: long-term unemployed people; low-skilled workers; older workers; and displaced workers. The report was prepared by David Grubb and Kristine Langenbucher, economists in the Employment Analysis and Policy Division of the OECD, together with Matija Vodopivec, researcher at the University of Primorska, under the guidance and supervision of Christopher Prinz. Statistical assistance was provided by Dana Blumin and editorial assistance by Jade Baker and Gabriela Bejan. Comments were provided by Mark Keese and Stefano Scarpetta. The report benefited greatly from discussions with experts, government officials, employer federations, trade unions, academics and businesses during an OECD mission to Slovenia in late 2015, and from comments on a draft version provided by several Slovene ministries and stakeholders.

Table of contents

Tables

Figures

Acronyms and abbreviations

ALMPs	Active Labour Market Programmes
CEE	Central and Eastern Europe
CRECs	*Comités d'aide au reclassement à entrées continues*
CSP	Career Path Security Contract *(Contrat de sécurisation professionnelle)*
CSW	Centres for Social Work
CV	Curriculum Vitae
DKK	Danish Krone
EC	European Commission
EFSA	Emergency Financial Social Assistance
EPL	Employment Protection Legislation
ERD	European Regional Development Fund
ESC	Economic and Social Council
ESF	European Social Fund
ESS	Employment Service of Slovenia
EU	European Union
EUR	Euro
FSA	Financial Social Assistance
GDP	Gross Domestic Product
GFC	Global Financial Crisis
GZS	Chamber of Commerce and Industry of Slovenia (*Gospodarska zbornica Slovenije*)
HRDSF	Slovene Human Resources Development and Scholarship Fund
IAP	Individual Action Plan
IMAD	Institute of Macroeconomic Analysis and Development
IRSSV	Social Protection Institute of the Republic of Slovenia (*Inštitut republike Slovenije za socialno varstvo*)
JSC	Job Security Council
LFS	Labour Force Survey
MDDSZ	Ministry of Labour, Family, Social Affairs and Equal Opportunities
MF	Ministry of Finance
NAIRU	Non-Accelerating Inflation Rate of Unemployment
NVQ	National Vocational Qualifications
OZS	Chamber of Craft and Small Businesses of Slovenia (*Obrtno-podjetniška zbornica Slovenije*)
PDIA	Pension and Disability Insurance Act
PES	Public Employment Service
PIAAC	OECD's Survey of Adult Skills
SA	Supplementary Allowance
SDS	Slovenian Democratic Party
SORS	Statistical Office of the Republic of Slovenia
SOS	Student Organisation of Slovenia
TWA	Temporary Work Agency

UB	Unemployment Benefits
UI	Unemployment Insurance
UISA	Unemployment Insurance Savings Accounts
VAT	Value Added Tax
ZDR-1	Employment Relationships Act (*Zakon o delovnih razmerjih*)
ZPIZ	Pension and Disability Insurance Institute of Slovenia (*Zavod za pokojninsko in invalidsko zavarovanje*)
ZSSS	Association of Free Trade Unions of Slovenia (*Zveza svobodnih sindikatov Slovenije*)
ZSVarPre	Social Assistance Act (*Zakon o socialno varstvenih prejemkih*)
ZUJF	Public Finance Balance Act (*Zakon za uravnoteženje javnih finance*)
ZUTD	Labour Market Regulation Act (*Zakon o urejanju trga dela*)

Executive summary

Labour market and activation policies are well developed in Slovenia and generally quite effective in connecting people with jobs and, thereby, contributing to economic growth and wellbeing. However, the global financial crisis hit Slovenia hard and revealed some structural weaknesses in the system, which have contributed to a high level of long-term unemployment, low rates of employment for some groups such as those who are older or low-skilled and poor reemployment chances for workers who have been made redundant. Recognising these challenges, the Slovenian government has commissioned this review as one strand of its plan to strengthen its activation and labour market policies. By encouraging greater labour market participation of disadvantaged groups stronger activation policies also contribute to Slovenia's National Development Strategy 2030 which aims at building social cohesion and ensuring that no one in society is left behind. Such stronger policies also contribute to Slovenia's goal of improving all citizens' access to education and training in every stage of life.

While the overall employment rate in Slovenia is around the OECD average, and was even higher than that before the crisis, some labour market outcomes are striking. The employment rate of people aged 55-64 is the third lowest in the OECD, the employment gap between high-skilled and low-skilled people is among the highest, and the share of long-term and very long-term unemployment (unemployed for more than one and several years, respectively) is exceptionally high. Slovenia will need to address these structural weaknesses in its labour market which are in part related to the policy setup, including the weak links between the Employment Service and the Centres of Social Work.

Strategic decisions will have to be taken by Slovenian policy makers about how much and where to invest in stronger activation policies in order to increase employment and generate longer-term gains from benefit savings. The system in Slovenia is geared well to help jobseekers who are readily employable but performs much less well in helping harder-to-place jobseekers who are often and increasingly parked on social assistance and more recently also partial disability benefits. With the size of this group gradually increasing, a better approach is needed to help them into work.

The OECD analysis infers that the most important areas for change in Slovenia are to:

- Strengthen the connection between the Employment Service and the Centres of Social Work by shifting responsibilities to overcome the separation of benefit administration and counselling, or even partially merging the two authorities.
- Tackle long-term unemployment by enforcing job-search requirements, benefit conditionality and benefit sanctions also for social assistance clients.
- Enable the Employment Service to help harder-to-place jobseekers by freeing up time for caseworkers to counsel these jobseekers and help them into training and work, and by improving the competence of caseworkers to deal with additional social and health problems.

- Make work pay for benefit recipients through lower taper rates and time-limited into-work benefits.
- Promote longer working lives through further and compatible changes of regulations in the unemployment system, the pension and the disability benefit system as well as the labour law to encourage later retirement.

Assessment and recommendations

The global financial crisis revealed important weaknesses and rigidities in Slovenia's social and labour market policies which hindered rapid adjustment. Among those are: a strong labour market dualism with a high share of temporary employment especially among young people; a high minimum wage relative to the average wage which was further increased in 2010, coupled with high taxes on labour; some tendency for growth in repeat unemployment with short intermittent employment periods; and a high level of long-term dependence on social assistance benefits.

In response to the crisis, a number of important but also difficult reforms have been implemented in Slovenia, including a major pension reform and a comprehensive overhaul of the labour law in 2013. Both have contributed to the recent return to economic growth. Despite these reforms, Slovenia continues to be a country with high spending on social benefits, especially pensions, and relatively low spending on active labour market programmes. Consequently, the Slovenian government is considering further reform. In the case of the labour market, the aim now is to strengthen policies to address some of the long-standing performance issues, in particular the high level of long-term unemployment and the low employment rate of older and low-skilled people and the limited support provided to redundant workers.

Slovenia's labour market was performing well before the crisis but has since fallen behind the OECD average

Slovenia's employment rate grew gradually since the early 1990s to reach the OECD average of around 65% in 2004 and then rapidly surpassed this level after the country's accession to the European Union, largely as a consequence of strong economic growth in the period 2004-08. The unemployment rate continuously declined during the same period to reach an all-time low of 4.4% in 2008 – among the lowest in the OECD area at that time.

However, Slovenia was hit very hard by the global economic and financial crisis that began in 2008. The unemployment rate more than doubled to almost 10% in 2013 and the employment rate fell by more than five percentage points while labour productivity initially also dropped. Only in 2014 did the situation slowly start to improve. Nevertheless, despite substantial fiscal stimulus and the important contribution of economic stabilisers, real GDP at the end of 2015 was still some 5% below its 2008 level, unemployment was still higher and employment still lower. On a positive note, Slovenia maintained the lowest degree of income inequality across OECD countries, despite the protracted drop in economic activity. And, maybe somewhat surprisingly, rather modest economic growth rates in the past year or so immediately translated into a fall in registered unemployment. However, at least initially, most of the new vacancies were for lower-level jobs.

A number of structural factors may have deepened and prolonged the recession, some of which are related to features of Slovenia's social and labour market policy. Among those characteristics are: a strong labour market dualism with a high share of temporary employment especially among young people; a high minimum wage relative to the average wage which was further increased in 2010, coupled with high taxes on labour; some tendency for growth in repeat unemployment with short intermittent employment periods; and a high level of long-term dependency on social assistance benefits.

Specific groups are at risk of long-term labour market disadvantage

In the context of its recent but still modest recovery, Slovenia is trying to rectify a number of structural labour market weaknesses and address the weak employment situation (in 2014, unless otherwise noted) of some groups of the population including:

- *Older workers*: the employment rate of people aged 55-64 is only 35% and thus 20 percentage points below the OECD average for this group. Only 18% of those aged 55-59 who were employed in 2009 were still employed when aged 60-64 in 2014 – the lowest retention rate among all OECD countries (the OECD average is 44% and the rate for the Nordic countries 70%). As a result, one in three jobseekers in Slovenia is older than 50 years.
- *Low-skilled workers*: the employment gap between high-skilled and low-skilled people (with employment rates of, respectively, over 80% and less than 50%) is among the highest in OECD countries, only topped by Poland, the Czech Republic and the Slovak Republic. Consequently, a high share of jobseekers has only poor educational attainment: one-third among all jobseekers, and around half of those who are long-term unemployed.
- *Long-term unemployed*: one in two jobseekers has been unemployed for more than a year and one in three for more than two years; both percentages are well above the OECD average. This is a long-term structural problem that has characterised the Slovenian labour market for 20 years and is indicative of structural problems related to work incentives and activation policies.
- *Redundant workers*: since 2011, the share of unemployed dismissed or made redundant has been higher in Slovenia than in other European countries. One in five of all jobseekers had previously been displaced, rising to one in three of those newly unemployed. Many displaced workers subsequently leave the labour force. Policy has so far paid little attention to early intervention for this group.

The characteristics of long-term unemployment, job displacement and a lack of skills overlap considerably. Of the 91 000 unemployed individuals in Slovenia aged under 55, 72% belong to at least one of these critical groups; and of the 8 000 unemployed individuals aged 55-64, this proportion rises to 86% (see Figure 0.1). Many jobseekers therefore suffer from at least two and often three of these risk factors and older jobseekers in particular are at the same time often workers who have previously been displaced, have been unemployed for a long time and lack adequate labour market skills. Accordingly, better labour market policies will need to address multiple problems concurrently.

Figure 0.1 **Multiple unemployment risks overlap considerably in Slovenia**

Distribution of unemployed people by age group and additional individual characteristics, 2014

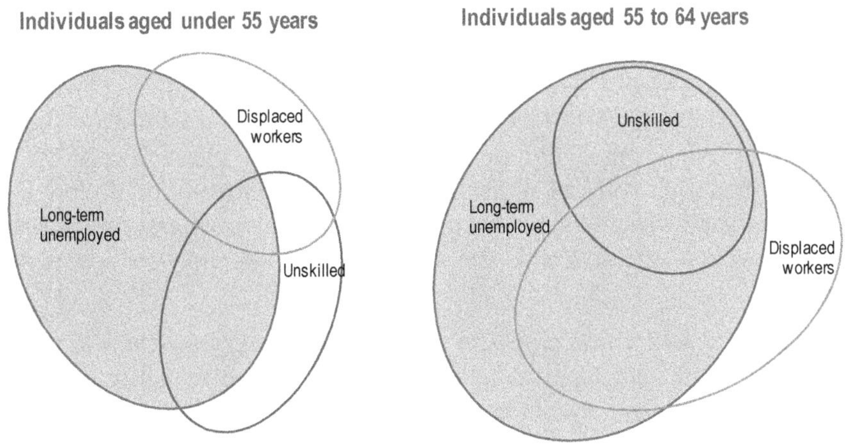

Source: Statistical Office of the Republic of Slovenia (SORS), Labour Force Survey data.

StatLink http://dx.doi.org/10.1787/888933415061

Unemployment insurance protects incomes of job losers and is quite generous in certain circumstances

Slovenia's unemployment benefit system provides decent income security for people becoming involuntarily unemployed or ending a temporary work contract. Displaced workers will usually be eligible for unemployment insurance while those quitting their job or not having worked and paid contributions for nine of the past 24 months are ineligible. Unemployment insurance benefit payment duration increases with the length of the prior work period so that those with contribution periods of less than five years will receive benefits for no more than three months while the maximum period of benefit receipt is 25 months for workers with over 25 years of contributions. Overall, one in three newly registered and one-fifth of all unemployed at any moment receive unemployment insurance benefit. This is a low share in international comparison, but many of the others receive other social benefits; in total, two in three unemployed receive a social benefit.

Initial income replacement rates are high in comparison to other countries: Replacement rates fall from 80% of past earnings initially to 50% in the second year for people entitled to such payment. However, there is a benefit ceiling which is only slightly above the national minimum wage. Other aspects make the unemployment benefit system in Slovenia potentially generous relative to systems in other countries: First, during benefit receipt people only have to accept jobs one level below their current qualification which is quite a lax condition for those entitled to payments for a longer period. Secondly, it seems relatively easy to negotiate dismissal for reason of incompetence with an employer to generate benefit entitlement – to the benefit of the worker or the employer, who can rehire the same worker on conditions more beneficial to the company (e.g. via a temporary contract). Thirdly, the system subsidises repeat unemployment in seasonal and temporary work contracts (e.g. in the tourism industry).

Social assistance and partial disability benefit receipt is high and becoming more frequent

The recent economic recovery has led to a fall in unemployment. However, there are two contrasting developments: short-term unemployment and the number of unemployment benefit recipients are falling while long-term and very long-term unemployment remains unchanged. In fact, the number of registered jobseekers receiving social assistance is increasing, especially among prime-age and older workers. This shift from unemployment benefit to social assistance, or from shorter-term to longer-term unemployment, is especially problematic because of the weaker effort that is made in Slovenia to help those on social assistance or long-term unemployed people more generally to find work.

Not only is the social assistance caseload increasing among jobseekers but also an increasing proportion of them are receiving partial disability benefits while being on the unemployment register: currently, one in ten jobseekers falls into this group up from one in twenty ten years ago. A large proportion of them are placed into a client segment of the employment service where regular support is not guaranteed. Hence, most of these people never return to work and more than 80% have been unemployed for over two years. Among the unemployed who were made redundant, as many as one in five receives a partial disability benefit, suggesting that labour market exit is frequent in this group. The Employment Service of Slovenia has yet to develop ways of dealing with these groups.

Making work pay for benefit recipients is a challenge

Incentives for recipients to move off benefit and into work are sometimes low in Slovenia, as in many OECD countries. For a one-earner couple with two children, for example, some 88% of the additional income is taxed away when moving from unemployment benefit into work paying two-thirds of the average wage. For a job paid at the average wage the ratio is 74% – i.e. the loss of benefits and taxation wipe out three-quarter of the additional earnings. The corresponding marginal effective tax rates are similar for a single person with two children and somewhat lower for people, singles or couples, moving from social assistance into work. Making work pay and worthwhile for these people is not always easy and also requires a strong enforcement of benefit conditionality, as discussed further below. In addition, lower taper rates, temporary in-work or into-work benefits or hiring subsidies can help provided they are not creating artificial behaviour such as working only short hours to receive the in-work payment. Effective in-work payments may have to be conditional on the job being full-time.

Low employment rates of older people reflect work disincentives embedded in welfare benefits

One reason for the low employment rate for older people relates to the special provisions in the unemployment benefit system for older unemployed people. First, they receive such benefit for much longer periods: 19 or 25 months if aged 50-54 or 55+ and having a prior work period of over 25 years, compared to a maximum of 12 months for those with an equally long prior work period but being under age 50. Secondly, the insurance clock is not reset to zero for beneficiaries over age 57 (or those with at least 35 years of paid contributions) who therefore requalify more easily for unemployment benefit. And thirdly, the latter group can also be granted an additional two years of pension contributions. As a result, work incentives for unemployed people aged 55 and over are weak and, not surprisingly, de facto one in three pensioners enter retirement through unemployment.

Recent pension reform has made early retirement less attractive and the employment rate of people in the 55-64 age group has indeed increased from 23% to 35% from 2005 to 2015. However, further progress is being undermined by the special rules in the unemployment insurance scheme for older people, which should be dismantled in order to overcome the widespread early retirement culture in Slovenia. Most OECD countries that had similar special rules have abolished those rules. Additional pension reform can also support the move away from early retirement practices, by using lifetime earnings as a reference for pension entitlements and introducing a link with annual increases in life expectancy through an automatic mechanism that affects one or several of the pension system parameters – be it the legal retirement age and/or other elements in the pension formula – as is now common practice in more than half of all OECD countries.

In view of the recent trend increase in partial disability benefits, future pension reform will also have to include modifications to the disability benefit system. Suggestions in this regard in a recent White Paper on Pension Reform to make vocational rehabilitation mandatory for people entitled to a partial disability benefit are welcome. In addition, the eligibility criteria to qualify for a partial disability benefit may need to be reconsidered and tightened; today eligibility is assessed mainly against job requirements and hazards in the previous job position rather than the general labour market.

Labour market institutions do little to address job displacement early

All unemployed people in Slovenia can register with the Employment Service and use its services, and those entitled to unemployment benefit must register within 30 days starting from the termination of their employment contract. There is no incentive or obligation for dismissed or displaced workers to register with the Employment Service and look for work earlier, as for example in Germany or Switzerland. This is unfortunate in view of the better reemployment chances for those seeking a new job quickly. A simple solution would be to introduce mandatory registration within three days after being given notice of job loss and four weeks before the expiry of a temporary contract, enforced through benefit cuts, say, of one week for people registering later.

More generally, the system in Slovenia pays little attention to helping displaced workers quickly. In fact, a recent change went in the opposite direction of encouraging early search for a job or for help since the maximum notice period for both collective and individual dismissals was shortened from 150 days to 60-80 days in exchange for lengthening the unemployment benefit payment period by one month. The Employment Service has few tools aimed at helping displaced workers early. Examples from other countries, such as Sweden, show how a longer notice period can be used effectively to speed up reemployment and prevent long-term unemployment and how rapid response services reaching out to dismissed workers (often in the workplace) can make a difference in helping them back into work. In addition, the current entitlement of dismissed workers to paid leave during the notice period to engage in job search should be extended and take-up encouraged.

The Employment Service of Slovenia is a good job broker and online services are well developed

While the Employment Service does not reach out to displaced workers prior to their actual dismissal unless employers are seeking advice, it is a well-functioning and modern service, managed through performance targets as is now common practice in successful public employment services around the OECD. The vast majority of jobseekers are registered with and about one-third of all vacancies in the job market are handled by the Employment Service. Acquisition of vacancies has become more difficult since the abolition of mandatory notification of vacancies in 2012, but the Employment Service still plays an important role for many employers and offers extensive recruitment services for all employers who wish to use them.

Online services for employers and jobseekers are well developed and the aim currently is to increase the use of these services, similar to what is happening in many other OECD countries. Moving forward it will be important to target online services to people who are able to help themselves and to keep the possibility of face-to-face client contact for those who need it. Use of online employment services could even be made mandatory for employable jobseekers, thereby facilitating the monitoring of job-search obligations and freeing resources for more individual counselling for harder-to-place jobseekers.

The capacity of the Employment Service to support harder-to-place jobseekers is limited

During the first counselling interview, jobseekers are assigned to one of three client segments: *directly employable* (motivated jobseekers with relevant skills); *employable with additional activities* (jobseekers lacking skills or motivation or having additional barriers); and *employable with intensive support* (jobseekers with complex barriers to employment). The client segment can be changed any time. The purpose of the segmentation is to facilitate better targeting of support by the Employment Service of Slovenia. However, segmentation is at the discretion of the employment counsellor as there is no formal profiling procedure in place.

Perhaps the biggest problem for the Employment Service is that it cannot help all clients to the same degree or to the degree necessary. Resources are limited and the average caseload per counsellor is high. As a result, harder-to-place clients in the second and third segments – the majority of whom receive social assistance or a partial disability benefit – are likely to be parked instead of receiving intense support. With limited resources and capacity, this may have been a reasonable strategy to reach overall employment targets and especially so in periods of slack labour demand. Recently the focus of the Employment Service was predominantly on job-search monitoring and frequent counselling of the most employable. This approach will need to be expanded in the future, as the share of employable jobseekers is currently declining and the share of harder-to-place clients increasing. Investments in activating this group will be needed to generate savings in the longer run. The current parking of clients is also reflected in statistics showing that certain groups are less likely to be referred to active labour market programmes, often groups that would in fact need such programmes most. For example, while overall 13% of jobseekers participate in a programme, this share is only 4% among older jobseekers and 6% among low-skilled jobseekers.

Slovenia has comprehensive administrative statistics on post-programme employment outcomes for different client groups. This is useful in choosing a suitable programme for a client depending on his or her needs and barriers to finding employment. However, rigorous impact evaluation with a comparison group and randomised controlled trial is lacking. It would be advisable to put pilot schemes in place more frequently to test new forms of interventions and to devote a certain share of spending by the Employment Service to the evaluation of programmes and trials to be able to judge which interventions should be maintained, extended or abolished. Something similar was done in the course of labour market reforms in Germany where evaluation of all programmes is fixed in legislation.

The connection of the Employment Service with the Centres for Social Work is weak and ineffective

A key issue that may be preventing more intensive and effective help being given to jobseekers that are harder to place, and to the long-term unemployed in particular, is the weak and not very effective link in Slovenia between the Employment Service of Slovenia and the Centres for Social Work. The latter are responsible for paying social assistance and improving the social integration of their clients and are managed on the local level, with each Centre reporting directly to the Ministry. First, the exchange of information is unbalanced: registration with the Employment Service is a prerequisite for social assistance entitlement, but the Centres for Social Work will not know when the social-assistance client fails to live up to the job-search or training participation requirements. Secondly, the work culture of the two institutions is quite different: while the Employment Service strongly believes in the effectiveness of activation, conditionality and the enforcement of sanctions, the Centres for Social Work still apply a largely social model looking after the complex needs and barriers of their clientele. A new remit of the Centres for Social Work is their central role for the implementation of *social activation*, a holistic approach to enabling individuals and families to resolve their problems and empower them to actively participate in society and integrate into the labour market. At the time of writing of this report, the final approach to social activation, the actors involved and their responsibilities were not fully defined. But during meetings of the OECD team with various stakeholders it became clear that the current discussion focusses on measures to resolve social problems with little attention to labour market activation as the ultimate goal. This is problematic for clients with weak but nevertheless considerable employability who can both play the system (knowing that there are no benefit sanctions on social assistance entitlements) or fall between the cracks (not receiving the support by the Employment Service they need to find employment).

These issues can be addressed in several ways. First, benefit sanctions are important for an effective activation regime and they need to be applied systematically and consistently for all jobseekers and across all regions in the country. This is not the case due to the sanctions which are supposed to be applied being very harsh and therefore needing strong administrative justification but also creating barriers towards their actual use. Lower-level sanctions initially which are tightened with every breach of an obligation would allow for a simplification of administrative procedures for establishing proof and strengthening compliance with the law, both among caseworkers and jobseekers.

Secondly, the connection between the Employment Service and the Centres of Social Work must be improved. It is not ideal that jobseekers claiming social assistance are required to deal with both the local Centre for Social Work (to claim benefit) and the Employment Service (to be activated). One way to address this separation is to merge the two institutions, fully or partially. A full merger would mean creating one single institution responsible for most of the income-replacement benefits and the activation of the working-age population. Such a merger would achieve the full integration of job broking, benefit administration and referral to active measures for employable social assistance recipients. At the same time, it would also bring not immediately employable recipients within the remit of the same institution, helping to establish a clearer path back into the labour market for individuals who are temporarily not employable. Alternatively, the Employment Service could be made responsible for the administration of social assistance benefits for registered clients – a partial merger. If both options are not immediately feasible, co-operation between the Employment Service of Slovenia and the Centres for Social Work must be formalised instead, or as a first step in preparing an eventual (full or partial) merger. For instance, the new regional Centres of Social Work which are currently established could become responsible for benefit administration and co-operation with the Employment Service, leaving only the frontline client services to the local Centres of Social Work.

Labour market duality remains a significant problem in Slovenia

Activation policy is not operating in isolation. To make the above recommended changes work, labour market and wage policies conducive to high employment are essential. The focus of this review is on activation policy but attention also has to be given to removing labour market distortions.

Recent labour market reform has sought to address the strong duality in type of employment by contract in the Slovenian labour market but with only limited effect. Terminating temporary employment contracts has become more costly, initially with some effect, but more recently much of new employment is once again non-standard, especially but not only among younger people. Reforms have not gone far enough in removing the differences in employment protection and overall costs between permanent and temporary or other non-standard forms of employment.

In view of the large number of different contracts used in Slovenia, including student work with its special regulations but also various forms of civil law contracts, moving towards fewer and less differentiated work contracts and thereby abolishing student work, for example, might be considered. This would do away with any incentives for either employers or workers to play the system or use inappropriate contracts. The exact regulations to reduce the differences between employment contracts would have to be determined in a tripartite process.

Pay systems, allowances and minimum wages can hinder the hiring of disadvantaged workers

Such a tripartite process will also be needed to remove other labour market distortions resulting from earnings components that are not treated in the same way as the regular wage. Meal and travel allowances are an important and, by international standards, exceptional component of earnings in Slovenia and up to a ceiling they are not taxable, explaining their popularity among workers. Both allowances together can add up to 10% of net earnings on average and 15% for lower-paid workers, and significantly more than this for those with expensive commutes. The current regulation has a number of drawbacks: it is open to some tax fraud; it is a disincentive to part-time work which is indeed rare in Slovenia compared to other OECD countries because the travel allowance has to be paid in full; and it distorts minimum wage benchmarking because the statistical concept of gross earnings in Slovenia excludes these allowances, whereas minimum income statistics include them.

Another peculiarity in Slovenia is the so-called seniority bonus paid in addition to the wage, which contributes to the lower employment potential of older workers to a certain degree. The seniority component is typically 0.5% of the wage for each year of service (although lower rates can be determined in collective agreements, depending on the economic sector) thus making older workers roughly 15% more expensive than younger workers. This contributes to hindering new hires of older jobseekers and locking some older workers into their current jobs.

Finally, special attention should be paid to the impact on both wage structures and employment of Slovenia's minimum wage. Relative to the average wage, the minimum wage was already high before its exceptional increase in 2010, and is now among the highest in the OECD. A high minimum wage can result in job loss and poorer hiring chances among the weakest segment of the workforce but also in employers preferring non-standard over regular employment to ensure they are only paying for actual hours worked. Rigorous and repeated evaluations of the impact of the minimum wage are therefore important. Making meal and travel allowances taxable, while setting a minimum for the total taxable wage, could clarify social dialogue, limit possible associated tax evasion, and rebalance the incentives for long commutes. In the short term, the tax deductibility of meal and travel allowances could be reduced with the maximum tax-deductible allowance set to what are currently the minimum prescribed rates.

From parking to actively helping high-risk jobseekers

One of the biggest strategic decisions to take for Slovenia in making its activation policy regime work better is about how much to invest and where to invest in order to increase employment and generate benefit savings in the medium and longer term. Slovenia does well in helping employable jobseekers into work but has not yet been willing to invest sufficiently in helping harder-to-place clients who end up being out of work for a long time. So-called social activation is still only starting and is not necessarily aimed at employment and therefore not a sufficient solution. Like in other OECD countries, also in Slovenia the group of high-risk jobseekers is increasing as a share of all jobseekers. Helping this group and increasing their labour market participation requires i) investments in early intervention as soon as people are displaced; ii) investments in continuous learning and skills upgrading to assure employability along the lifecycle; and iii) investments aimed at improving the ability of the Employment Service to help jobseekers with multiple risks, both through lower caseloads for and better competences among employment counsellors co-ordinated with social service work to resolve barriers to employability. Such investments will be needed, in addition to further structural adjustments, to increase the low employment rates of older and unskilled workers, cushion the consequences of job displacement and lower long-term unemployment.

Key policy recommendations for Slovenia

Enabling the Employment Service to help harder-to-place jobseekers

- Introduce a profiling tool to be used by caseworkers in a systematic manner to segment jobseekers into the three pre-defined risk groups and thereby assure that harder-to-place jobseekers are given extra help faster and more consistently.
- Increase the number of employment counsellors to reduce their caseload and free time to support harder-to-place jobseekers into training and work.
- Bring sufficient competence into the Employment Service to deal better with additional labour market barriers related to social and health problems.

Strengthening the link between the Employment Service and the Centres of Social Work

- Improve the connection between the Employment Service of Slovenia (ESS) and the Centres of Social Work (CSW) to prevent social assistance recipients with the capacity to work from falling between the cracks (i.e. not getting the employment support they need) and from misusing the system.
- Introduce lighter sanctions which are increased with every breach of an obligation and apply sanctions systematically and consistently by both the ESS and the CSW.
- Consider the following options to strengthen the links between the ESS and the CSW:
  - Make the ESS responsible for the administration of social assistance payments, at least for clients who have to register with the ESS;
  - Make the regional CSW offices responsible for the administration of social assistance payments (leaving only the frontline client services to the local CSW/ESS offices) and align their regional structure with that of the regional ESS;
  - Merge the ESS and the CSW at both the regional and local level.

Addressing job displacement early on

- Make registration with the ESS mandatory within a few days after being given notice of dismissal and four weeks before the end of a fixed-term contract, with benefit sanctions in case of late or non-registration.
- Equip the ESS with the means and tools to react promptly in case of collective as well as individual dismissal, through rapid response units in the regional offices, to facilitate and encourage quick job-to-job transitions.
- Consider increasing again the only recently shortened notice period to give the Employment Service more time for a rapid response before the actual dismissal.

Doing more to tackle long-term unemployment

- Enforce conditionality, job-search obligations and sanctions for social assistance clients in the same way as for jobseekers who receive unemployment benefit.
- Develop activation programmes for the increasing number of jobseekers receiving partial disability benefit who are currently exempt from participation requirements.
- Make work pay especially for longer-term unemployed people, e.g. by lower taper rates and expanded time-limited into-work benefits that encourage taking up work.

Key policy recommendations for Slovenia *(cont.)*

Keeping older workers in employment longer

- Consider abolishing the special rules for older workers in the unemployment system (the longer payment duration, the easier re-entitlement, and the granting of two years of pension contributions) which are conducive to early retirement.
- Further reduce and eventually abolish the seniority bonus in the Slovenian labour law.
- Continue with pension reform that promotes longer working lives, including by using lifetime earnings as a reference base and introducing an automatic mechanism that takes the annual increase in life expectancy into account.
- Reform the partial disability benefit system to prevent it being used as a pathway into retirement including by, as suggested in a recent White Paper, making vocational rehabilitation mandatory and reconsidering and tightening benefit eligibility criteria.

Assuring employability over the lifecycle

- Evaluate training programmes rigorously to identify interventions that best help those with poor or outdated skills.
- Invest in career and training counselling as well as continuous learning and skills updating or upgrading to keep people employable.

Removing labour market distortions

- Consider further changes in the labour law to eliminate existing differences between different types of contracts to avoid tactical behaviour, and explore in a tripartite process the options for and potential of a more unified work contract.
- Roll back unnecessary peculiarities in the pay system, in particular the non-taxable travel allowance which invites misuse and tax fraud and discourages part-time work.
- Continue evaluating the impact of the minimum wage legislation and consider carefully whether its high level is a barrier to employment of disadvantaged groups.

Chapter 1

Key labour market outcomes in Slovenia: Tackling some long-standing issues

Before the onset of the global financial crisis in 2008/2009, Slovenia experienced a period of considerable and stable economic growth, including a large increase in employment. However, the crisis hit Slovenia hard, resulting in a large drop in employment and record levels of unemployment, often the result of jobs wiped out by firms closing or down-sizing. Only in 2014 did the situation slowly start to improve. Nevertheless, levels of long-term unemployment remain high and there is a considerable risk for some of the cyclical unemployment to translate into a structural one. In the context of its recent but still modest recovery, Slovenia is trying to rectify a number of the structural labour market weaknesses and address the weak employment situation especially of low-skilled and older workers who have very low labour market attachment by international standards.

The statistical data for Israel are supplied by and under the responsibility of the relevant Israeli authorities. The use of such data by the OECD is without prejudice to the status of the Golan Heights, East Jerusalem and Israeli settlements in the West Bank under the terms of international law.

During the 15 years until the onset of the Global Financial Crisis (GFC), in 2008, Slovenia experienced a period of considerable and stable economic growth, allowing the country to gradually close the income gap with the OECD average and move from a low-employment to a high-employment country. The GFC hit Slovenia hard, harder than most other OECD countries, with labour market indicators deteriorating quickly to record levels (in case of unemployment) or levels observed ten years earlier (in case of employment). With a second recession in the years 2012-13, as in many OECD countries, the recovery was slow and labour market indicators only started to swing back onto a good path as of 2014.

This chapter describes and discusses the overall labour market trends as well as developments for particular groups of the population; long-term unemployed people, displaced workers, low-skilled workers, and older workers. For the future, Slovenia faces three intrinsically related labour market challenges: first, in the short run, to sustain economic growth in order to return to its employment growth path; secondly, in the medium run, to address a range of long-standing issues masked by the steady pre-GFC growth and uncovered again after 2008; and thirdly, in the long run, to maximise labour market potential of all groups in order to respond to the rapid ageing of the population projected for the coming decades.

Overall labour market trends

Employment rates are recovering slowly since 2014 after a big dint following the GFC

The Slovenian employment rate saw a steady increase from around 60% in 1994 to a historical peak of 68.8% in 2008, well above the OECD and EU22[1] averages at the time. After the onset of the GFC, however, the employment rate fell quickly again to a level below the OECD and EU22 averages, with a trough of 63.3% in 2013 (Figure 1.1, Panel A). Only in the past two years has the employment rate increased again: quite significantly so, despite only relatively modest economic growth.

The economic crisis did not impact on all age groups in the very same way. While there has been a significant decline in employment rates for young adults under age 30, the losses were less pronounced for prime-age workers aged 30-49. In an international comparison, employment rates of older workers aged 55-64 are low in Slovenia. However, employment rates for this age group fell less after the GFC than for young adults and rates were higher in 2014 than back in 2008 (Figure 1.1, Panel B).

Figure 1.1. **Employment rates in Slovenia fell sharply since the onset of the global financial crisis, especially for young adults**

Employment rates (employment as a share of the population) in the OECD, European Union and Slovenia, 1993-2015

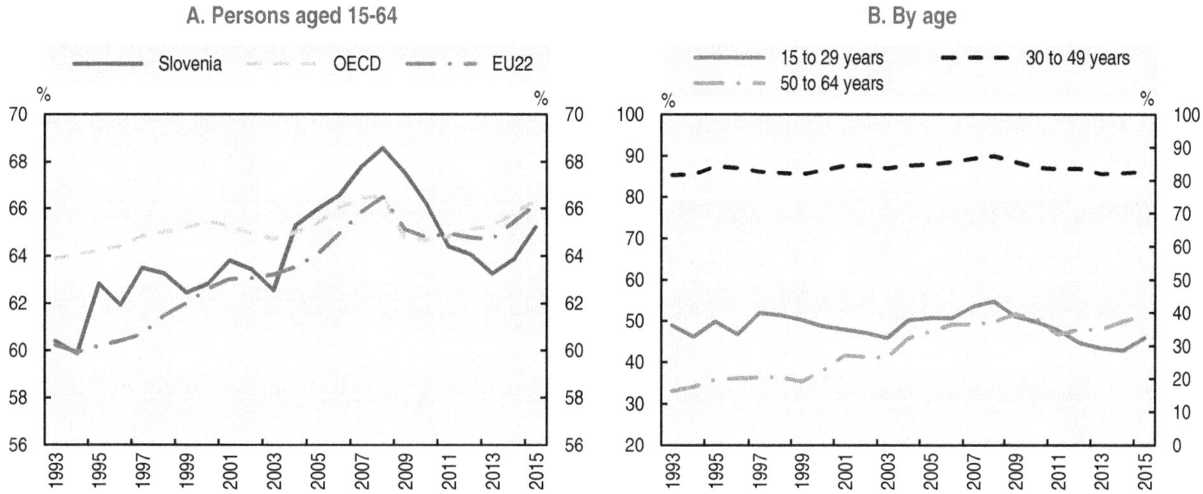

Note: OECD and EU22 are weighted averages. EU22 includes all EU countries which are also OECD members.

Source: *OECD Employment Database* (*LFS by sex and age dataset*) www.oecd.org/employment/database.

StatLink http://dx.doi.org/10.1787/888933414948

The "disappearing middle" of the wage distribution in Slovenia

There is some discussion on the extent to which Slovenia is suffering from job polarisation, a phenomenon that has been observed for a considerable period of time in many OECD countries and which is characterised by a loss of jobs in the middle of the income and skills distribution. Job polarisation is quite strong in the United States and in Japan and also in some European countries, including Belgium, the Netherlands and Spain (Eurofound, 2016), and presents a new mismatch problem for employment services across the OECD.

Prior to the GFC, in the period 1995-2007, Slovenia belonged to a group of countries (including Austria, Belgium, Germany, and the United Kingdom) where growth in the top quintile of the wage distribution – i.e. upgrading – was combined with little change in medium-paid jobs and some gains in lower-paying jobs. These developments can be best described as "hybrid polarisation/upgrading" (Eurofound, 2011). Since 2010, this pattern has clearly consolidated in Slovenia: employment growth continued in the top quintile, while there were was little change in the bottom quintile of the wage distribution. However, there have also been heavy losses in the middle quintiles (Figure 1.2). Similar patterns are observed in Denmark and Estonia. Going forward, workers in the middle of the distribution will need more support through measures such as education and training to increase their productivity and competitiveness. This is necessary both from a national and individual perspective to stop this hollowing out in the middle of the wage distribution.

Figure 1.2. **The Slovenian labour market is becoming more polarised**

Employment change (in thousands) by job-wage quintile, Q2 1996-Q2 2015

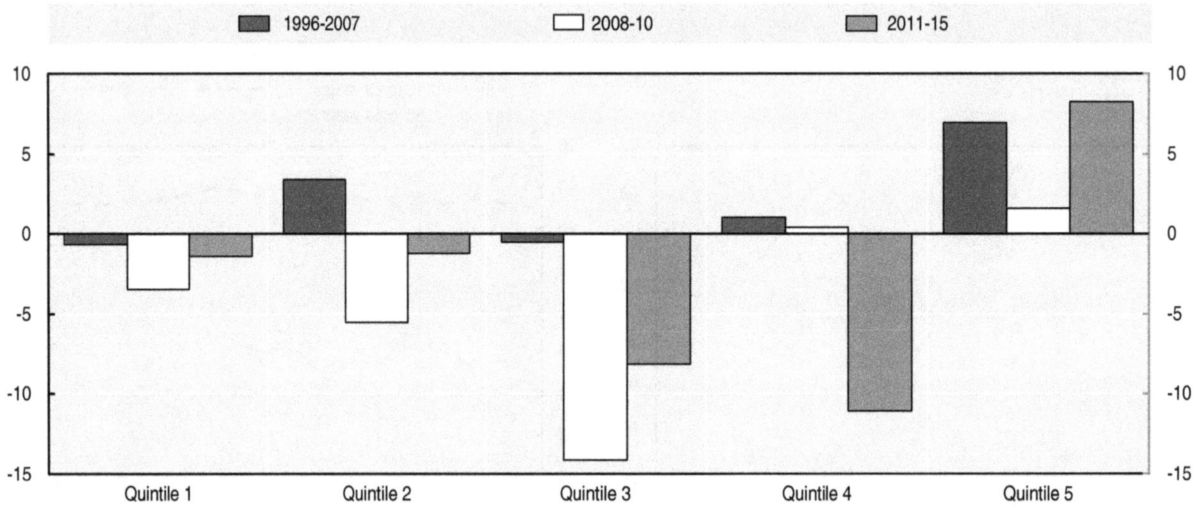

Source: Eurofound (2013), "Employment polarisation and job quality in the crisis: European Jobs Monitor 2013", Dublin; and Eurofound (2016), "What do Europeans do at work? A task-based analysis: European Jobs Monitor 2016", Publications Office of the European Union, Luxembourg.

StatLink http://dx.doi.org/10.1787/888933414957

Unemployment levels have reached historical peaks in 2013

The post-2008 fall in employment rates in Slovenia is mirrored in an equally sharp increase in unemployment since the onset of the GFC. The unemployment rate peaked in 2013, at over 10%, and in 2015 the rate stood at 9% – still well above the trough of 4.4% in 2008 (Figure 1.3, Panel A). The unemployment rate was below the OECD average in the period 2001-10 but is again above that average since 2011.

The increase in unemployment was most dramatic for young adults aged 15 to 29 years, with the rate increasing from 8.3% in 2008 to 19.0% in 2013, but unemployment rates in Slovenia also doubled to 8% and over for all other age groups (Figure 1.3, Panel B). The recent recovery has only reached young adults with a two percentage point drop in the unemployment rate to 16.2% in 2015, whereas unemployment rates have fallen only marginally for both prime-age and older workers.

Unemployment in Slovenia is projected to continue its recent decline through to the end of 2017 to around 7.7%. With unemployment rates staying on such a high level for such a long time there is a considerable risk for some of the cyclical unemployment to translate into a structural one. Following the pre-recession decline of structural unemployment, measured by the non-accelerating inflation rate of unemployment (NAIRU), to a trough in 2008, structural unemployment started to rise again from 2009 and has now stabilised at just below 8% (Figure 1.3, Panel A). According to OECD projections, little change in structural unemployment is foreseen until the end of 2017. Structural reforms – including labour market reforms – will have to continue in Slovenia to ensure that unemployment does not consolidate on a new higher level.

Figure 1.3. **Structural unemployment grew sharply in Slovenia since the onset of the global financial crisis and remains high**

Unemployment rates (unemployment as a share of the labour force) and estimates of NAIRU in the OECD and Slovenia, 1999-2015

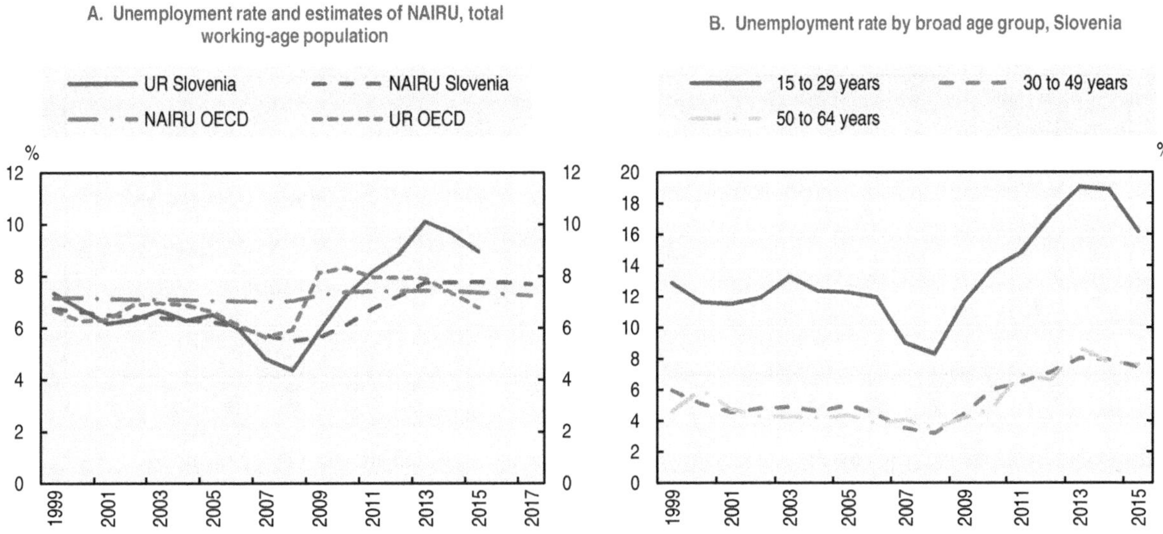

NAIRU: Non-Accelerating Inflation Rate of Unemployment; UR: Unemployment rate.

Note: OECD unemployment rate is a weighted average; the NAIRU estimate for the OECD is an unweighted average.

Source: *OECD Employment Database (LFS by sex and age dataset)* www.oecd.org/employment/database and *OECD Economic Outlook 99 dataset.*

StatLink http://dx.doi.org/10.1787/888933414966

Long-term and very long-term unemployment remain key challenges

Following the increase in unemployment levels, the incidence of long-term unemployment (people unemployed for 12 months and more) also saw a steep increase from 2010 onwards. In 2014, more than one in two jobseekers has been unemployed for more than a year (Figure 1.4, Panel A). This is close to the very high level more than ten years ago and significantly above the OECD average of around one-third. Even worse, *very* long-term unemployment is frequent in Slovenia: almost 60% of those unemployed for more than a year have in fact been unemployed for more than two years and around 20% for more than five years; these are very high shares in international comparison and they have been at this high level for the past two decades.

The risk of long-term and very-long term unemployment is highest for older workers but also high for prime-age workers: two-thirds of workers aged 50-64 and more than half of those aged 30-49 are long-term unemployed (Figure 1.4, Panel B). Structural long-term unemployment is a big concern. Improving active labour market policies will be critical to prevent the crisis-induced rise in (very) long-term unemployment from transforming into structural unemployment and permanent exclusion from the labour market.

Figure 1.4. **High levels of long-term unemployment in Slovenia reveal structural problems**

People unemployed for more than one year as a share of all unemployed people: Slovenia, OECD and EU22 and Slovenia by age group, 2000-15

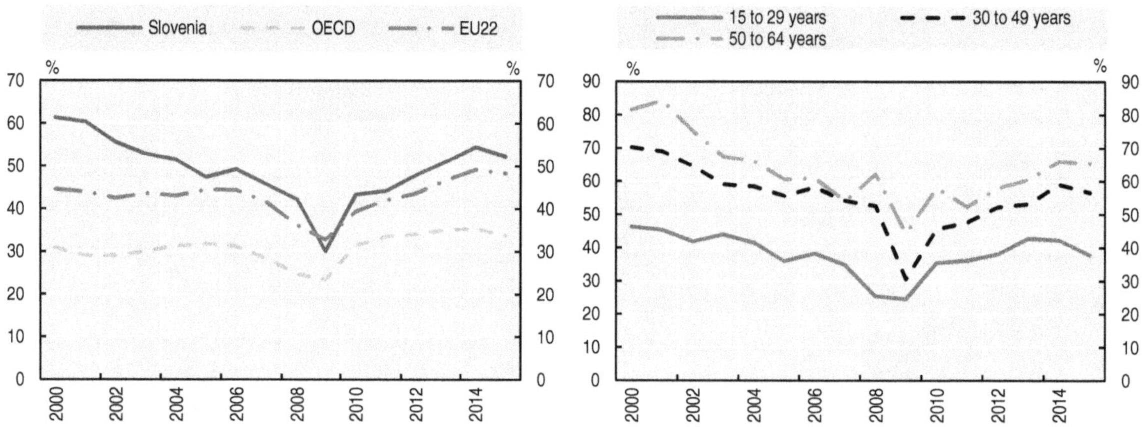

Note: OECD and EU22 are weighted averages. EU22 includes all EU countries which are also OECD members.

Source: *OECD Employment Database* (*LFS by sex and age dataset*) www.oecd.org/employment/database.

StatLink http://dx.doi.org/10.1787/888933414976

The high risk of permanent labour market exclusion for Slovenians over age 50 is reflected in high rates of inactivity relative to both OECD and EU22 averages for this age group (Figure 1.5). On the contrary, inactivity levels are comparatively low in Slovenia among prime-age workers and similar to the OECD and EU22 averages for young workers under age 30.

Figure 1.5. **Inactivity in Slovenia is high among older workers and low among prime-age workers**

Share of the population by labour force status and age group, OECD, European Union and Slovenia, 2015

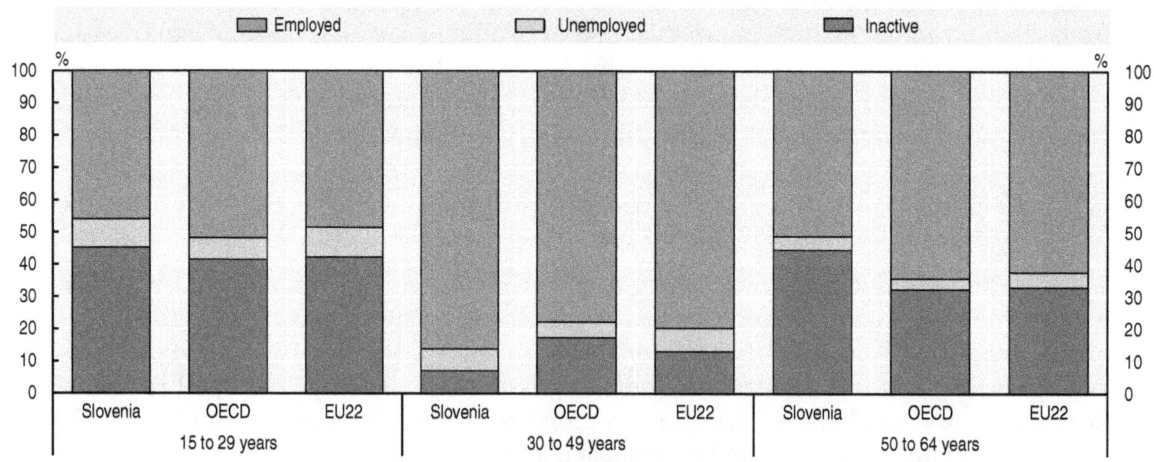

Note: OECD and EU22 are weighted averages. EU22 includes all EU countries which are also OECD members.

Source: *OECD Employment Database* (*LFS by sex and age dataset*) www.oecd.org/employment/database.

StatLink http://dx.doi.org/10.1787/888933414988

Involuntary job loss is coming down gradually since 2009

The drop in employment and the increase in unemployment in Slovenia since the onset of the GFC were to a considerable extent the result of jobs wiped out by firms closing or down-sizing. Workers "displaced" involuntarily from these jobs often have been in their jobs or occupations for a long time and have never experienced unemployment before. Some will find comparable jobs quickly but many others face long periods of unemployment, during which time their skills depreciate. Even when they find a new job, it may have lower pay or inferior working arrangements in comparison to their pre-displacement job. As such, the personal costs of job displacement can be substantial and long-lasting (OECD, 2013).[2]

Table 1.1 shows the share of employees dismissed or made redundant between time t-1 and t for European countries from 2006 to 2013. In most countries, dismissals peaked in 2009-10, but they remained high or even continued to rise in a number of countries, including Greece, Italy, Portugal, Spain and also Slovenia. Dismissal rates in Slovenia in 2013 were still three times higher than prior to the recession and Slovenia now ranks among European countries with relatively high annual dismissal rates.

Table 1.1. **Dismissal rates in Slovenia are still two to three times higher today than before the global financial crisis**

Workers dismissed or made redundant as a share of all workers, Slovenia and European countries, 2006-13

	2006	2007	2008	2009	2010	2011	2012	2013
Norway	0.5	0.4	0.4	0.8	0.6	0.6	0.4	0.4
Iceland	0.5			1.7	1.0	0.8	0.7	0.7
United Kingdom	1.2	1.1	1.3	2.8	2.0	1.8	1.7	1.1
Netherlands	..	..	0.5	1.2	1.2	0.6	0.9	1.2
Switzerland	1.0	0.7	0.7	1.1	1.3	0.7	1.0	1.2
Sweden	1.3	1.0	0.9	2.8	1.8	1.2	1.4	1.4
Luxembourg	1.1	1.1	1.0	1.4	1.0	1.2	1.1	1.4
Belgium	1.3	1.2	1.2	1.8	1.6	1.4	1.5	1.7
Austria	2.2	2.2	1.9	2.5	2.1	1.5	1.5	1.7
Germany	2.4	2.0	1.9	2.7	2.1	1.8	1.7	1.7
Finland	1.1	1.1	1.0	3.1	2.4	1.5	1.8	2.1
France	1.6	1.5	1.4	2.2	2.3	0.8	..	2.1
Slovak Republic	1.6	1.2	1.3	4.2	3.3	2.3	2.3	2.3
EU average	**1.5**	**1.3**	**1.4**	**3.0**	**2.7**	**2.1**	**2.4**	**2.3**
Estonia	1.2	0.9	2.0	8.1	7.3	3.0	2.0	2.5
Slovenia	**1.2**	**0.8**	**0.8**	**2.2**	**2.4**	**2.5**	**2.2**	**2.6**
Czech Republic	1.7	1.2	1.2	3.6	3.1	2.7	2.8	2.7
Poland	2.2	1.4	1.3	2.6	2.8	2.5	2.5	2.7
Denmark	1.4	1.3	1.6	3.8	3.8	3.2	3.1	3.1
Portugal	1.9	2.0	2.0	3.5	2.8	2.9	4.2	3.5
Italy	1.5	1.6	1.9	2.7	2.7	2.5	3.0	3.8
Hungary	2.5	2.6	2.8	5.4	4.9	4.5	4.8	3.9
Spain	1.7	1.5	2.9	6.3	5.3	4.6	5.5	4.8
Greece	1.2	1.2	1.1	2.2	3.2	4.5	5.7	4.8

Note: The EU average is an unweighted average.

Source: OECD estimates based on the European Labour Force Survey.

StatLink http://dx.doi.org/10.1787/888933415288

Measured over the entire past decade, roughly one in five newly-registered unemployed in Slovenia had lost their job for economic reasons. Prior to the GFC this share had fluctuated around 15%, then jumped up to over 25% in 2009 and since then came down again gradually to just over 15% (Figure 1.6). The largest group of newly-registered unemployed, however, is people whose fixed-term contract has ended. This reflects the very frequent use of temporary employment in Slovenia, especially among young workers.

Figure 1.6. **In Slovenia, around one in five new jobseekers have been displaced from their job**

Number of newly registered unemployed by reason of job loss (left-hand scale; in thousands) and share of job displacements among newly registered unemployed (right-hand scale; as a percentage)

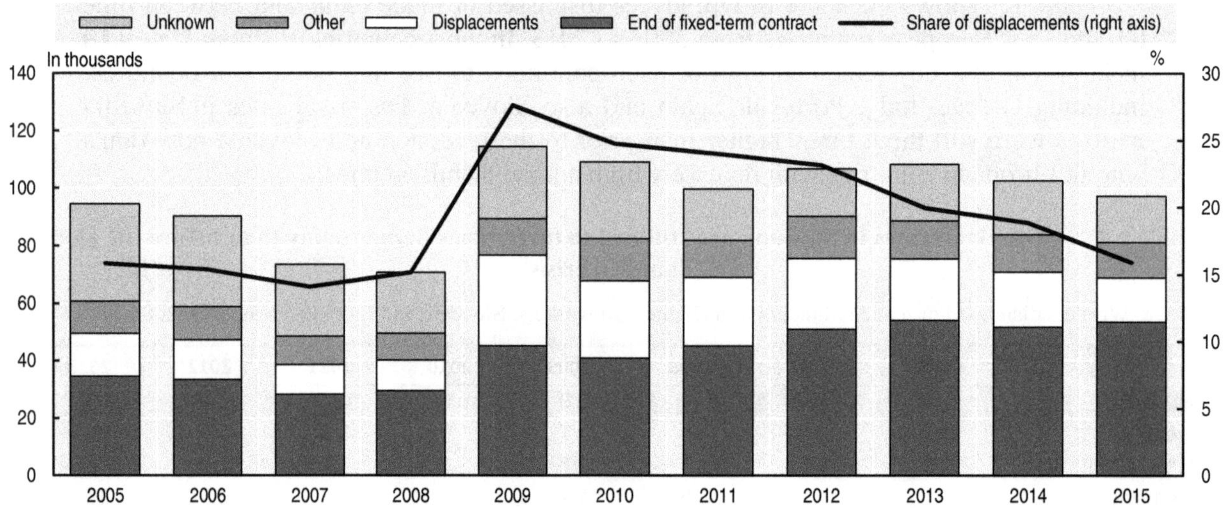

Note: "Displacement" includes bankruptcy of employers and permanent redundancies; "Other" includes serious misconduct, ban due to inspection, expiry of public works, sentence over six months, separations due to employer not fulfilling obligations, worker incompetence, unsuccessful probationary work (first six months of indefinite contract), termination with an offer of a new contract, written agreement, transition between registries within the ESS and termination of operations.

Source: Employment Service of Slovenia.

StatLink http://dx.doi.org/10.1787/888933414997

Labour market participation of special groups

In the context of this review of activation policies in Slovenia, two groups of workers with low labour market attachment by international standards deserve special attention because their rates of employment are very low in Slovenia compared to other OECD countries: low-skilled workers and older workers.

Low-skilled workers face a large and persistent employment gap in Slovenia

In Slovenia, a higher proportion of the working-age population has upper secondary education than in the EU on average. The recent decline in the share of this group has been more than off-set by the continuous rise in the share of people with tertiary education, closing the gap with the EU average on this account. As a result, the share of people with less than upper secondary education is lower in Slovenia than on average in the EU. And similar to the trend for the EU as a whole, the proportion of low-educated people has been shrinking in Slovenia from just over 20% in 2004 to around 13% in 2015 (Figure 1.7, Panel A).

This is important, as educational attainment and skills have a large impact on the likelihood of being employed.

Employment rates are much lower for people with less than upper secondary education than those with higher education in both Slovenia and the EU as a whole. In Slovenia, the rate for people with low education is just below 50% with a gap of about 20 percentage points to those with upper secondary education and about 35 percentage points to those with tertiary education (Figure 1.7, Panel B). After the GFC, employment rates have declined in Slovenia for all groups but most so for those with below upper secondary education, with some recovery recently. Some of this decline can be explained by a substantial decline of employment in the construction sector after 2008, which was also driven by major public infrastructure projects in motorway construction coming to an end in 2008.

Figure 1.7. **Employment of the low-skilled population in Slovenia is low and has fallen further**

Working-age population (25-64) shares and employment rates by level of educational attainment, Slovenia and EU28, 2004-15

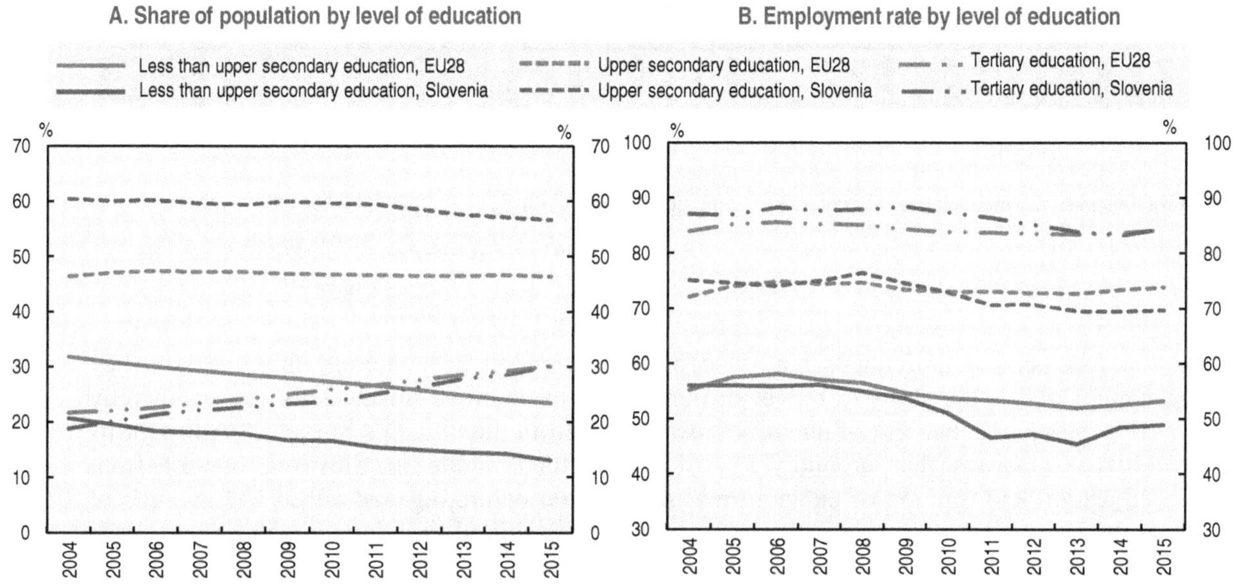

Note: Unweighted EU averages.

Source: Eurostat.

StatLink http://dx.doi.org/10.1787/888933415008

Poor employment outcomes for individuals with less than upper secondary education are also reflected in high unemployment rates. In Slovenia, 17.8% of these individuals were unemployed in 2014, in comparison with 13.5% in the OECD on average and 5.8% for individuals with tertiary education (Figure 1.8). This is in addition to the large share of individuals with low educational background who have withdrawn from the labour market, as reflected in their low employment rates.

Figure 1.8. Unemployment is at least twice as high for the low-educated population in most OECD countries, including Slovenia

Unemployment rates (as a share of the labour force) by level of educational attainment, Slovenia and selected OECD countries, 2014

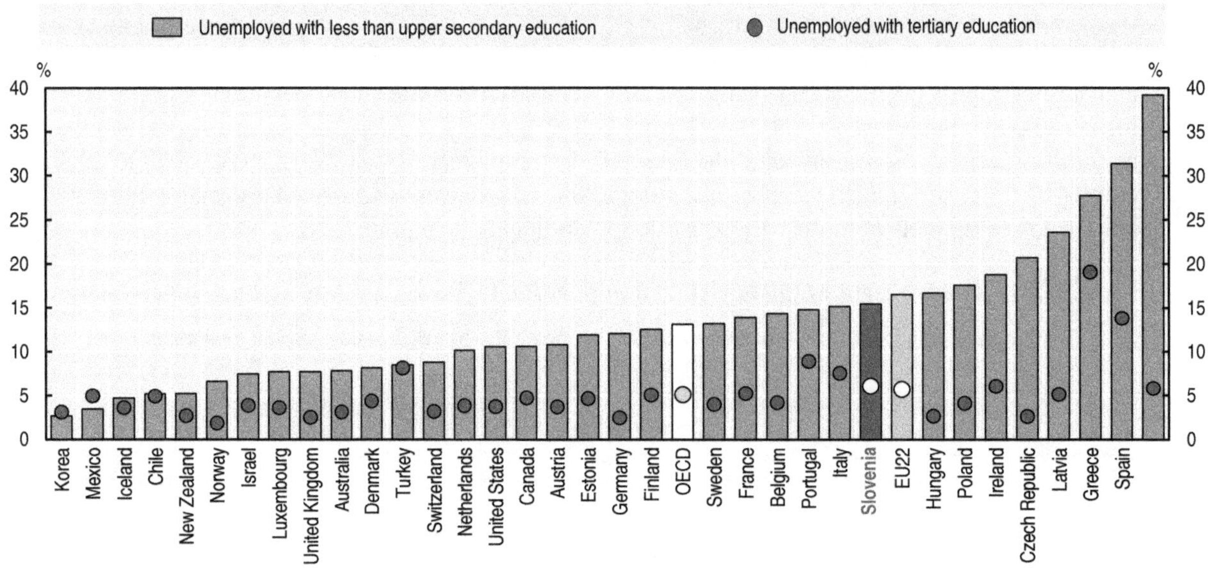

Note: OECD and EU22 are weighted averages. EU22 includes all EU countries which are also OECD members.

Source: OECD (2015), *Education at a Glance* (www.oecd.org/edu/education-at-a-glance-19991487.htm).

StatLink http://dx.doi.org/10.1787/888933415018

Low-skilled individuals may also often be trapped in a vicious circle, where they cannot obtain the skills to move into employment or move up the jobs ladder, thereby also facing a higher risk of unemployment. Data from the OECD's Survey of Adult Skills (PIAAC) shows that around 78% of high-skilled adults in Slovenia benefit from education and training of either formal or informal nature, against an OECD average of only 72%.[3] The education and training rate of low-skilled individuals is at around 30%, similar to the OECD average. However, Slovenia has a particularly large skills gap in education and training rates between low-skilled and high-skilled workers (Figure 1.9).

Figure 1.9. **Participation in continued training is low for the low-skilled population, also in Slovenia, adding to the persistence of skills gaps**

Percentage of adults who participated in adult education and training during year prior to the survey, by level of proficiency in literacy, 2012 and 2015[a]

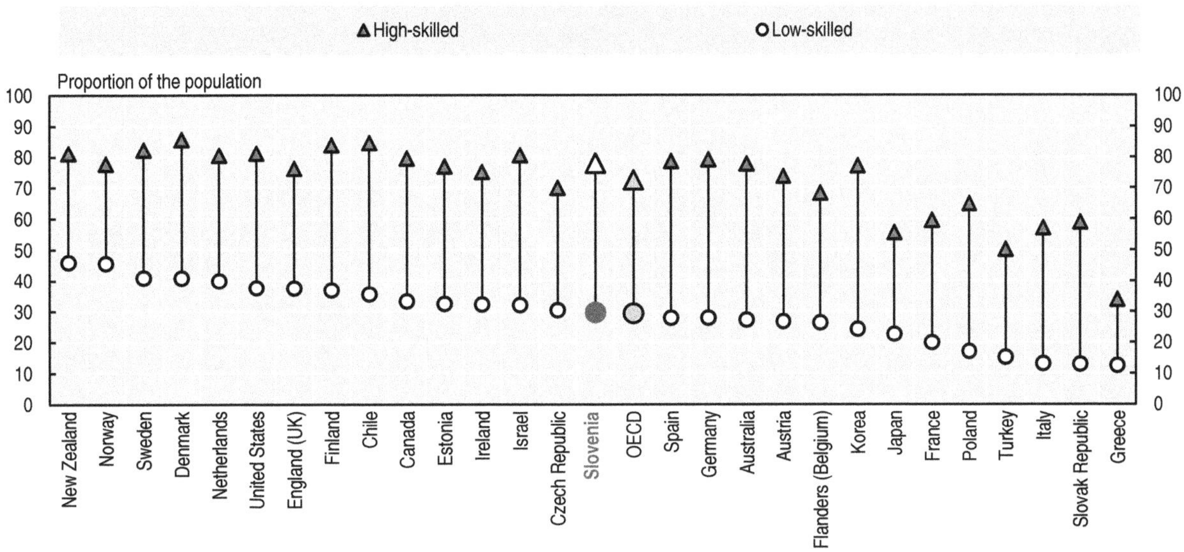

Note: High-skilled individuals are those with a literacy proficiency score at level 4 or 5. Such adults can integrate, interpret and synthesise information from complex or lengthy texts that contain conditional and/or competing information. Low-skilled individuals are those with a literacy proficiency score at level 1 or below. Such adults can read short texts on familiar topics and locate a single piece of information that is identical to or synonymous with the information given in the question.

a) Year 2015 for Chile, Greece, Israel, New Zealand, Slovenia and Turkey; for all other countries, 2012.

Source: Survey of Adult Skills (PIAAC) 2012, 2015.

StatLink http://dx.doi.org/10.1787/888933415024

Older worker employment has improved, but retention rates remain low

One group stands out in Slovenia as the one which is left behind more than any other group, compared with other OECD countries: older workers. The employment rate of workers aged 55-59 is around 55% and for those aged 60-64 only around 15% (Figure 1.10, Panel A). This compares with corresponding employment rates of over 80% (age 55-59) and over 50% (age 60-64) in the vanguard countries including the Nordic countries, Switzerland, New Zealand and Japan. The low employment rates are also reflected in the low share of workers aged 55-59 years who continue to work for another five years: it is only 17.7% in 2014 and thus lower than in any other OECD country. In vanguard countries in the north of Europe, this share is as high as 65-70% (Figure 1.10, Panel B).

Figure 1.10. **Employment rates for older workers in Slovenia are lower than in other OECD countries**

Employment rates and retention rates for older workers, Slovenia and OECD countries, 2015

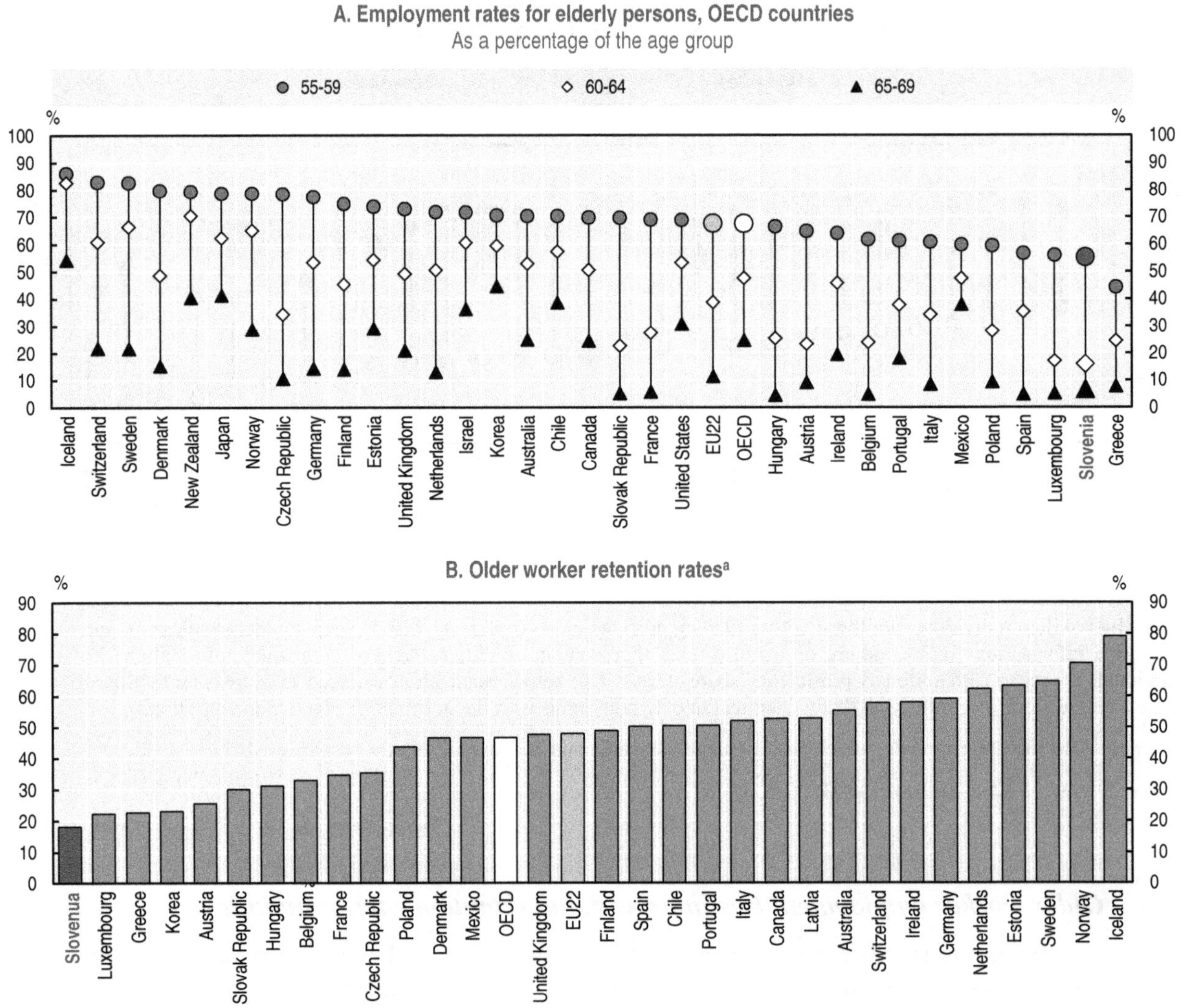

a) Employees aged 60-64 with job tenure of five years or more as a percentage of employees aged 55-59 five years earlier.

Source: *OECD Employment Database* (*LFS by sex and age dataset*) www.oecd.org/employment/database (Panel A) and *Job Tenure dataset* (Panel B).

StatLink http://dx.doi.org/10.1787/888933415036

Apart from disincentives in the benefit system for older workers to remain longer in the labour market (see Chapter 3), older workers may often not be attractive to employers due to their lower skill levels, especially given the high seniority bonuses in Slovenia (see Chapter 2). Across OECD countries, proficiency in literacy, numeracy and problem solving in technology-rich environments typically peaks among 25-34 year-olds while the proficiency of 55-64 year-olds is generally the lowest of all age groups. This is also the case in Slovenia, where 25-34 year-olds have the highest proficiency scores and 55-65 year-olds the lowest. However, older Slovenians score significantly lower in literacy, numeracy and problem solving in technology-rich environments than their peers across other OECD countries (Figure 1.11).[4]

Figure 1.11. **Older Slovenians have lower skills proficiencies than their peers in other countries**

Trend scores by age, foreign-born adults excluded

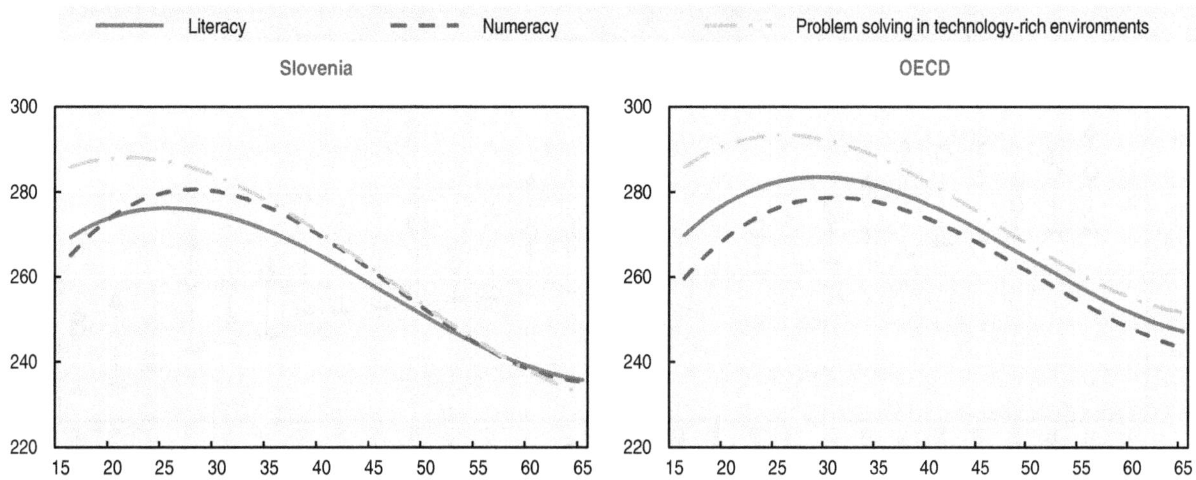

Source: OECD (2016), *Skills Matter: Further Results from the Survey of Adult Skills*, OECD Skills Studies, OECD Publishing, Paris, http://dx.doi.org/10.1787/9789264258051-en.

StatLink http://dx.doi.org/10.1787/888933415049

Again, like for the low-skilled population, the low share of older people seeking to upskill by participating in education or training programmes contributes to their low employment potential. Only around a third of Slovenes aged 50 to 65 years participate in formal or informal training, compared to over half in many other OECD countries, especially those countries with high employment rates among older workers (Figure 1.12). Among Slovenes aged 30 to 49 years, the corresponding share in formal or informal training is 56%, compared to Denmark, Finland, New Zealand, Norway and Sweden where 70% or more of prime-age adults participate in education and training. Again, these figures suggest that more can be done in Slovenia to upskill the population continuously to promote longer working lives.

Figure 1.12. **Only a third of older workers in Slovenia seek to improve their skills to remain employable**

Percentage of adults who participated in adult education and training during year prior to the survey, by level of proficiency in literacy, 2012 and 2015[a]

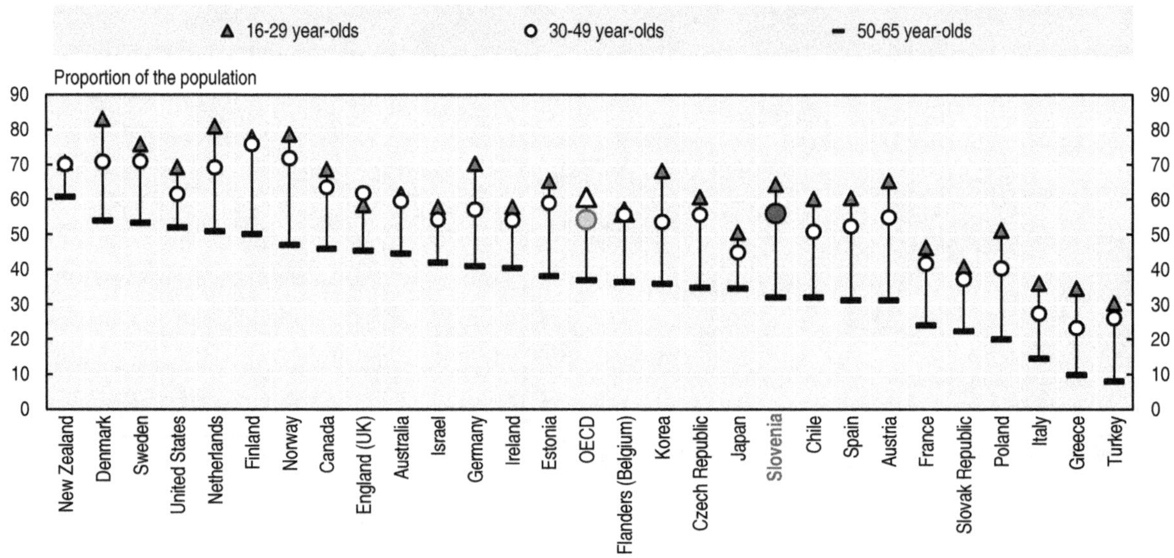

Countries are ranked in descending order of persons aged 50-65.

a) Year 2015 for Chile, Greece, Israel, New Zealand, Slovenia and Turkey; for all other countries, 2012.

Source: Survey of Adult Skills (PIAAC) 2012, 2015.

StatLink http://dx.doi.org/10.1787/888933415059

Key findings

In conclusion, the following are the main labour market challenges which Slovenia will have to address in the coming decade:

- Exceptionally low rates of employment of older workers aged 55 years and over.
- Low rates of employment and high rates of unemployment for the low-skilled population.
- High rates of long-term and very long-term unemployment for all age groups but especially older workers.
- Relatively high rates of involuntary job loss and job loss among those with a fixed-term contract.
- Low training participation for the most vulnerable groups and increasing job polarisation, creating new mismatch problems in the labour market.
- And more generally, very slowly improving labour market outcomes since the onset of the GFC, with considerable risk of a higher level of structural unemployment going forward.

Notes

1. EU22 includes: Austria, Belgium, Czech Republic, Denmark, Estonia, Finland, France, Germany, Greece, Hungary, Ireland, Italy, Latvia, Luxembourg, the Netherlands, Poland, Portugal, Slovak Republic, Slovenia, Spain, Sweden and the United Kingdom.
2. The term "job displacement" refers to involuntary job separations for economic or technological reasons. Ideally, the exact reason for each job separation would be observed for job displacements to be distinguished from other forms of job separations. In practice it is often difficult to accurately measure the true reason for job separations. In the following, two types of data are used measuring self-defined displacement or involuntary job loss. The first is from the European Labour Force Survey (EU-LFS) which includes a retrospective question about the main reason for leaving the last job. Workers who have been "dismissed or made redundant" can be distinguished from other types of separations. The EU-LFS, however, does not allow distinguishing dismissals for economic reasons and therefore underestimates job displacement. The second set of data is derived from administrative records of the Employment Service of Slovenia (ESS). These data measure the share of inflows to overall registered unemployment that is due to dismissal as against other reasons for job separation. ESS data are also imperfect, however. The end or non-extension of a fixed-term contract that is related to economic restructuring cannot be identified and is therefore not classified as job displacement.
3. The OECD Survey of Adult Skills (PIAAC) assesses the proficiency of adults from age 16 in literacy, numeracy and problem solving in technology-rich environments. The point-based results of these assessments are grouped into six different proficiency levels ranging from very low ("below level 1") to very high ("level 5").
4. Interestingly, unlike the profile found in most countries, in Slovenia, there seems to be very little improvement in proficiency in literacy and problem-solving skills between the ages 16 and 30. Younger Slovenians (25-34 year-olds) underperform their peers across OECD countries in literacy and problem-solving, but score similarly to their peers in numeracy.

References

Eurofound (2016), *What Do Europeans Do at Work? A Task-based Analysis: European Jobs Monitor 2016*, Publications Office of the European Union, Luxembourg, www.eurofound.europa.eu/publications/report/2016/labour-market/what-do-europeans-do-at-work-a-task-based-analysis-european-jobs-monitor-2016.

Eurofound (2013), *Employment Polarisation and Job Quality in the Crisis: European Jobs Monitor 2013*, Dublin, www.eurofound.europa.eu/publications/report/2013/labour-market-business/employment-polarisation-and-job-quality-in-the-crisis-european-jobs-monitor-2013.

Eurofound (2011), *Shifts in the Job Structure in Europe during the Great Recession*, Publications Office of the European Union, Luxembourg, www.eurofound.europa.eu/publications/report/2011/labour-market/shifts-in-the-job-structure-in-europe-during-the-great-recession.

Database references

OECD Employment Database (*LFS by sex and age dataset*) www.oecd.org/employment/database.

Chapter 2

Opportunities: The Slovenian labour market and policy environment

This chapter discusses some key features of the policy environment in Slovenia, to help understanding of current labour market outcomes and activation policy challenges and of the large impact of the recent recession. These features include among other things the relatively high minimum wage; legally required or tax-exempt allowances paid to employees; and non-standard forms of work and their regulation. The chapter looks at how these issues as well as benefits and benefit conditionality may interact, e.g. the minimum wage may encourage the use of fixed-term contracts, while benefit entitlements from fixed-term contracts encourage repeat unemployment. The chapter also describes the social and labour market reform path Slovenia has followed since its independence and the recent partial breakdown of social dialogue.

The statistical data for Israel are supplied by and under the responsibility of the relevant Israeli authorities. The use of such data by the OECD is without prejudice to the status of the Golan Heights, East Jerusalem and Israeli settlements in the West Bank under the terms of international law.

This chapter describes some key features of the institutional and political background in Slovenia, to help understanding of current labour market policy issues: these include the breakdown of social agreement and wage restraint after adoption of the euro in 2008, and falls in union membership and collective bargaining coverage. It discusses some issues that fall outside the scope of the next two chapters but remain important for labour market and activation policy more broadly. These include the minimum wage; allowances paid to employees (some of which are not taxed and/or have undefined status in relation to the minimum wage), which are tending to obscure policy analysis and social dialogue, and involve some economic distortion; and non-standard forms of work and their regulation. The chapter also looks at how these issues as well as benefits and benefit conditionality may interact, e.g. the minimum wage may encourage the use of fixed-term contracts, while benefit entitlements from fixed-term contracts encourage repeat unemployment.

A brief history of Slovenian labour market policy

Slovenia's gentle post-socialist transition

From the time it declared its independence from Yugoslavia in 1990 until the beginning of the global recession in 2008 Slovenia was one of the most successful of the post-socialist transition countries and featured both strong economic growth and a comparatively high standard of living. It was also amongst the first of the onetime Eastern Bloc territories to enter the European Union, the first of these newcomers to preside over the EU and the first to enter the Eurozone. As described by Hrast and Raker (2015):

> *...in the transition period in the 1990ies, contrary to some other post-socialist countries, Slovenia did not experience a so called 'welfare gap' (Kolarič et al., 2009, 2011). Instead, the country's welfare reforms followed a gentler path, maintaining strong state involvement in the provision of services and in regulating the economy through state ownership of a many companies and banks. Bohle and Greskovits (2007) claim that the Neo-corporatist regime established after Slovenia's independence has exhibited a firmly institutionalised balance between marketisation, i.e. liberalisation, privatisation and market-oriented institution building, and social protections (based on a welfare system and economic protectionism) and that this balance differs markedly from the Neoliberal brand of capitalism that emerged concurrently in the Baltic and Visegràd states.*

As often in Nordic countries, the Slovenian labour market, characterised by social partnership and a large government sector, achieved positive labour market and social outcomes with high employment, low unemployment and low levels of income inequality. However, it cannot be assumed that tripartite governance is uniformly successful as, for example Austria's older-worker employment rate has at times been far below the EU 28 average, because the social partners too often solved labour market adjustment problems by transferring workers to disability and early retirement benefits. Guardiancich (2011) argues that Slovenia developed a thick web of political checks and balances, with a moderately pluralist party system and powerful social partners, especially the Association of Free Trade Unions of Slovenia (ZSSS). Although on the positive side Slovenia avoided the social disruption that ravaged post-socialist countries, on the negative side, there were repercussions on the type of capitalism and on policymaking procedures that Slovenia developed:

> *Slovenia revelled in insider privatisation... A national economic elite formed through the appointment of politically loyal cadres in top economic positions and the creation of quasi-state-owned investment funds following the Ownership Transformation Act... Slovenian politicians were forced into lengthy and cumbersome negotiations, had problems in facing organised interest groups. A perennially quarrelling and factionalist political class exhausted, after two decades, the initial advantages and failed to implement structural reforms. The result is widespread immobilismo, the exacerbation of the insider-outsider problem and agenda-hijacking by some interest groups... the single-issue, Democratic Party of Pensioners of Slovenia took part in all coalition governments since 1997 (in 2000 it gave external support to Premier Andrej Bajuk). This probably qualifies it as the most successful pensioner party in the world. Owing to its pivotal role in coalition governments, DeSUS more often than not prevented even slight changes to the country's retirement system.*

The impact of the global financial crisis

The recession from 2008 was a setback for political governance, social partnership, economic outcomes and the welfare system, but at first each area could perhaps too easily blame its problems on developments in the other areas. As described by Hrast and Rakar (2015), it put the country's well-developed social systems under increasingly significant pressure:

> *...Slovenia faced one of the most pronounced recessions in the OECD... Its GDP growth rate after 2008 was negative, and the country has been slower to recover than others in the EU-28... The government's gross national debt (as a share of GDP) has risen sharply, growing from 22% of GDP in 2008 to more than 80% of GDP by the last quarter of 2014 (IMAD, 2015). The crisis has revealed critical weaknesses in Slovenia's pre-crisis economic performance, structural inconsistencies within its welfare system and the country's limited ability to innovate (OECD, 2011). This has forced its government to take significant steps to restructure the welfare system, while restructuring has in turn produced discontent amongst Slovenia's citizenry.*

The social partners and their institutional role

Slovenia has a long tradition of social partner regulation of the labour market and guidance of broader social and economic policy. However, in the 2000s, the membership of union and employer organisations and the coverage of employees by collective agreements began to decline. Social agreements on disinflationary wage policies helped Slovenia to qualify for membership of the Eurozone in 2007, but this consensus broke down and positions polarised around topics such as the minimum wage, employment contracting and pension reform, which are more controversial and influenced also by political pressures, popular opinion, and economic analysis.

Unions

As described by Guardiancich (2011), Slovenian trade unions strengthened during transition, securing a uniquely firm socioeconomic role among post- socialist countries. They are at the same time key civil society representatives as well as defenders of the state bureaucracy. Nevertheless "...the labour movement split along pro- and anti-communist lines. The successor union ZSSS retained one third of the labour force, maintaining its primacy during the last two decades… Other left-leaning unions, i.e. Pergam and Konfederacija '90, distanced themselves from ZSSS."

More than half of all public sector employees are members of the Confederation of Trade Unions of the Public Sector, KSJS, created in 2006 with 81 000 members (39 000 of them in the Education, Science and Culture Trade Union: www.sviz.si/eng/). However, overall union density has fallen sharply, from 44% in 2003 to 22% in 2013 (Ignjatović and Mrčela, 2015).

Employers

As described by Guardiancich (2011), on the employer side:

> *During 1991-2006, two employer organisations – the Chamber of Commerce and Industry of Slovenia (Gospodarska zbornica Slovenije, GZS) and the Chamber of Craft and Small Businesses of Slovenia (Obrtno-podjetniška zbornica Slovenije, OZS) – represented all entrepreneurs due to compulsory membership. Since 2006, membership has been voluntary and employer associations' density decreased, as they now employ some 80-90% private sector employees. Since collective agreements require a density threshold of 50% for automatic extension, further declines may be detrimental.*

Collective agreements

Despite falls in union membership, in 2005 still 96% of employees were covered by collective agreements. Collective agreements at industry level can be extended by the minister of labour to all the companies in an industry if the union signing the agreement is representative and the employers in the employers' association employ more than half the employees in the industry. In 2005 all employers had to be members of chambers of commerce and industry, but the 2006 Collective Agreements Act provided that only employers or employers' associations with a voluntary membership could sign collective agreements. According to one source (www.worker-participation.eu/National-Industrial-Relations/Countries/Slovenia/Collective-Bargaining) still around 90% of employees are covered by collective bargaining, due the use of extension mechanisms. However, the European Company Survey reports a decline in coverage rate from 90% in 2009 to 78% in 2013 (Mrčela, 2015). Another source, the Wage Dynamics Network survey, reports that in 2013 "68.8% of firms apply collective agreements to at least some of their workers... and these firms employ 79.4% of all workers" (although this survey covers approximately 300 000 workers, not including agricultural, self-employed and non-profit entities where coverage would tend to be lower), but coverage has decreased only slightly compared to 2006 (Jemec and Vodopivec, 2016).

Although firms' survey responses indicate that around 20% of employees are not covered by a collective agreement, it seems likely that in about half these cases the employees are in a firm that (although not actively engaged in bargaining) is legally subject to an extended collective agreement that could in principle be enforced by the labour inspectorate. At the same time, since extension procedures are only in place for certain sectors of activity, plausibly 10% of employees (in addition to managers, who in any case have individual agreements) are not covered even in principle.

The institutional roles of the social partners

After the transition recession was over, Slovenia started a long tradition of concertation. The social partners drafted every year or two a social agreement outlining their mutual obligations and broad guidelines for the direction of labour market policy and reforms. Collectively-negotiated social agreements on economic, social and wage policy, notably agreements on disinflationary wage policies, played a crucial role in satisfying the Maastricht criteria and subsequent euro adoption (Banerjee, Vodopivec and Sila, 2013).

Guardiancich (2011) describes the social partnership institutions:

> *The social partners have a dual role in welfare state matters in Slovenia: i) an advisory role through the Economic and Social Council (Ekonomsko-socialni svet, ESC); ii) an administrative role through their own representatives in the tripartite boards of the Institute for Pension and Disability Insurance, the Health Insurance Institute of Slovenia and the Employment Service of Slovenia... In general, the New Right tried to change the composition of these administrative boards to significantly weaken the role of social partners. As for the ESC, this has 15 seats, five for each partner. The Council is not underpinned by any legal act, apart from government regulation, but it nonetheless holds disproportionate power: the Parliament only discusses socioeconomic legislation that had already been debated by ESC members.*

However, since 2009, this tradition of concertation has largely broken down. Some elements have been revived, but the government more often has to decide.

The breakdown of dialogue and the blockage of necessary reforms

Prior to the recession, at the political level, as Guardiancich (2011, 2012) explains:

> *..the real break with the socialist past happened only with the ascendancy in late 2004 of Janez Janša, leader of the conservative Slovenian Democratic Party (SDS). The Slovenian New Right fully applied its imperative policymaking style and adversarial stance to uproot the ruling socio-economic elites, among others the so-called rdeči direktorji (red directors). Despite four years of heightened domestic political confrontation, the country successfully integrated into the European Union, adopted the Euro, and presided over the European Council.*

Despite the good intentions of government, since 2009 social dialogue has been erratic and attempts at reviving the tradition of social agreements have been ineffective. The 2007-09 social agreement was, according to the employers, initially agreed upon under favourable economic conditions, and therefore by 2009 needed a substantial update. The starting points of the social agreement were presented to the Economic and Social Council only in November 2009. The measures included restrictive income policy, reduced public spending, and lowered non-wage labour costs to improve competitiveness and introduce more flexibility into the labour market. "In order to convince the unions to continue negotiating, the Government guaranteed that the minimum wage would be valid for all workers (also those not covered by collective agreements), and withdrew the idea of a packaged solution... with such grim prospective, in the face of the multiple structural reforms ahead, the National Assembly unanimously approved the Minimum Wage Act on 14 January 2010." (Guardiancich, 2012). However, since then the minimum wage has been the topic most disputed between the social partners.

In 2010 and 2011, the government attempted to pass reform legislation on other matters (regulation of mini-jobs, pension reform, etc.) but this legislation either was withdrawn due to popular protests organised by particular interest groups, or was actually passed but then later defeated in a referendum. As the severity and depth of the recession – which had at first been partly masked by employment policy measures delaying layoffs – became clear, a consensus around the need for crisis measures emerged in 2012. Speculation that an international bailout would be needed to recapitalise the banking system – itself still largely state-owned – peaked only in late 2013.

The tradition of social agreements was partly revived from 2012 onwards when Janez Janša's executive gained approval for short-term savings measures as well as the Starting Points for the Social Contract 2012-16. A tangible breakthrough was achieved in May 2012 by passing the Public Finance Balance Act (ZUJF) – a super-law that modifies as many as 39 other laws - and amendments to the state budget and public sector collective agreement which reduced wages by 8%.

Following six years without a valid agreement, and after over a year of negotiations, Slovenia's social partners signed a new Social Agreement for 2015-16 in February 2015. However, the various stakeholders failed to reach a meaningful consensus on the direction for necessary reforms, and thus this Social Agreement arguably offers little substantive guidance. Its most specific, notable provision stipulates that the government will not increase nominal tax revenue in 2015 (although this does not rule out redistributing the tax burden, e.g. via the introduction of a real estate tax). Regarding areas that may be relevant for activation policy, the Social Agreement mentions the following actions to be taken:

- Identifying the causes for the low employment rate of older workers and conducting an impact assessment of recent legislative changes; based on this assessment, developing further measures that will contribute to longer labour market attachment for older workers.
- Strengthening the role of the social partners in the implementation of active labour market policy measures.
- Creating a mechanism for the promotion and effective training of workers and the unemployed.
- In the area of active labour market programmes, conducting a comprehensive analysis of the efficacy and efficiency of the measures implemented in the 2007-13 Financial Perspective (expenditures until 2015); on this basis, in consultation with the social partners, developing active labour market policy measures which aim to facilitate and encourage faster entry into the labour market for young people and other disadvantaged groups, with a particular emphasis on the long-term unemployed, the elderly and persons with disabilities.
- Evaluating the institution of temporary lay-offs, with the possibility of increasing the involvement of the Employment Service of Slovenia.
- Preparing a proposal to establish a severance pay fund.
- Reforming policies regarding the employment of pensioners.

One of the most contentious issues – relating to the minimum wage – was left out of the final Social Agreement for 2015-16, and in September 2015 the labour unions submitted into parliamentary procedure reforms to exclude bonuses for unfavourable working hours from the definition of the minimum wage, and the coalition government passed this into legislation. On 27 November, all but one of the employer associations withdrew from the social agreement on the grounds that the change represents a violation of the social pact, stating that it undermines trust among social partners and prevents the continuation of social dialogue (Lukic, 2016; www.sloveniatimes.com/employers-withdraw-from-social-pact-after-minimum-wage-hike).

Erratic policy developments in 2010-11

The government in 2010 planned to pass four major reforms: the 2010 Minimum Wage Act, the Labour Market Regulation Act (which deals with benefits and active labour market programmes, ALMPs), the Employment Relationship Act (which deals with employment protection legislation, EPL) and the Mini-Jobs Act which sought to regulate fixed-term work and particularly student work. These reforms were negotiated as a package but "following the protests of the unions... with the great irritation of all employers' associations, the four laws were treated separately... Whereas the two acts increasing security (Minimum Wage Act and the Labour Market Regulation Act) are now in force, those promoting greater flexibility were either withdrawn (Employment Relationships Act) or defeated at a referendum (Mini-Jobs Act)." (Guardiancich, 2012). A similar development was that in 2010 the government bypassed the tripartite Economic and Social Council to legislate a new Pension and Disability Insurance Act (PDIA-2), but the union association ZSSS gathered the 40 000 signatures necessary to hold a referendum on the whole Act, and a large majority voted against the reform.

Ticar (2014) remarks that the Employment Relationship Act as enacted in September 2010 was changed three times and voted as a wholly new law in March 2013. Stropnik (2013) says that in the field of social assistance "we could speak of a comprehensive policy design only if we include - besides the relevant legislation in force - the new/amended legislation that was first passed and then rejected in the referendums in 2011, and those important pieces of legislation that had been drafted several years ago but have not yet been submitted."

The labour market programme response to the crisis in 2010-11

In 2009 and 2010, Slovenia introduced two measures aimed at limiting job-losses due to temporary, negative demand shocks (Kajzer, 2010):

- Partial Subsidising of Full-Time Work Act (January 2009), which allowed firms to reduce full-time working hours from 40 to 32 hours per week (upon agreement with the representative trade unions) and entitled them to receive subsidies of up to EUR 120 per worker per month (thus not fully compensating firms for the decrease in hours worked, even for workers being paid the minimum wage).
- Partial Reimbursement of Payment Compensation Act (May 2009), which reimbursed firms which placed workers on forced temporary leave and provided funds for training such workers. Up to half of a firm's workers could be placed on temporary leave at a time, and firms were required to pay 85% of the workers wage for the duration of the forced leave (half of which was then reimbursed to the firm).

Funding for these measures was available through to March 2011 and September 2011, respectively. The measures were utilised fairly extensively in sectors where the impact of the economic crisis was most immediate, and arguably stemmed job losses in the short-term, but their broader effects have not been studied in detail. The measures may have only postponed the necessary labour market adjustment and caused labour hoarding (Kajzer, 2010). Expenditure on labour market training and direct job creation was also increased in 2009 and increased further in 2010, but it fell in 2011 and again in 2012 (source: OECD/EC database on labour market programme expenditure and participants), and in these years the employment rate declined somewhat further.

After the onset of the economic crisis, Slovenia increased the generosity of unemployment benefits (UB) and relaxed eligibility criteria (in January 2011; ZUTD). Generosity was reduced again as part of the 2012 fiscal consolidation package (ZUJF). The 2011 reform decreased the minimum employment period required for UB eligibility to nine months in the preceding two years (previously, the requirement was 12 months in the preceding 18 months). An analysis of the 2011 law by Dolenc et al. (2012) showed that it significantly increased unemployment benefit generosity in practice, especially for younger workers and women.

Policy developments after 2012

In December 2012, the Slovenian National Assembly passed a revised pension reform, which from 2013 applies to a progressively increasing proportion of new claims. The April 2013 labour market reform (Employment Relationships Act) reduced the disparity in firing costs between fixed term and permanent contracts (see Box 2.1 below).

In order to reduce the relative tax advantages of hiring workers via student employment agencies, in June 2012 the concession fee paid to the agencies was increased from 12% to 23% (an additional 2% being earmarked for the construction of student dormitories), and in February 2015 mandatory social security contributions were applied to student earnings. Student work retains its appeal to employers as an extremely flexible form of employment.

The post-2012 policy developments are described in more detail below.

Causes of the depth of the recession

Slovenian analysts blame current labour market and social problems on the recession and call for additional measures to relieve social distress. However, it is important to assess the likely causes of the depth of the recession. Although the recession has bottomed out and some recovery has taken place, in 2015, GDP was still 4.5% below its 2008 level, the employment rate was 3.4 points below its peak level of 68.6%, and the unemployment rate was still close to 10% rather than 5%. This has happened despite the massive use of fiscal stimulus and stabilisers, reflected in the increase of the debt/GDP ratio (only about 10 points of the increase being attributable to the recapitalisation of major banks). The continuation of a recession that started in 2009 is likely to reflect structural more than cyclical factors. This section outlines the main candidates.

Industrial structure and management

According to Guardiancich (2011), Slovenia prior to 2004 suffered delayed privatisation, inefficient buy-outs, hybrid Privatisation Investment Funds and quasi-state funds, and excessive gradualism in the development of financial services, which "show Slovenian policymakers will continue managing state-owned enterprises. This generated distrust towards institutional investors, kept foreign owners out of the country, and created powerful yet inefficient majority shareholders of the Slovenian enterprise sector."

Although a right-wing government was elected in 2004, public opinion soon turned against plans to privatise and liberalise markets, and instead of introducing structural reforms policy veered towards economic populism. "The global financial meltdown then exacerbated all the negative traits of the Slovenian economy and its unresolved structural problems."

Banking sector crisis

The banking-sector crisis arguably originated in excessive optimism about economic growth following EU and Euro Area accession and poor governance of state-owned banks and lax lending standards. Much of the credit went to the construction sector, and this exacerbated the boom-bust cycle. Loans to the corporate sector declined continuously after 2010, with the sharpest fall in 2014, tending to forestall recovery (Bank of Slovenia, 2016a; 2016b).

High minimum wage

As discussed below, since it was increased in 2010 the ratio of the minimum wage to the average wage in Slovenia has been among the highest in Europe. This may have partly reduced total employment directly, and partly increased segmentation as employers became more cautious about hiring low-paid workers on a permanent contract; as outlined below, segmentation may in a less-direct way also reduce total employment.

Labour market dualism

Labour market dualism is regulated by the social partners through collective agreements and by employment protection legislation, and it is influenced by tax and benefit incentives. Excessively strict regulation of non-standard forms of work can reduce employment, because many potential workers do not want a full-time permanent position, and in rigid labour markets older or displaced workers find it difficult to re-enter employment, and this in turn encourages the provision of early retirement benefits. But an artificially high incidence of non-standard work can also reduce employment. Temporary workers, in particular, suffer repeat unemployment and are first out in a recession. Keeping in mind that both the causes and the consequences of labour market dualism are complex, factors increasing labour market dualism in Slovenia have been:

- In the 2000s and 2010s, union membership has sharply declined, which makes it more difficult to enforce wage restraint on "insiders" through national social agreements.
- In the 2000s, student work increased, as employers (and students) increasingly exploited its exemption from regulation and taxation.
- The minimum wage increase of 2010 and the associated labour costs make employers more reluctant to hire on permanent contracts.

Factors reducing labour market dualism include the 2013 labour market reform, which increased the cost of fixed-term contracts relative to permanent contracts, and activities of the labour inspectorate which suppress inappropriate forms of non-standard work.

Benefit coverage of repeat unemployment and long-term unemployment

Adaptation to benefit system parameters can be a long-term process. Repeat unemployment with a benefit claim in Canada increased for 10 to 20 years after a 1971 unemployment insurance reform (Riddell and Kuhn, 2010). After the introduction or easing of access to assistance benefits, their caseloads often started at a low level but then increased rapidly for 15 years or more (OECD, 2003). Effective public employment service management and interventions in Slovenia have slowed any increases in benefit dependency of this kind, but may not have prevented them entirely:

- The 1998 cuts in unemployment insurance (UI) durations did not affect short (three month) benefit claims based on 12 months of contributions. Employers and employees have probably to some extent adapted to the employment conditions for benefit coverage. In 2011, the reduction of the minimum contribution requirement to nine months increased the incentive for temporary or seasonal work with a three-month break.
- The current minimum income level is seen as inadequate (Stropnik, 2013). From 1993 to 2001, the guaranteed minimum income level (social assistance) was very low and social assistance beneficiaries were not really pulled out of poverty. Following amendments to the Social Assistance and Services Act 2001, minimum income levels were gradually increased. From 2001 to 2005 the caseload more than tripled despite relatively strong economic conditions. In 2006 time-limited unemployment assistance paid as an extension to UI benefits was replaced by financial social assistance, which itself was normally time-limited (OECD, 2009a). A reform in 2007 which increased behavioural obligations, and a reform in 2012 changing the asset tests, were followed by short-term falls in the caseload, but by 2015 the total number of recipients was again slightly higher than in 2005. Social assistance is rarely now described as temporary, and the share of long-term claims in the total has increased, while also some very-long-term unemployed are covered by partial disability insurance benefits rather than social assistance.

Trade-offs and feasibility of policy measures

As discussed below, quantitative estimates for the impact of the minimum wage hike (IMAD, 2012; Laporšek et al., 2015) suggest it is at least partly responsible for the fall in employment. In this way, the minimum wage could be a factor increasing long-term unemployment among low-productivity workers. But it may also motivate the use of non-standard contracts, which increases short-term unemployment. In principle, activation measures, raising worker motivation and productivity, could counteract the increase in long-term unemployment and stricter regulation of non-standard contracts could counteract the increase in short-term unemployment, restoring full employment at the new higher minimum wage. However, policy advisers need to assess the operational and political feasibility of different measures and advise politicians and the public about the trade-offs. For example, strict regulation of all fixed-term contracts is a blunt instrument if the problem it tackles is specific to low-wage workers.

The minimum wage increase

The minimum wage was arguably high before the 2010 increase: OECD (2009b) argued that "Although the minimum wage has declined relative to the average wage in recent years, it is still fairly high by OECD standards. The ratio of the minimum wage to the average wage should not increase and preferably be further reduced in order to improve the employment prospects of the low-skilled young workers". However, early in 2010 it was decided to increase the minimum wage by 23% by 2012 at the latest, with also an indexation mechanism. Most of the increase was in place by 2011, with further 5% increase from 2011 to 2013 while average earnings hardly changed, but since 2013 average earnings have increased marginally faster.

The impact of the minimum wage on the structure of earnings

The number of minimum wage recipients increased from about 20 000 in the years 2005 to 2009 to about 45 000 by mid-2010 and further to 50 000 in 2013, but fell back to 37 000 by September 2015. The number of minimum-wage workers in the public sector increased from near zero in 2009 to 8 600 in 2015, while the number in the private sector had fallen back to about 28 000 (Ignjatović and Mrčela, 2015) and data for March 2016 show a further decrease to 23 000, which is not much higher than in 2009. The decrease may reflect slight increases in average earnings relative to the minimum wage since 2013, or statistical quirks given that minimum wage status is reported by employers and legislation does not exactly define which allowances and bonuses should be included.

According to data from the Pension and Disability Insurance Institute of Slovenia, the minimum wage hike created a spike at the bottom of the wage distribution, with a large number of workers close to the new minimum wage level (Laporšek et al., 2015). However, employers are obliged to pay social insurance contributions corresponding to the legal monthly minimum wage. They could increase the base for social insurance contributions to the level of the minimum wage, or slightly above, by including more expenses and bonuses in the wage as observed by Ignjatović and Mrčela (2015), or by increasing the formal but reducing the informal part of the total wage as discussed below.

For large employers and their employees, collective agreements are implemented reliably, and following the increase in the minimum wage "In sectoral collective agreements of the private sector the lowest basic wage is determined according to nine different tariff classes ranging from the lowest I. simple work to the highest IX. extremely important and most demanding work. However, the first five or more tariff classes in many of these collective agreements are squeesed into one because the employer is not allowed to pay lower wages than the statutory minimum wage." (Kovačič, 2014).

For small firms, the impact may be quite different as compared with larger firms if they underreport income from sales and use the concealed income from sales to pay employees partly in cash. OECD (2004) notes evidence for under-declaration, citing an assessment that "envelope salaries" exist in practically all of the CEE countries, although sometimes only in particular sectors, and that this is the largest component of undeclared work in some countries. When the minimum wage is declared for tax purposes but true wages are higher, the authorities may increase the minimum wage not mainly for reasons of employment policy but in order to increase tax receipts, and the higher minimum wage may increase the employer and employee social security contribution payments with less impact on the true level of wages. Along these lines, Feldina and Polanec (2012) cite an official estimate that in Slovenia the informal economy was 8.3% of GDP in 2007 with the largest contribution coming from underreporting of output, and they estimate that job destruction caused by minimum wage hikes was lower in small sole proprietorships which tend to be more involved in informal economic activities. Small firms may also have greater flexibility for including expenses or making adjustments to allowances and bonuses, which are more difficult for large firms covered by collective agreements.

Employment impact of the minimum wage increase

Analysis by economists of the minimum wage increase was generally pessimistic:

- Lindič (2011), analysing a smaller minimum wage increase that took place early in 2008, using data up to December 2009, estimated that it had a negative effect on employment in real estate, renting and business activities, which was the industry sector with the highest share of minimum wage employees (over 6%) prior to the 2008 increase.
- OECD (2011) commented "Overall, the decision to increase the minimum wage… reveals how much more weight Slovenia's social consensus model places on equity considerations in wage determination than on efficiency. Indeed, the main argument raised to justify the hike in the minimum wage was to operate an adjustment with the cost of living... Now that Slovenia is a member of the euro area, the focus of the authorities and social partners will need to shift if Slovenia is to maintain its competiveness".
- IMAD (2012) predicted a negative employment impact from the increase in the minimum wage: "the significant increase in the minimum wage also contributed to job loss. In the short term around 5 000 persons are estimated to have lost work due to the higher minimum wage, and in the long term around 17 000." The latter figure corresponds to about 2.5% of dependent employment (1.2% of the population of working age).
- Laporšek et al. (2015) estimate that for a "sub-minimum" group of individuals (probably over 50 000) with wages below the new minimum at the time of its introduction, the probability of staying employed one year after the minimum wage increase was reduced – in a sense that arguably allows for a causal interpretation – by about 6%, with also some reduction for those earning slightly more. This finding is consistent with the Institute of Macroeconomic Analysis and Development's (IMAD) estimate for the short-run employment impact.
- Stoviček (2013), although not quantifying the impact, warned that "*...the minimum wage can even prove counterproductive if it is set so high that efficiency costs become large. While the minimum wage may increase the probability of working-poor households escaping poverty, it may also increase the probability of non-poor households entering poverty due to a loss in employment or a decline in hours worked. As the main reason for poverty is unemployment (45% of unemployed persons are at the risk of poverty in Slovenia), an excessive increase in the minimum wage, which aims to reduce in-work poverty but actually raises unemployment, may even contribute to the risk of poverty.*"

The employment rate for ages 15-64 fell by over five percentage points (about 8%) from 2008 to 2013 and recovered by nearly two percentage points from 2013 to 2015, leaving a net fall to 2015 of about 3.5 percentage points, the largest net fall after Denmark and four Eurozone crisis countries, Greece, Ireland, Portugal and Spain. With cyclical recovery some optimism has returned, but the outcomes remain consistent with the predictions of a (modest) negative impact.

Substitution towards non-standard forms of employment

A high minimum wage may provoke a shift away from regular full-time employment towards temporary or part-time employment, as employers comply with the minimum wage but take more care to pay only for the hours of work that they most need, or they shift to non-standard forms of employment which escape the minimum wage or lower labour costs in other ways (e.g. reduced social insurance contributions, other labour rights and restrictions on termination). For example:

- Among OECD countries with high minimum wage ratios over 20% of employment is temporary in the Netherlands; about 30% of part-time work is involuntary in Australia, 40% in France and 60% in Portugal (OECD Employment Database);
- In Poland, which had the highest minimum wage in terms of relative labour costs (according to Stoviček, 2013), 20.9% of workers in 2010 had civil law contracts not subject to the minimum wage or many of the regular social insurance contributions and worker rights (Clauwert and Schomann, 2013); in Chile and Turkey, with the highest ratios of the minimum wage relative to median earnings, 20% or 30% of dependent employment is informal (Jütting and Laiglesia, 2009; OECD, 2013).

In some cases, the authorities reduce employer costs for minimum-wage workers intentionally (e.g. exemptions from social insurance contributions for employers of young people or new hires of young unemployed are provided as a labour market measure). In other cases, the (unintended) artificial usage of contracts that offer reduced costs is tolerated to some extent, as arguably has been the case with student work in Slovenia.

Non-standard work

Non-standard forms of work include part-time work, temporary work (fixed-term contract work and temporary agency work – although Slovenia also has a specific legal status for student work some agency workers have a permanent contract), and self-employment, including "bogus" self-employment when an employee is paid through a contract for services. Several types of labour regulation and their enforcement, as well as the structure of non-wage labour costs, and entitlements to in-work and out-of-work benefits can influence the incidence of particular types of non-standard employment.

Active labour market policy needs to achieve placements primarily into regular work, which provides benefit coverage in the case of involuntary layoff and at the same time supports benefit sanctions in cases of voluntary quit. Other forms of work either are not covered by benefits, or if they are covered they are likely to pay benefits out of proportion to contributions:

- Benefits act as a subsidy to temporary contracting combined with short unemployment spells particularly because in the case of temporary contract employment, it is difficult to enforce conditionality. If a claimant could have got a new temporary (or a permanent) contract, but claimed benefit instead, this is de facto not documented and a sanction for voluntary quit is applicable in theory but not in practice. Also, jobseeker requirements are limited due to the principle that job search should be mainly independent in the initial phase of unemployment; and since inflows are high, the Employment Service of Slovenia lacks resources to intervene effectively in each case. Repeat temporary contracts, which allow UI to be combined with employment on a long-term basis subject to the defined contribution requirements, are difficult to control.
- Part-time work, by heads of household who need full-time work to achieve a minimum income level, involves similar problems: if the part-time earnings are not deducted from benefits, part-time status is subsidised, and in theory the PES can oblige part-time workers to take a full-time job but in practice this is difficult.
- For the self-employed and informal workers, the PES lacks reliable short-term information even about employment status and earnings, and in most countries the PES provides basic information services but no cash benefits. Self-employed workers with low earnings are often not entitled to assistance benefits until they have closed their business completely.

Except for informal work, most types of non-standard work have some real business and labour market function and fit the preferences of certain workers, so an effective labour market policy aims to keep the incidence of non-standard work at a reasonable level rather than eliminate it completely. This implies offering regular work as the main solution for workers who are not making an adequate income from temporary work, part-time work or self-employment.

Where the incidence of non-standard work is low, a large proportion of vacancies may still be for temporary jobs, but unemployed workers should most typically get work experience through several short contracts and after some time take a permanent and stable job. Where the incidence of temporary work is high, many unemployed workers are rotating in and out of temporary contracts for years before starting a permanent job: the temporary contracts can no longer be seen as useful work experience, the unemployment is anticipated and not exactly involuntary, and the labour market settles into a bad equilibrium with high unemployment, high benefit costs and ineffective activation measures.

A better equilibrium can be promoted partly by direct activation measures but also by some other measures that promote regular employment contracts – regulating non-standard contracts and taxing their identified costs (e.g. costs for the benefit system), and ensuring that regular contracts are competitive for employers - not giving insiders too-high minimum wages or employment protection. Arguably labour market policy in the Nordic countries was most successful in terms of keeping unemployment low when they combined relatively strict employment protection with national-level wage agreements: wage agreements kept their industries competitive, maintaining employer demand for labour despite the potential costs of retaining less-productive workers implied by employment protection. However, consensus around wage agreements is not always achievable at national level, and when national agreements exist they can become difficult to enforce at local level.

Student work

Student work was introduced in Slovenia in 1959 and could be described as a form of temporary agency work where there are three parties: students and pupils as workers, employers, and agencies (student services) which act as mediators between students and employers. A student must be referred by a student service before the start of work. In this relationship, student services receive a large concession fee (formerly 14%, increased to 25% in June 2012), the student only needs proof of student status, and employers do not have to go through lengthy procedures to hire or fire workers. Until recently neither students nor their employers had to pay pension, health or other social insurance contributions, making student workers much cheaper than regular full-time workers (Ignjatović and Mrčela, 2015; Suklan and Golob, 2015; Šušteršič et al., 2010)

Temporary employment in Slovenia for 15-24-year-olds mainly takes the form of student work, although for 25-29-year-olds it more often takes the form of fixed-term contract work (Kajzer, 2013; Ignjatović and Mrčela, 2015). In 2013 the share of temporary employment in total employment for young people aged 15-24 stood at 73.2%, the highest incidence in the EU (IMAD, 2014). For comparison, the incidence of temporary contracts among the total population is only marginally higher in Slovenia than the OECD average (see below).

In 2008, student services issued 1 180 000 receipts for 84 258 616 hours of work: this is equivalent to about 5% of employment on a full-time equivalent basis, consistent with it being the main employment status for 10% or 15% of workers if the work is part-time. "Second, these jobs do not guarantee basic social security rights, and are subject to very low taxation (14%). Third, a precondition for eligibility is to be enrolled as a student in university, de facto prolonging the time spent in undergraduate studies (the average peaked at 6.8 years). Fourth, given the limited number of universities, student jobs create regional employment disparities. Fifth, employers who employ students have an unfair advantage over firms that do not. Finally, student services get a huge slice of the cake (37.5% of the concession fees; some EUR 15 million) and their spending record is not spotless…" (Guardiancich, 2012). Students have many benefits, including state-funded tuition fee waivers for over 80% of students, subsidies for living expenses (meals, accommodation, transportation and cultural activities), state scholarships and the flexibility of student work. The in-study benefits that are not tied to progress of studies and the shortage of workplaces for youth attract "fake students", who would not normally go into tertiary education, estimated to be as high as one third of tertiary students (Šušteršič et al., 2010; Eurydice, 2011).

Against the background described above, a major reform of student work was attempted with the 2010 Mini-Jobs Act, which restricted the new mini-jobs to students, the unemployed (who inform the employment service of their activities, which can earn them up to EUR 200 gross per month), the retired and other inactive persons, capped mini-job work at 60 hours per month for a given individual, limited total hours of mini-job work for larger employers, and required the payment of social security contributions. However, the Student Organization of Slovenia (ŠOS) and ZSSS collected votes for a referendum, in which this law was defeated.

In autumn 2014, student work was partly regulated in the framework of additional austerity measures and of the balancing of the 2015 state budget by amendments to the Public Finance Balance Act. According to the new regulation, implemented on 1 February 2015, and following the principle that "any work counts", social security contributions are paid on student work; this has eliminated the major characteristic that made it the most precarious form of temporary and occasional work. Student work is now taken into account in the calculation of the pension and disability insurance period: the student is credited one month of insurance period for each 0.6 Slovenian average wage in earnings from student work. As well as an 18% concession fee on student work, employers have to pay 8.85% in pension contributions and 6.36% in healthcare insurance contributions, and students will have to make a 15.15% contribution to the pension system. The student minimum hourly wage rate (EUR 4.50 or EUR 3.80 net of pension insurance) is about 10% below the regular minimum wage (Stropnik, 2015).

According to the labour force survey, the share of student work in total employment increased continuously from 0.9% in 2000 to 3.8% in 2009 and 2010 before falling to 2.5% in 2013, due probably to the recession and the 2012 increase in the concession fee. The number of persons performing student work according to the labour force survey declined from 37 000 in 2009 and 2010 to 23 000 in 2013, but recovered to 31 000 in 2015, possibly due to supply-side factors (the minimum wage for student workers has increased, and the pension reform creates an incentive for students to make pension contributions) and employer demand factors (substitution away from fixed-term contract employment). However, students are working fewer hours than before, due perhaps to the increase in employer cost and more-effective limitation to occasional and temporary work (Ignjatović and Mrčela, 2015).

Fixed-term contract work

In Slovenia in 2015, according to the national labour force survey, 12.8% of employees had a fixed-term contract. Including other contractual situations, 17.8% of employees had a contract of limited duration, above the European average of 14.2% (http://appsso.eurostat.ec.europa.eu/nui/show.do?dataset=lfsa_etpga). According to unpublished administrative statistics, inflows to registered unemployment with an unemployment insurance (UI) claim based on expiry of a fixed-term contract have greatly increased since the 2000s, from around 14 000 in 2005 and 11 000 in 2006-08, to 15 000 annually in 2009-11, 21 000 in 2012 and 23 000 in 2015. Total inflows to registered unemployment in 2015 were about the same as in 2005, so these UI claims have also increased sharply as a share of total inflows. This is likely to reflect in some combination employer response to the increased minimum wage and regulatory changes, learning effects (adaptation of contracting behaviour to the UI contribution requirements), and the relaxation of contribution conditions for unemployment benefit entitlement in response to the recession. From 2011, only nine months of employment in the last 24 months are required for a repeat claim. If a worker repeatedly claims three months of benefit with a replacement rate of 80% after nine months of work, the UI payments total about 27% (=80%/3) of the wage payments, which may be seen as a relatively large public subsidy.

Slovenia's April 2013 labour market reform increased regulation and taxation of fixed-term contracts and slightly reduced them for permanent contracts (Box 2.1). In the first year after these changes, rates of transition into permanent jobs from fixed-term contracts and unemployment increased. However, the net and longer-term impact remains uncertain, and the use of several forms of non-standard work increased again in 2015.

Box 2.1 The 2013 labour market reform

Slovenia's revised Employment Relationships Act of March 2013 restricted the use of fixed-term contracts by requiring severance payments upon contract termination, increasing the employer UI contribution rate for fixed-term contracts (although the increase was small, from 0.06% of earnings to 0.30%), and limiting the maximum duration of fixed-term contracts for the same work position to two years. At the same time, for permanent contract notices and severance pay requirements for layoffs were eased, and employers were exempted from UI contributions for the first two years.

A Working Group for Monitoring the Effects of Labour Market Legislation reported in 2014 that in the short term the legislative changes had contributed to achieving the stated goals of reducing labour market segmentation and increasing flexibility, to a limited extent. The changes stimulated the employment of younger workers (those under 30 years) on indefinite contracts, but not older workers (those over 55 years). Labour market flows – from employment to unemployment, and vice versa – increased, consistent with increased flexibility. However, the report cautions that the decrease in the share of employment via fixed-term contracts – one of the stated goals of the reforms – may have come at the expense of an increase in employment via alternative forms of flexible employment: student work and contracting via sole proprietorships.

In terms of specific suggestions for future reforms, the Working Group (2014) report recommends:

- Analysing how to improve the inclusion of displaced workers in employment services during their notice periods (a new stipulation in the Labour Code, which gave workers on notice the right to use employment services, was little used).
- Examining measures that could increase participation in the newly-instituted work schemes for retired workers, including the possibility of mentoring programmes that link retirees and younger workers.
- Examining a unified framework of financial incentives for the employment of younger and older unemployed workers (social contribution waivers and subsidies), re-evaluating the existing social contribution waivers for older workers which are not targeted at the unemployed.
- Examining the tax benefits of alternative forms of work commonly utilised by employers, e.g. student work and contracting with sole proprietors.

A Bank of Slovenia survey following the enactment of the 2013 reforms found that their perceived effects amongst employers were relatively small (Schnattinger et al, 2015). In an ad-hoc survey of 1 285 firms, only 14% reported that the reforms had affected their hiring or firing policies. For those that were affected, the intended decrease in labour market segmentation seems to have been achieved. The survey also queried firms regarding obstacles to hiring workers on permanent contracts. Amongst successful firms which had increased employment in recent years, the most important factors cited were i) taxation of labour and ii) uncertain macroeconomic conditions, followed by iii) a lack of suitably skilled workers and iv) the inability to unilaterally lower wages in the event of shocks (Jemec and Vodopivec, 2016). High firing costs and hiring costs were next in terms of relevance, out of a total of ten possible factors. Less than one tenth of firms reported that they had to resort to worker dismissals in response to the increase in the minimum wage, but almost a quarter of firms reported that they hired fewer workers.

The revised Act also introduced indefinite-term employment with temporary work agencies, limiting the number of temporary agency workers to 25% of the final user's total employment but excluding workers employed by the agencies from the quota (Ticar, 2014). This is seen as a decrease in restrictions on the use of temporary work agencies. The 2013 labour market reform reduced the OECD index of the strictness of employment protection legislation against individual dismissals from 2.39 to 1.99 and it also reduced the index for temporary contracts from 2.50 to 2.13, because the decrease in restrictions on the use of temporary work agencies (particularly in cases where the workers are employed by the agency under a permanent contract) outweighed the increased restrictiveness on fixed-term contracts. These two index values are now both close to an unweighted OECD average (Vodopivec at al., 2016).

Temporary work agency work

Ignjatović and Mrčela (2015) report that according to administrative reports the number of workers provided by agencies increased from 9 898 in 2009 to 15 198 in 2013. These annual data overstate the numbers employed in a given month, and Lukic (2016) reports that the number of people employed by or through temporary work agencies (TWA) increased from 6 819 in October 2013 to 14 937 in October 2015, an increase roughly from 1% of dependent employment to 2%.

Ignjatović and Mrčela (2015) state that the temporary worker is insured against all labour risks (unemployment, health, pension, etc.) and the "temporary worker's rights also include the right to use the benefits that the client company provides to its own workers". The TWA may pay meal and travel allowances based on the worker's travel to the client company place of work.

Self-employment

The share of self-employment in total employment increased from 9.9% in 2008 to 12.6% in 2011 (Lukic, 2016), partly due to the sharp fall in dependent employment. However, there was also a fall in self-employment incomes which according to Ignjatović and Mrčela (2015) corresponds with the increased activity of the Employment Service of Slovenia offering a subsidy (a grant of EUR 4 500 if the person remains self-employed for at least two years) for becoming self-employed. Due to concerns about the impact on poverty this subsidy was abolished in 2014. Lukic (2016) reports a further slight increase in self-employment in 2014.

The use of civil law contracts (contracts for service) is prohibited if the relationship between the employer and the independent contractor has elements of an employment relationship. The number of violations of this sort detected by the labour inspectorate increased in the 2010s reaching 237 in 2014, but this may reflect increased enforcement activity, and "the reference on the growing trend and share of bogus self-employment in the Slovenian labour market is only anecdotal" (Ignjatović and Mrčela, 2015). The 2013 Employment Relationships Act extended employment protection rights to sole proprietors whose revenues at a single client exceed 80% of their total.

Undeclared work

Despite a generally high quality of public governance, Slovene literature identifies a significant incidence of grey economy work. Indeed the Social Contract for the 2015-16 period (ESC, 2014) refers to "The crisis of values in Slovenian society, which manifests itself disrespect for laws and regulations, corruption, undue accumulation of wealth by individuals, growing inequalities, a systematic destruction of enterprises, the transferring of cash to tax havens, and the evasion of tax and social security contributions".

Feldina and Polanec (2012) note that the official estimate for the share of informal economy in Slovenia, 8.3% of GDP in 2007, is significantly higher than the corresponding values for established market economies (e.g. 6.5% in neighbouring Austria in 2004) and lower than the corresponding values for the majority of transition economies (e.g., 15.3% in Hungary in 2004; 9.5% in Estonia in 2000).

Only a fraction of the informal economy in financial terms represents undeclared work, but undeclared work even with low earnings becomes costly when by supplementing benefits it increases replacement rates to around 100%, increasing the incentive for repeat UI claims and long-term social assistance benefit claims. Although undeclared work has probably declined in at least some sectors of the economy since the 1990s, undeclared work by social assistance recipients may have become a more significant issue as assistance benefits are no longer conditional on the contribution record or effectively time-limited. Ignjatović and Mrčela (2015) note that "strong dependence on the activity status and the high at risk-of-poverty rate for unemployed people are somewhat alleviated by the strong involvement of household/family/relatives assistance in different activities (food, clothes, care) and the relatively high share of undeclared work in local communities". Agencies delivering activation programmes encounter reluctance to take work which they attribute primarily to undeclared work.

Slovenia is perhaps an example of good practice in terms of tackling undeclared work, since information systems allow linking of administrative records to detect inconsistencies, and many measures have been introduced over the years:

- A taper was introduced in the 1990s because the difference between low wages and the minimum income has acted as a strong disincentive to look for work. Tapers are also considered an incentive for social assistance beneficiaries to try to find work in the formal economy. This is particularly important in countries with a relatively large grey economy. (Stropnik, 2013a).
- Unions supported more severe sanctions for the informal economy, but had some reservations regarding the Prevention of Work and Hiring Labour in Informal Economy Act (2011), which contributed to its rejection in a referendum … This led analysts to conclude that this reflects "their short-term interests, neglecting possible medium- and long-term positive consequences for employment and the employed". (Stropnik, 2013a).
- The recently-enacted Prevention of Undeclared Work and Employment Act (Official Gazette of the Republic of Slovenia, No. 32/2014) and the new Labour Inspection Act (Official Gazette of the Republic of Slovenia, No.19/2014) tighten the state's relationship towards offenders in the labour market. "*Slovenia has been facing problems of high unemployment and low law enforcement for quite some time. Labour rights violations and, equally, unemployment rates increased during the evolution of the crisis. Therefore, the state wanted to liberalise labour legislation on one and improve its enforcement on the other hand.*" (Ticar, 2014).
- A "personal supplementary work" voucher, which costs EUR 9 per months, was introduced in 2015. The voucher should be purchased for or by individuals who work as domestic helpers, and individuals who produce art and craft products or harvest and sell forest fruits and herbs. Their annual personal income from personal supplementary work may not exceed two average monthly wages for the preceding year. Individuals must be registered with the relevant national agency and are under these circumstances insured for work injury and occupational disease, and recognised for entitlement to pension and disability insurance.
- From 2016, cash transactions in the economy are more strictly controlled through a requirement to use fiscal cash registers, which is expected to increase VAT income by EUR 70 million per year (Vidmar, 2015).

Tax and social insurance contribution rates

In Slovenia, total tax revenue since 2011 has been about 37% of GDP, higher than in the Czech Republic, Slovak Republic and Poland but lower than in several other European countries. Social security contribution revenues are relatively high, representing about 15% of GDP and 40% of total tax revenue (among the highest levels, together with the Czech Republic, Slovak Republic, Poland and several other European countries).

However, unemployment insurance (UI) contribution rates are low at 0.14% of salary for the employer and 0.06% for the employee. With a combined contribution rate of 0.2%, UI contributions covered less than 25% of expenditure in the 2000s and only about 8% in 2011-13. From 2011-13, UI expenditure totalled about 0.8% of GDP and social assistance and disability benefit payments to the registered unemployed were probably about the same amount. By 2015, UI claims had fallen, but the number of registered unemployed on other benefits had increased.

Many other countries partly fund UI benefits through general taxation and this is not necessarily problematic. A principle that UI benefits should be wholly funded from contributions, at least on average over the cycle, arguably has some symbolic or ideological impact on system management, but it can be negative (e.g. when workers think that the contributions "entitle" them to benefits without conditionality) or positive (e.g. when areas of unwarranted cost growth attract attention, and are intensively analysed and debated). If low UI contribution rates in Slovenia are concealing the true cost of the benefits from stakeholders, but nevertheless promoting an entitlement mentality, reform is desirable. Contribution rates could be raised to cover costs while also emphasising some version of a principle stated in the Swiss unemployment insurance law (and applied by courts, when assessing appeals against benefit sanctions). "The insurance benefit claimant must, with the assistance of the competent employment office, undertake everything that can reasonably be expected of him to prevent unemployment or shorten it". (www.admin.ch/opc/fr/classified-compilation/19820159/, Article 17).

In Slovenia, revenue from income taxes as a percentage of GDP is below the OECD average, but about the same level as in Visegrad countries. Revenue from property taxes is particularly low, 0.6% of GDP in 2013 whereas the OECD average is 1.9% (OECD, 2015). Property tax reform should be pursued as one measure that could slightly shift the tax burden away from labour.

Seniority allowances

Older-worker employment rates tend to be high in countries with flexible labour markets, where workers find it easier to change jobs and average earnings peak in middle age and fall for the 55-59 and 60-64 age groups. Against this background, seniority allowances, which increase indefinitely with years employed, are a likely cause of low older-worker employment rates in Slovenia.

Strategies encouraging firms to retain incumbent older workers encounter employer resistance on labour cost grounds. Some policy measures focus on this cost issue. For example, in Japan an older worker's unemployment benefit entitlement can be paid to the firm as a subsidy for retaining them past the company standard retirement age; in Korea, the government promotes a "wage peak" system where wages can decline after age 55; in the 2000s, the Netherlands reduced employer social security contributions for workers hired after age 50, or retained by same employer after age 55.

The Employment Relationships Act 2013 specifies that "The amount of the seniority bonus shall be laid down in a branch collective agreement". Kump (2008) reported that the allowance was 0.5% of basic salary for each year of service, and OECD (2009a) reported that it was previously mandated at a minimum 0.5% per year of service. This percentage still applies in most private sector agreements, although the public sector agreement now specifies 0.33% for each completed year of service (www.mp.gov.si/fileadmin/mp.gov.si/pageuploads/mp.gov.si/zakonodaja/angleski_prevodi_zakonov/Collective_Agreement_070311.doc). Vodopivec (2014) finds that in 2001 workers aged over 50 enjoyed a 18% wage premium, reflecting mandated seniority pay, but their relative marginal productivity had fallen since 1994, and was no longer higher than for younger workers. He concludes that mandated seniority pay may play an important role in hindering the employability of older workers in Slovenia.

New hires are entitled to a seniority allowance based on their previous years employed (which are documented from pension contribution records or similar) at the rate defined in their new employer's collective agreement, so this bonus increases the employer cost of a new hire of an older worker relative to a younger worker. Employer reluctance to hire older workers may lock them into their current job even when they are dissatisfied with it. In a 2011 survey, in Slovenia 46% of workers strongly agreed "I am satisfied with my job" (EU average: 69%) and 72% strongly agreed that they "wish to retire as soon as possible" (EU average: 43%). Older workers with tertiary education or higher were more often satisfied with their job, but still relatively anxious to retire (Damjan et al., 2016).

In 2003, annual new hires of 55-64-year olds totalled only 2% of the stock of 55-64-year old workers, compared with an EU average of 5%, rising to about 8% in Denmark and the United Kingdom. By 2014 Slovenia's older-worker hiring rate had increased to 4%, closer to the European average of 6% (www.oecd.org/els/emp/OW2014.xlsx). This might reflect increased layoffs of older workers in the recession. At the same time, it might indicate that Slovenia's labour market is becoming less rigid. When the wage for new hires can be individually negotiated, any obligation to pay seniority allowances is not such a significant constraint. To facilitate retention in current jobs under collective agreements, seniority bonuses could be capped after a certain number of years, in line with private-sector practices for tenure-related pay bonuses in other countries.

High labour costs for older workers also increase the employer's incentive to dismiss them, at ages where extended unemployment benefit and related entitlements represent a route into early retirement. The employer needs to lay them off for incompetence, since if they quit they will not be eligible for benefits. This clearly happened in 2010 and 2012 when inflows to unemployment peaked with 10% of inflows being due to "worker incompetence", and coinciding with peaks in first-time requests for calculations of pension eligibility (MDDSZ, 2016).

Travel and meal allowances

Along with the seniority allowance and an annual holiday bonus, meal and travel allowances are an important component of wages in Slovenia. Meal and travel allowances (unlike other allowances) are not taxable. Perhaps as a legacy from the operation in former Yugoslavia of co-operative enterprises in a quasi-market environment but under worker self-management, important features of these allowances in Slovenia are internationally exceptional:

- The allowances are paid to the employee directly with their regular salary, not as reimbursements of actual costs (e.g. travel passes), direct purchases (e.g. meal vouchers) by the employer, or as allowances that can be claimed by employees in their tax returns.
- The Employment Relationships Act requires employers to pay these allowances, whereas such employer payments in other EU countries are not required by law (Korpič-Horvat et al., 2009), although the rates of allowances can vary depending on the employer's collective agreement.

In some other OECD countries, the tax system provides quasi-fixed deductions that nominally represent work-related costs, but direct reimbursements of actual commuting costs by the employer or the regular costs of meals as a cash payment are treated largely as a taxable salary. In New Zealand, meal allowances are non-taxable only when the employee has worked two hours of overtime on the day of the payment (www2.deloitte.com/nz/en/pages/tax-alerts/articles/collective-agreements-and-employee-allowances.html). In the United Kingdom, employers may provide luncheon vouchers (spent only in restaurants) but the ceiling on tax relief available for them was not updated since 1948 and was abolished in 2013, i.e. employer funding of the vouchers is treated as taxable salary https://en.wikipedia.org/wiki/Meal_voucher; HMRC, 2012). In France, by contrast, employer contributions to the cost of meal tickets – which can be spent on fruit and vegetables and prepared meals, or in restaurants – are tax exempt up to EUR 5.37 per working day, not including holidays, or around EUR 1 200 per year.

As regards travel costs, the Italy, Spain and the United Kingdom provide no income tax reduction for commuting costs; in Ireland (only in the case of a travel pass paid by the employer) and the Netherlands public transport costs can be deductible; Germany provides an (employee) tax allowance of EUR 0.30/km of the simple distance between home and workplace regardless of the mode of transport or total distance, and also a reduced (15%) employer tax rate if an employer pays a travel allowance (up to this limit) to employees. Several more European countries allow deduction of car costs at a similar rate but only if public transport is not available (ECF, 2014; EY, 2015). In France, travel allowances for home-to-workplace commuting are tax exempt up to the value of 50% of the cost of cheapest method of public transport (only reimbursements of the cost of travel passes, not individual tickets), on up to EUR 200 per year of employer contributions to petrol costs (if the employee voluntarily uses their own car). The whole cost (based on distance and standard kilometric rates) of travel by car is tax exempt if the public transport option is unavailable: however, this excludes situations where home and workplace are in the same transport region (the Ile de France which covers more than half the area of Slovenia is counted as a single transport region: www.service-public.fr/particuliers/vosdroits/F19846), and cost savings from car-sharing are not allowed (www.urssaf.fr/portail/home/employeur/calculer-les-cotisations/les-elements-a-prendre-en-compte/les-frais-professionnels/les-frais-de-transport.html). Another factor is that several countries (e.g. Austria, France, Sweden) provide a fixed tax allowance or deduction for commuting costs or the overall costs of employment or they disallow itemised claims below a certain threshold, so that only taxpayers with lengthy or expensive commutes gain by itemising their commuting distance or costs (ECF, 2014).

Level of the allowances

In Slovenia, the consolidated Regulation on the tax treatment of reimbursements and other income from employment dating from 2006 and 2008 (www.pisrs.si/Pis.web/pregledPredpisa?id=URED4359) limits tax deductibility to:

- Meal allowance: EUR 6.12 for each day an employee is present at work for four hours or more.
- Travel allowance: if the habitual residence is more than 1 km from the place of employment, the cost of public transport; plus, if the closest station(s) for the public transport are more than 1 km from the habitual residence and/or the place of employment, EUR 0.18 for each full kilometre of travel to the closest stations. If the employee "for justified reasons" cannot use public transport, the allowance is EUR 0.18 per full kilometre according to normal minimum road links.

Since 2014, employers have to report the amount of exempt meal and travel allowances, along with their reports of withholding tax on salaries paid. Under the Employment Relationships Act, the allowances are to be paid under the conditions and in the manner determined by collective agreements, or the collective agreement for comparable activities. Court decisions have confirmed that the employer must reimburse the costs of adequate meals during working time.

In 1996, in a typical-case calculation travel allowance payments totalled 2.3% of employer labour costs, or 3.7% of gross earnings (therefore, a higher percentage of net earnings) for a secretary, a lower-paid employee (OECD, 1997). In 2010, travel allowance payments averaged EUR 834 per year, about 4.7% of average gross earnings or 5.8% of median gross earnings (SORS, 2013a). In 1996 typical-case calculations, travel allowances were determined as 60% of the cost of public city transport (OECD, 1997). According to 2012 information, transport allowances covered 60-80% of the cost of public transport, and some collective agreements fixed the allowances for commuting distances over 2 km by car at 8% of the cost of petrol; Guardiancich, 2012; Unilang, 2012). In the 1996 typical case calculations cited, meal allowances were five times the size of travel allowances but in the 2010 statistics they averaged nearly the same. Travel and meal allowances together may therefore amount to over 10% of net earnings on average and 15% for lower-paid workers, with considerable variation across individuals.

Meal and travel allowance payments are not strongly correlated with gross earnings by occupation or firm size. By level of educational attainment, annual payments increase in absolute terms but fall sharply as a proportion of gross earnings (EUR 1 306 or 11.6% of gross earnings at less-than-secondary level, EUR 1 723 or 6.3% of gross earnings at tertiary level). They therefore increase the employer cost of low paid work relative to gross earnings, but reduce the combined (employee plus employer) tax rate on low-paid work relative to labour cost.

Administration, incentives and interaction with the minimum wage

General incentives

The tax-exempt status of travel allowances in principle subsidises employees' use of their own time and other resources for commuting. In depressed regions it increases incomes and it may reduce unemployment, although it also reduces the incentive for businesses to locate in the depressed regions, rather than for example in Ljubljana. It is open to some tax evasion, where an employee lives not far from their workplace but is registered at a distant address (e.g. their parents' home). For employers who precisely comply with specified principles of calculation, as employees relocate and petrol prices change each month, travel allowances also involve administration costs.

Part-time work

Travel allowance payments might increase the employer cost of part-time (more precisely, part-day) work relative to full-time work, if two part-time workers replace one full-time worker and the employer pays a travel allowance to both workers. The incidence of part-time work in total dependent employment in Slovenia has increased from about 3.5% in 2000 to 7% in 2014, which is higher than in several other CEE countries, but remains far below the OECD average. The proportion of part-time work under a regular employment contract seems to be considerably lower than this, since about a third of all part-time work is student work (SORS, 2013b) for which meal and travel allowances are not paid.

Interactions with the minimum wage

The statistical concept of annual gross earnings in Slovenia does not include meal and travel allowances (SORS, 2013a). Average meal and travel allowances for a worker with less-than-secondary education in 2010 (EUR 1 306) were 14.5% of an annual gross minimum wage in 2011 (after the 2010 increase). These allowances are normally payable in addition to the minimum wage (although according to Ignjatović and Mrčela, 2015, there are "known cases where some employers also include various bonuses belonging to the worker from work…in the prescribed minimum wage").

Feldina and Polanec (2012) identify minimum-wage workers as those with a total annual gross wage within EUR 5 of the minimum, so that people who are paid a seniority or other allowance in addition to a basic wage at the minimum rate are by definition not minimum-wage workers. On this basis, the incidence of minimum-wage work is close to zero in firms with 30 or more employees, but it reaches 6% to 7% for sole proprietorships with 1-3 employees. Other studies (Schnattinger et al., 2015; Laporšek et al., 2015) allow more variation above the minimum, and therefore identify more people as minimum-wage workers, but they do not at all mention the treatment of allowances.

In the case of employees not covered by any collective agreement, paying some employees more as a regular wage and less as a seniority or meal allowance (or perhaps, other expense) may to some extent be legitimate. In the dispute over the 2015 Act Amending the Minimum Wage Act (which requires that bonuses for night shifts and work on Sundays and public holidays should be paid as compensation additional to the minimum wage), a "hidden agenda" for both employers and unions may be the prospect that the authorities will supervise and enforce other bonuses and allowances, whereas currently the *de facto* main requirement is payment of taxes on at least the minimum wage.

Making meal and travel allowances taxable, at the same time as incorporating them with other allowances into the minimum wage, would clarify social dialogue, limit possible associated tax evasion, and rebalance the incentives for long commutes. Short of this, the size of the allowances treated as tax-exempt might be further standardised. The 2012 Public Finance Balance Act (ZUJF) reduced the meal allowance in the public sector to EUR 3.52 (www.sloveniatimes.com/sweeping-changes-on-the-table), well below the current limit on tax deductibility (see above).

Statistical basis of the minimum wage increase legislated in 2010

The 2010 increase in the minimum wage was a response to the findings of a study which identified the minimum cost of living in Slovenia as EUR 562.02 per month (Stropnik et al., 2009; Stropnik, 2013a; Ignjatović and Mrčela, 2015). In 2009 the net minimum wage (about EUR 460 net per month) was only about 82% of the minimum costs of living, and it was also below the 2007 at-risk-of-poverty threshold (about EUR 495). "As a consequence of all this, and in order to maintain a work-incentive ratio between the minimum wage and the minimum income after a foreseen increase in social transfers, in March 2010 we witnessed the biggest increase in the minimum wage in Slovenia ever (by 23%), to EUR 734 gross (Minimum Wage Act 2010), or EUR 562 net". More specifically, in negotiations between the social partners, the net minimum wage of EUR 562.07 was set at the minimum cost of living estimated from the spending of the 20% of non-agricultural households with the lowest incomes (Stropnik, 2013b).

An expenditure survey would not directly identify the items of expenditure covered by meal and travel allowances (a worker's itemised travel expenses can legitimately be far different from their travel allowance, e.g. if they car-share or bike). Workers with less than secondary education in 2010 received meal and travel allowances averaging EUR 109 per month from their employer (SORS, 2013a), which suggests that minimum cost of living, net of these allowances when they are paid, would have been around EUR 453 per month, which was covered by the net minimum wage even before the increase.

International comparisons and the at-risk-of-poverty rate

When wage statistics do not include meal and travel allowances but labour costs do include these allowances the ratio of the minimum to the average wage in labour costs terms will exceed the ratio in gross earnings terms (assuming that the allowances do not vary strongly with the wage).

At the same time, ratios between the minimum wage and household incomes will be understated, since bonuses and allowances are recorded as income in household income statistics. Inconsistent treatment of these allowances between the numerator and denominator of various minimum wage ratios can account for extreme variations in Slovenia's position in international comparisons of the minimum wage. Stovičet (2013) reports that the ratio of minimum wage to average earnings in 2011 was 0.49 in terms of gross earnings, slightly higher than in any other EU country, and 0.52 in terms of labour costs, much higher than in any other EU country (the next-highest ratio was 0.44 in Poland). Stovičet (2013) also reports that the ratio of the net income of the minimum wage-worker to the at-risk-of-poverty threshold was 0.98, the fourth-lowest ratio among the 18 EU countries. Stovičet attributes the difference to Slovenia's relatively-equal income distribution (which reduces the ratio of average to median incomes), but this factor could only explain a fraction of the difference: Slovenia's ratio is about 30% above the EU average in labour cost terms and 10% below the EU average relative to the at-risk-of-poverty level. Two further factors likely to be involved are:

- Family (child) allowances in Slovenia are relatively high, which reduces the disposable income of a single-person minimum-wage household relative to (equivalised) median disposable income.

- In several other countries with a relatively-high minimum wage, labour costs for a minimum-wage worker are reduced by subsidies (e.g. reductions in employer social security contribution rates target on minimum-wage workers).

However, the most important factor is likely to be that the at-risk-of-poverty threshold is calculated as 60% of national median equivalised disposable income after social transfers including meal and travel allowances, whereas the calculated net income of the minimum-wage worker excludes these allowances. Reworking Stoviček's estimates to include average allowances, the net income of a minimum wage worker in 2011 may have been nearly 1.2 times the at-risk-of-poverty level, the third-highest ratio in the EU (after the Netherlands and the United Kingdom) or not much lower.

Support for education and training

Education and training are key determinants of productivity and competitiveness at the national and individual levels. They are a key factor increasing individual productivity. Investment in worker skills can help companies to adapt to high labour costs. At the national level, GDP per hour worked only recovered to its 2008 level in 2015, and even partial restoration of previous growth rates would do much to resolve macroeconomic problems. Since 2006, the Slovene Human Resources Development and Scholarship Fund (HRDSF) has become the central public institution promoting youth education and skills, workplace skills development and human resources management at company level.

Scholarships

In 2006 the HRDSF took over the programmes of the former Science and Education Foundation, a public fund established by the Slovene Government in July 2001. Through the HRDSF, Slovenia provides the resources for the development and mobility of its intellectual capital, funding studies by Slovenes abroad and by foreigners in Slovenia, and supporting the international mobility of students and researchers from and to Slovenia (www.culture.si/en/Slovene_Human_Resources_Development_and_Scholarship_Fund). The scholarships include funding for the best students in the country to study at foreign universities, with an obligation to return to the country and be employed in Slovenia for at least as many years they have received scholarship support. Over 2008-14 HRDSF disbursed over EUR 100 million in scholarships for tertiary and post-graduate education and over EUR 10 million for co-financing of company scholarships. The European Social Fund (ESF) co-funds further company scholarships through Single regional scholarship schemes implemented by regional development agencies (RDAs) (EUR 14.7 million) (HRDSF, 2015).

In the 2015-19 period, MDDSZ and the ESF will provide up to EUR 1.2 million to fund up to 1 000 scholarships of EUR 100 per month for youths training for undersubscribed professions. Priority areas with an anticipated gap between labour demand and labour supply related to the retirement of qualified workers include handcraft, computer science, mechanical engineering, electrical engineering, food processing, construction, forestry, wood processing, chemical technologies and services (hotel management, catering and chimney sweeping). The shortage fields will be determined yearly by the responsible ministry in co-operation with the social partners and youth representatives (www.cedefop.europa.eu/en/news-and-press/news/slovenia-scholarships-shortage-occupations).

European Social Fund and national funding and programmes

Of the ESF 2007-13 planned funding for Slovenia (EUR 756 million), more than 20% was allocated to the human resource development and lifelong learning function (EUR 165 million). It may be noted that 2007-2013 funding supported expenditure into 2014 and 2015. Of the 2007-13 funding mediated by MDDSZ (EUR 404 million), the largest share was implemented by the Employment Service of Slovenia. By this route, the ESF provided about half (or more, in some years) of the total funding for ALMPs; the balance has varied significantly by year, with mainly government funding of job-creation measures and ESF funding of other measures (see Chapter 4).

In the coming years, ESF funding will be somewhat lower. The MDDSZ 2014-20 Operational Programme totals over EUR 600 million EUR for employment, supporting transnational labour mobility, social inclusion and the fight against poverty. This includes about EUR 180 million from the ESF and EUR 56 million from the European Regional Development Fund (ERDF). The Employment Service of Slovenia implements programmes targeted at the unemployed and the more-recent European Youth Employment Initiative (EUR 9.2 million for 2014-20, with matching ESF funding), while HRDSF has the key role in implementing programmes targeted at employed persons and young people in school.

HRDSF non-scholarship programmes

In addition to its disbursements for university scholarships, over the period 2008-15 the HRDSF ran eight human resources development programmes. The earliest and largest HRDSF programmes in terms of ESF funding were Practical Training with Work (with EUR17.7 million disbursed to end 2014), Qualification and Training of Employees (company training, EUR 11.0 million), and Reducing the Education Deficit (completion of secondary education and the retraining of adults, EUR 9.9 million). Programmes implemented from 2010 or later include Diversifying the School Programmes (EUR 3.7 million), Lifelong Career Guidance for Companies and Employees (EUR 3.5 million), Competence Centres for Human Resources (EUR 5.6 million), and Youth Mentorship, for a total of over EUR 70 million of ESF funding from 2007 or 2008 to end 2014. The investment in human resources managed by the HRDSF in these areas exceeded EUR 80 million in 2015, reflecting the build-up of programmes and co-funding.

Among the 2007-15 ESF-funded programmes, Practical Training with Work, where vocational and technical school children implement projects on employer premises, cost about EUR 700 per participant on average and the Qualification and Training of Employees cost about EUR 300 per participant.

HRDSF programme content and implementation

The number of grant applications approved by the HRDSF per programme ranged from over 10 000 for Practical Training with Work, applicants being mainly small employers offering places to children in vocational education, to 19 for the Competence Centres for Human Resources, which were industry centres promoting collaboration between companies by exchanging expertise, defining competences and assisting companies with the design and organisation of their specific training courses. Lifelong Career Guidance for Companies and Employees, with 370 approved applications, provided support at company level to human resources departments to engage with employees and invest in their development. Companies were encouraged to open up opportunities and set the right challenges for staff, and measures delivered included profiling, career plans, training in personal and career development and "soft" skills.

The first and largest of the employee development programmes, Qualification and Training of Employees, provides co-financing for companies to set up training courses with more employees participating longer-term than would normally be the case. The content of training may vary widely, e.g. emotional intelligence, building relationships and management of stress for sales workers; or the management and retrieval of documentation, for workers manufacturing technical equipment. This programme from 2011 was called the Training and Education Programme (UIZ 2011), which started with two calls for applications for company training of all employees, but narrowed the third call down to the co-financing of training for employees aged 50 or older, women who completed only primary school education and the disabled. Targeted measures to foster employability and job mobility contribute, in Slovenia as in other countries, to ongoing increases in older-worker employment rates.

The 2013-15 Youth Mentorship programme subsidised the hiring of 464 young workers, usually as their first job, to work with a skilled mentor for 6-12 months. At end 2015, 93% of the young workers were still employed. High cost, averaging EUR 6 700 per mentee participant (based on expenditure to end 2015), limited the participant numbers. A key objective of this programme was "the effective transfers of "secrets" or specific knowledge between employees… [b]y transferring knowledge internally, a company preserves, captures, improves and uses all of the available knowledge in order to achieve progress in terms of competitiveness and growth" (HRDSF, 2015).

Key findings and recommendations

Slovenia maintained effective social partnership arrangements through its gentle post-socialist transition and a period of national focus on the goal of EU and Euro Area membership in 2004 and 2007. However, the recession from 2009 was deep and cast a long shadow, exacerbated by structural problems that had not been fully addressed, the 2010 minimum wage hike, and social and political conflict over this change, employment regulation, and reforms to tackle growing pressures on the welfare state. Necessary reforms of employment regulation and pensions were subsequently implemented, and some labour market recovery is now under way. The minimum wage, high in international comparison, has probably led to some job loss and employer preference for non-standard forms of work, which avoid the potential cost of regular permanent contracts. Investments in skills, raising productivity, are essential to maintain cost competitiveness. As social assistance has become more like a long-term unemployment benefit, it needs to be managed appropriately. Other structural challenges persist, at least partly, calling for further reform. The rest of the report looks in depth at reform needs and possible policy solutions in relation to Slovenia's activation policy.

References

Banerjee, B., M. Vodopivec and U. Sila (2013), "Wage setting in Slovenia: interpretation of the Wage Dynamics Network (WDN) survey findings in an institutional and macroeconomic context", *IZA Journal of European Labor Studies*, 2013, Vol. 2, No. 9, http://izajoels.iza.org.

Bank of Slovenia (2016a), "Economics and Financial Developments", January, https://www.bsi.si/iskalniki/reports.asp?MapaId=1730.

Bank of Slovenia (2016b), "Economics and Financial Developments", April, https://www.bsi.si/iskalniki/reports.asp?MapaId=1730.

Bohle, D. and B. Greskovits (2007), "Neoliberalism, embedded neoliberalism and neocorporatism: Towards transnational capitalism in Central Eastern Europe", *West European Politics*, Vol. 30, No. 3, pp. 433-466.

Clauwaert, S. and I. Schömann (2013b), *The Crisis and National Labour Law Reforms: A Mapping Exercise. Country Report: Slovenia*, www.etui.org/Publications2/Working-Papers/The-crisis-and-national-labour-law-reforms-a-mapping-exercise.

Damjan, K. et al. (2016), "Active and Healthy Ageing for Active and Healthy Old Age: WP3 analytical report of the AHA.SI project", Institute for Economic Research, Ljubljana, www.staranje.si/sites/www.staranje.si/files/upload/images/analytical_report.pdf.

Dolenc, P., S. Laporšek, V. Špruk, Matija Vodopivec, Milan Vodopivec, B. Zupančič (2012), "Empirical Analysis of the Effects of the Labor Market Regulation Act", paper presented at the 22nd Statistical Days, Radenci, Slovenia, November, www.stat.si/StatisticniDnevi/Docs/Radenci%202012/prispevki/Dolenc%20-%20ZUTD.pdf.

ECF – European Cyclists' Federation (2014), "Commuting: Who pays the bill? Overview of fiscal regimes for commuting in Europe and recommendations for establishing a level playing-field", www.eltis.org/sites/eltis/files/trainingmaterials/141117-commuting-who-pays-the-bill_2.pdf.

ESC – Economic and Social Council (2014), *Social Contract for the 2015-2016 Period*, www.ess.si/ess/ess-eng.nsf/economic-and-social-council/social-agreement-for-the-period-2015-2016.

Eurydice (2011), "Student Fees and Support", Chapter 3 in: *Modernisation of Higher Education in Europe 2011: Funding and the Social Dimension*, http://eacea.ec.europa.eu/education/eurydice/documents/thematic_reports/131en.pdf.

EY – Ernst and Young (2015), "Response to consultation on tax treatment of expenses of travel and subsistence for employees and office holders (Department of Finance, Ireland)", www.ey.com.

Feldina, A. and S. Polanec (2012), "Underreporting and Minimum Wage", *LICOS Discussion Paper*, No. 324/2012, https://feb.kuleuven.be/drc/licos/publications/dp/dp324.

Guardiancich, I. (2012), "The case of Slovenia", in Guardiancich, I (ed.), *Recovering from the Crisis through Social Dialogue in the New EU Member States: The Case of Bulgaria, the Czech Republic, Poland and Slovenia*, www.ilo.org/wcmsp5/groups/public/---europe/---ro-geneva/---sro-budapest/documents/publication/wcms_203443.pdf.

Guardiancich, I. (2011), "Slovenian Social Policy in a Consensual Political System: The Dilemmas of a Delayed Transition", in Stambolieva, M. and S. Dehnert (eds.), *Welfare States in Transition: 20 Years after the Yugoslav Welfare Model*, Friedrich Ebert Stiftung, Sofia, http://library.fes.de/pdf-files/bueros/sofia/08711.pdf.

HMRC – Her Majesty's Revenue and Customs (2012), *Luncheon Vouchers: Repeal of Relief*, www.gov.uk/government/uploads/system/uploads/attachment_data/file/192150/ots_luncheon_vouchers.pdf.

Hrast, M. and T. Rakar (2015), "The Future of the Slovenian Welfare State and Challenges to Solidarity", Paper prepared for the Annual ESPAnet Conference: The Lost and the New Worlds of Welfare, 3-5 September, Odense, Denmark, https://blogs.kent.ac.uk/welfsoc/files/2015/05/Draft_Paper_FilipovicHrastRakar.pdf.

HRDSF – Human Resources Development and Scholarship Fund (2015), *With the Development of People – We Prosper: Collection of Programmes, Projects, Experience and Ideas* (available in Slovene via https://ec.europa.eu/epale/sl/resource-centre/content/z-razvojem-ljudi-uspevamo).

Ignjatović, M. and A. Mrčela (2015), *Reducing Precarious Work Through Social Dialogue: Slovenia, Draft Version October 2015*, European Commission, www.research.mbs.ac.uk/ewerc/Our-research/Current-projects/Reducing-Precarious-Work-in-Europe-through-Social.

IMAD – Institute of Macroeconomic Analysis and Development (2015), *Development Report 2015*, Ljubljana, www.umar.gov.si/en/publications/development_report.

IMAD (2014), *Economic Issues 2014*, Ljubljana, www.umar.gov.si/en/publications/economic_issues.

IMAD (2012), *Development Report 2012*, Ljubljana, www.umar.gov.si/en/publications/development_report.

Jemec, N. and M. Vodopivec (2016), *Labour Market Adjustment During the Crisis in Slovenia: Firm-Level Evidence from the WDN Survey*, www.ecb.europa.eu/home/pdf/research/wdn/WDN_Country_Report_SL.pdf.

Jütting, J. and J. de Laiglesia (eds.) (2009), "Is Informal Normal? Towards more and better jobs in developing countries", OECD Development Centre, OECD, Paris.

Kajzer, A. (2013), "Slovenia: Young people and temporary employment in Europe", www.eurofound.europa.eu/observatories/emcc/comparative-information/young-people-and-temporary-employment-in-europe.

Kajzer, A. (2010), "Can Simple Subsidy for Shorter Working Hours Efficiently Preserve Jobs in an Economic Crisis without Causing Labour Hoarding?", Mutual Learning Programme Peer Reviews, Paris, 27-28 September, http://ec.europa.eu/social/BlobServlet?docId=10550&langId=en.

Kolarič, Z., A. Kopač and T. Rakar (2011), "Welfare states in transition: the development of the welfare system in Slovenia", in S. Dehnert and M. Stambolieva (eds), *Welfare States in Transition: 20 Years after the Yugoslav Welfare Model*, Friedrich Ebert Foundation, Sofia, pp. 288-309, http://library.fes.de/pdf-files/bueros/sofia/08711.pdf.

Kolarič, Z., A. Kopač and T. Rakar (2009), "The Slovene welfare system: gradual reform instead of shock treatment", in K. Schubert, S, Hegelich and U. Bazant (eds), *The Handbook of European Welfare Systems*, Routledge, London: New York, pp. 444-461.

Korpič-Horvat, E., B. Tičar and R. Bohinc (2009), "The Salary System in the Private Sector in the Republic Slovenia", *Organizacija*, Vol. 42, No. 4, July-August.

Kovačič, H. (2014), "Slovenia: Changes to wage-setting mechanisms in the context of the crisis and the EU's new economic governance regime", Eurofound, www.eurofound.europa.eu/observatories/eurwork/comparative-information/changes-to-wage-setting-mechanisms-in-the-context-of-the-crisis-and-the-eus-new-economic-governance.

Kump, N. (2008), "Slovenia", in *Adjustment Capacity of Labour Markets of the West Balkan countries (Country Studies – Vol. II)*, European Economy Economic Papers No. 346, http://ec.europa.eu/economy_finance/publications/publication_summary13372_en.htm.

Laporšek, S., M. Vodopivec and M. Vodopivec (2015), "The Employment and Wage Spillover Effects of Slovenia's 2010 Minimum Wage Increase", Proceedings of the Australasian Conference on Business and Social Sciences 2015, Sydney (in partnership with *The Journal of Developing Areas*), www.aabss.org.au/system/files/published/000911-published-acbss-2015-sydney.pdf.

Lindič, M. (2011), "The impact of the irregular minimum wage increase on wages, employment and average hours paid (case study for Slovenia)", *IB Revija* 4/2011, www.umar.gov.si/avtorski_prispevki/ib_revija.

Lukic, G. (2016), *Annual Review of Labour Relations and Social Dialogue Slovenia*, Friedrich Ebert Stiftung, www.fes-socialdialogue.org/news-list/e/annual-review-of-labour-relations-and-social-dialogue-slovenia-2015.

MDDSZ – Ministry of Labour, Family, Social Affairs and Equal Opportunities (2016), *Bela knjiga o pokojninah* (White Paper on Pension System Development), Ljubljana, April, www.mddsz.gov.si/fileadmin/mddsz.gov.si/pageuploads/dokumenti__pdf/dpd/2Bela_knjiga_o_pokojninah.pdf.

Mrčela, A. (2015), "Slovenia: Working life country profile", www.eurofound.europa.eu/observatories/eurwork/comparative-information/national-contributions/slovenia/slovenia-working-life-country-profile.

OECD (2015), *Revenue Statistics 1964-2014*, OECD Publishing, Paris, http://dx.doi.org/10.1787/ctpa-rev-data-en.

OECD (2013), *Economic Surveys: Chile, 2013*, OECD Publishing, Paris, http://dx.doi.org/10.1787/eco_surveys-chl-2013-en.

OECD (2011), *Economic Surveys: Slovenia, 2011*, OECD Publishing, Paris, http://dx.doi.org/10.1787/eco_surveys-svn-2011-en.

OECD (2009a), *OECD Reviews of Labour Market and Social Policies: Slovenia*, OECD Publishing, Paris, http://dx.doi.org/10.1787/9789264068995-en.

OECD (2009b), *Economic Surveys: Slovenia, 2009*, OECD Publishing, Paris, http://dx.doi.org/10.1787/eco_surveys-svn-2009-en.

OECD (2004), "Informal Employment and Promoting the Transition to a Salaried Economy", *Employment Outlook 2004*, OECD Publishing, Paris, http://dx.doi.org/10.1787/empl_outlook-2004-7-en.

OECD (2003), "Benefits and Employment, Friend or Foe? Interactions between Passive and Active Social Programmes", *Employment Outlook 2003*, OECD Publishing: Paris, http://dx.doi.org/10.1787/empl_outlook-2003-6-en.

OECD (1997), *Labour Market Policies in Slovenia*, OECD Publishing, Paris.

Riddell. C. and P. Kuhn (2010), "The Long-Term Effects of Unemployment Insurance: Evidence from New Brunswick and Maine, 1940-1991", *Industrial & Labor Relations Review*, Vol. 63, No. 2.

Schnattinger et al. (2015), "Results of the 2014 Wage dynamics network survey in Slovenia", Banka Sloveniji, Prikazi in analize 2015:1, Ljubljana, www.bsi.si/en/publications.asp.

SORS – Statistical Office of the Republic of Slovenia (2013a), "Earnings (by the Structure of Earnings Survey), Slovenia, 2010 – Final Data", *Rapid Reports*, No. 3/2013, www.stat.si/doc/statinf/si-3placeporaziskovanjuostrukturiplace2010.pdf.

SORS (2013b), *From Traineeship to Retirement*, Ljubljana, January 2013, www.stat.si/doc/pub/07-RP-127-1301.pdf.

Stoviček, K. (2013), "Minimum wages in Slovenia: Reducing employment but not poverty?", *ECFIN Country Focus*, Vol. 10, No. 4, June, http://ec.europa.eu/economy_finance/publications/country_focus/2013/cf-vol10_4_en.htm.

Stropnik, N. (2015), "Improved regulation of student work in Slovenia", Flash report, ESPN, http://ec.europa.eu/social/keyDocuments.jsp.

Stropnik, N. (2013a), "Assessment of the implementation of the European Commission Recommendation on active inclusion: A Study of National Policies: Slovenia", EU Network of Independent Experts on Social Inclusion, http://ec.europa.eu/social/keyDocuments.jsp.

Stropnik, N. (2013b), "Minimalni življenjski stroški in minimalni dohodek" (Minimum cost of living and minimum wage), Institute for Economic Research, www.arhiv.ds-rs.si/sites/default/files/file/dokumenti/posveti/20130513-sociala/Nada_Stropnik.ppt.

Stropnik, N. et al. (2009), "Minimalni življenjski stroški" (Minimum costs of living), Inštitut za ekonomska raziskovanja (Institute for Economic Research), Ljubljana.

Suklan, J. and T. Golob (2015), "Student work in Slovenia", in J. Stroulhal (ed.), *Proceedings of the 4th International Conference on Economics, Law and Political Science*, Rome, 7-9 November, www.wseas.us/e-library/conferences/2015/Rome/EPLS/EPLS-21.pdf.

Šušteršič, J., B. Nastav and T. Kosi (2010), "Ekonomski vidiki študentskega dela" (Economic Aspects of Student Work), Faculty of Management Koper, University of Primorska, www.sizad.si/resources/files/Ekonomski_vidiki_studentskega_dela_POROCILO.pdf.

Ticar, L. (2014), "Recent developments of labour legislation in Slovenia within the context of economic crisis", International Society for Labour and Social Security Law, http://islssl.org/wp-content/uploads/2014/08/Slovenian-National-Report.pdf.

Unilang (2012), "Re: Minimum monthly wages in Slovenia", blog post, http://forum.unilang.org/viewtopic.php?t=37252.

Vidmar, N. (2015), "Tackling Undeclared work in Slovenia: Legal Frame and Main Goals", Ministry of Labour, Family, Social Affairs and Equal Opportunities, www.ijf.hr/upload/files/file/ENG/GREY-conf/vidmar.pptx.

Vodopivec, M. (2014), "Equal Pay for Equal Work: Wage and Productivity Differentials during Slovenia's Transition", *Eastern European Economics*, Vol. 52, No. 5, pp. 87-110.

Vodopivec, M., S. Laporšek and M. Vodopivec (2016), "Levelling the Playing Field: The Effects of Slovenia's 2013 Labour Market Reform", *IZA Discussion Paper*, No. 9783, Bonn, ftp.iza.org/dp9783.pdf.

Working Group (2014), "Report of the Working Group for Monitoring the Effects of Labour Market Legislation in 2013", IMAD, Ljubljana.

Chapter 3

Assuring work motivation and work incentives in the Slovenian benefit system

A critical component of activation policies concerns the incentives that individuals face to become formally employed or to remain in employment. To what extent does social policy in Slovenia strike the right balance between providing income support for vulnerable individuals while ensuring that such individuals are still motivated to seek employment? Do those receiving unemployment or social assistance benefit have strong financial incentives to engage in job search? What are the financial incentives for delaying retirement until the statutory retirement age – and how can individuals exploit the system of unemployment, disability and social assistance benefits to effectively exit the labour market at an earlier age? Finally, how did the 2009 recession and the subsequent austerity measures affect social policy, and what have been the effects of these changes on government expenditures and the number of benefit recipients? These questions are discussed in this chapter.

The statistical data for Israel are supplied by and under the responsibility of the relevant Israeli authorities. The use of such data by the OECD is without prejudice to the status of the Golan Heights, East Jerusalem and Israeli settlements in the West Bank under the terms of international law.

Throughout its gentle transition to a market economy following its independence from Yugoslavia, Slovenia retained a fairly egalitarian income distribution – indeed, by several measures, its income inequality is among the lowest in the OECD. Such low inequality has been achieved partly by a system of taxes and government transfers that are among the largest in the OECD. While such redistributive policies may foster social cohesion and contribute to low poverty rates, the combination of taxes, benefits and transfers decreases the appeal of taking up formal employment, particularly for low-wage earners.

Slovenia's social policy system was severely tested in the aftermath of the 2009 recession. The magnitude of the recession and the weak subsequent recovery has placed a significant burden on public finances. The government's initial response to the crisis was to increase benefit generosity, which was followed by retrenchment in 2012 as the necessity of reducing the government deficit became more urgent. In addition, as is discussed below, public expenditures are disproportionally spent on individuals no longer in the labour force. The large share of spending on old-age pensions largely reflects the early retirement of workers in the past; the 2013 pension reform has resulted in gradual increases in the age at which workers have been retiring and will continue to have a moderate effect as it comes into full effect by 2020. Nevertheless, further increases in the retirement age will be necessary to ensure the fiscal sustainability of the pension system. In addition, the existing system of partial disability benefits threatens to undermine the goal of increasing the employment rate of older workers, as such benefits have increasingly been used as a bridge to early retirement.

Key features of the Slovene tax and social benefits system

This section discusses Slovenia's well-developed social protection system and its strong role in reducing inequality, both across individuals and regions. Slovenia responded to the crises with a temporary expansion of the system's generosity. However, the latest trends suggest new and unexpected dynamics in the system that have yet to be addressed by policy makers.

The income distribution is very egalitarian, with a disproportionate share of social spending on individuals no longer in the labour force

Slovenia's public social spending is slightly above the OECD average, with a large share of spending going to pensions. In 2011, social spending amounted to 24% of GDP, compared to an OECD average of 21.4% (Figure 3.1). Expenditures on pensions account for almost half of public social spending, considerably above the OECD average. This outcome reflects a relatively low effective retirement age, especially when compared with a fairly long life expectancy (OECD, 2015). While spending on health is slightly above the OECD average, spending on incapacity and family benefits are comparable to the OECD average as percentage of GDP. On the other hand, spending on active labour market policies, unemployment benefits, housing and other social policies are comparatively low. As a whole, public social spending is thus disproportionately focused on individuals who are no longer in the labour force.

Figure 3.1. **A disproportional share of social spending in Slovenia goes to pensions**

Public social expenditure by broad social policy areas as a percentage of GDP, 2013

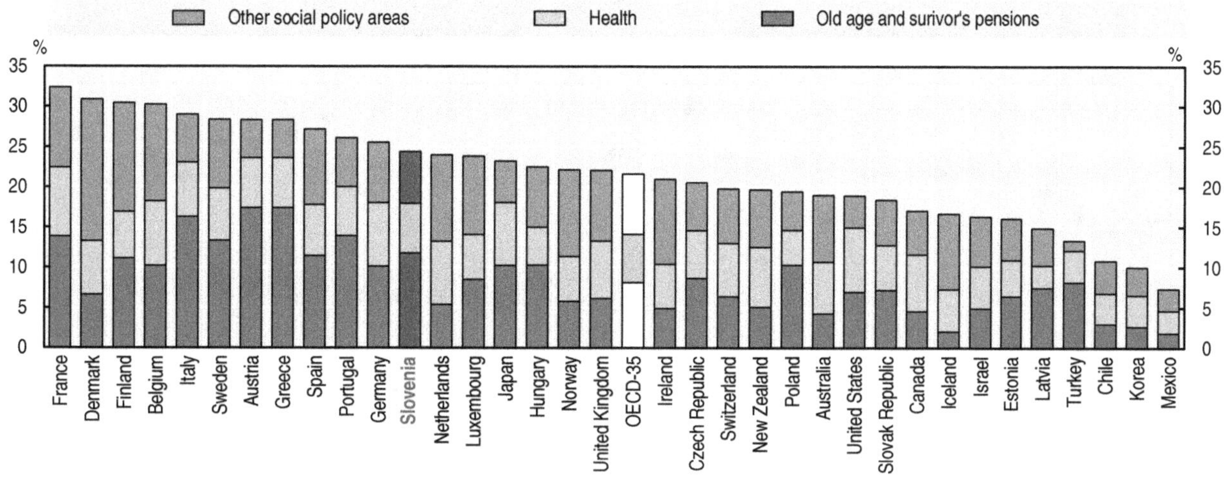

Note: Data for Australia, Canada, Chile, Israel, Korea and New Zealand refer to 2014, to 2012 for Greece and Poland and to 2011 for Mexico.

Source: *OECD Social Expenditure Database* (www.oecd.org/social/expenditure.htm) and *OECD/Eurostat Labour Market Programme Database*, http://dx.doi.org/10.1787/data-00312-en for ALMP expenditures.

StatLink http://dx.doi.org/10.1787/888933415070

The income distribution in Slovenia is very egalitarian; an outcome achieved partly by a system of taxes and government transfers that are among the highest in the OECD. In 2011, Slovenia had the lowest level of income inequality as measured by the Gini coefficient, which measures inequality along the entire income distribution and where lower levels represent greater equality (the Gini coefficient is normalised to range from 0 to 1). Because income inequality in Slovenia prior to taxes and transfers is on par with the OECD average, the low level of inequality can be largely attributed to government policies, which decrease the Gini coefficient by 0.21 in absolute terms (Figure 3.2).

Regional factors play a sizable role in explaining income inequality before taxes and transfers. An analysis by Banerjee and Jesenko (2015) finds a considerable disparity in per capita GDP across Slovenia's 12 regions. In 2008, per capita GDP in the richest region, the capital region, amounted to 142% of the national average, while in the poorest, the Pomurska region in the extreme east, it amounted to 65% of the average. After transfers, differences in per capita household incomes ranged from 112% to 82% of the national average, respectively, for these two regions. In addition to labour productivity, differing employment rates explain these discrepancies. Furthermore, commuting between regions plays a vital part in Slovenia in reducing disposable income inequality.

Figure 3.2. **Slovenia has the lowest income inequality in the OECD area, largely reflecting significant government taxes and transfers**

Differences in income inequality pre and post-tax and government transfers, 2011

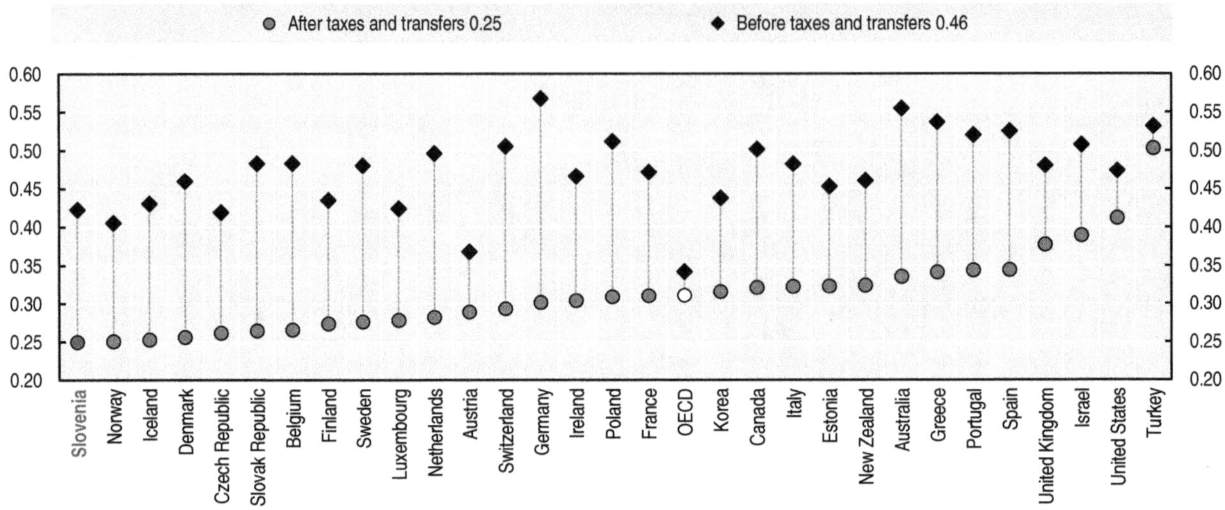

Note: Data refer to 2010 for Belgium and 2012 for Australia and the Netherlands.

Source: *OECD Income Distribution Database* (www.oecd.org/social/income-distribution-database.htm).

StatLink http://dx.doi.org/10.1787/888933415089

Despite the high degree of redistribution, Slovenia has a tax system that is only moderately progressive and is comparable to the OECD average. A single individual at 167% of the average wage faces a tax wedge as a percentage of total labour costs that is 7.9 percentage points higher than an individual at 67% of the average wage, compared to an OECD average of 8.3 percentage points (OECD, 2016).[1] For married individuals with children, the tax system is slightly more progressive in Slovenia than in other OECD countries. The level of the average tax wedge, on the other hand, is considerably higher in Slovenia than in other OECD countries, standing at 42.6% in Slovenia compared to 35.9% in the OECD on average.

Personal income taxes in Slovenia apply to an individual's income, with no taxation of spouses or a family as a whole (*Tax and Benefit Systems: OECD Indicators Database*, 2014). This is in contrast to means-tested social benefits, which are calculated taking into account all family members and their income. The taxpayer is entitled to the family allowance for a dependent child and other dependent family members – for example, a spouse without their own income. The family allowance for a dependent child is transferable between partners or spouses. The allowance for the same maintained family member in the tax year is granted only to one taxpayer, while another may be granted only the possible difference up to the total amount of the relief. The amount of the family allowance progressively increases with each additional child, amounting to EUR 2 437 for the first child (equivalent to 23.7% of the annual minimum wage) and EUR 2 649 for the second child (equivalent to 25.8% of the minimum wage).

Initial response to crisis of increasing benefit generosity was followed by retrenchment

Slovenia's initial public policy response to the 2009 recession was to increase the generosity and coverage of benefits. However, the subsequent imperative to reduce the government deficit resulted in cuts to unemployment and social benefits as well as increased enforcement of benefit conditionality. The initial round of reforms included the Labour Market Regulation Act, which came into effect in January 2011, as well as the Social Assistance Benefits Act, which parliament passed in 2010 but whose implementation was postponed until January 2012. The 2011 Labour Market Regulation Act increased the generosity of the unemployment insurance system: it increased the replacement rate (level of benefits compared to pre-unemployment wages) for unemployment benefits and reduced the required duration of employment necessary to be eligible for benefit. The Social Assistance Benefits Act increased basic social assistance by 13% and introduced systemic changes to social benefit entitlement, although the interaction of benefits resulted in a decline in many recipients' disposable income (Stropnik and Prevolnik Rupel, 2015). Many of the increases in benefits were short-lived: the May 2012 Fiscal Balance Act cut or froze benefits and entitlements across the board.

The combined effect of these various factors is that total expenditures on social protection have remained flat since 2012 despite an increase in pension outlays (Figure 3.3). After increasing by one percentage point from 2008 to 2010, spending on non-pension income support has remained level from 2010 onwards at approximately 5.5% of GDP. This has occurred even despite a considerable decrease in employment over the beginning of that period, during which employment declined from 966 000 in 2010 to a low of 906 000 in 2013 (SORS, 2016). The considerable increase in pension expenditures since 2008 has been almost entirely driven by growth in the number of old-age pension recipients, whose average annual growth rate increased from 3.1% before the crisis to 4% in 2009-13. The number of disability pension recipients has been gradually declining throughout this entire period.

Figure 3.3. **Old-age pension outlays have increased in Slovenia; other public social expenditures have not**

Public social expenditure by social policy areas as a percentage of GDP, 1996-2013

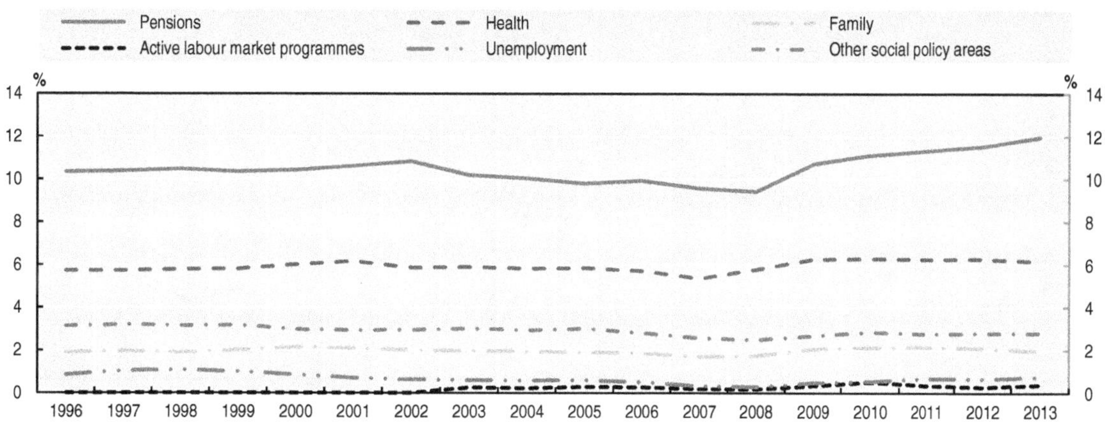

Note: Other social policy areas also includes Incapacity related benefits and Housing.

Source: *OECD Social Expenditure Database* (www.oecd.org/social/expenditure.htm).

StatLink http://dx.doi.org/10.1787/888933415092

Recent developments are remarkable and partly unexpected. The decline in the number of unemployed has been accompanied by an increase in social assistance and partial disability recipients (Figure 3.4). Following a delayed adjustment of employment after the sharp economic contraction in 2009, the share of registered unemployed receiving unemployment benefits peaked in March 2011, when 34.9% of the registered unemployed were receiving benefits. By 2015, as individuals exhausted their entitlements and employment began to recover, the share of unemployment benefit recipients among the unemployed decreased to 21%.

Figure 3.4. **Decrease in unemployment benefit receipt in Slovenia has been accompanied by increase in social assistance and partial disability benefits**

FSA, unemployment benefit and unemployed partial disability benefit recipients in Slovenia, 2005-15

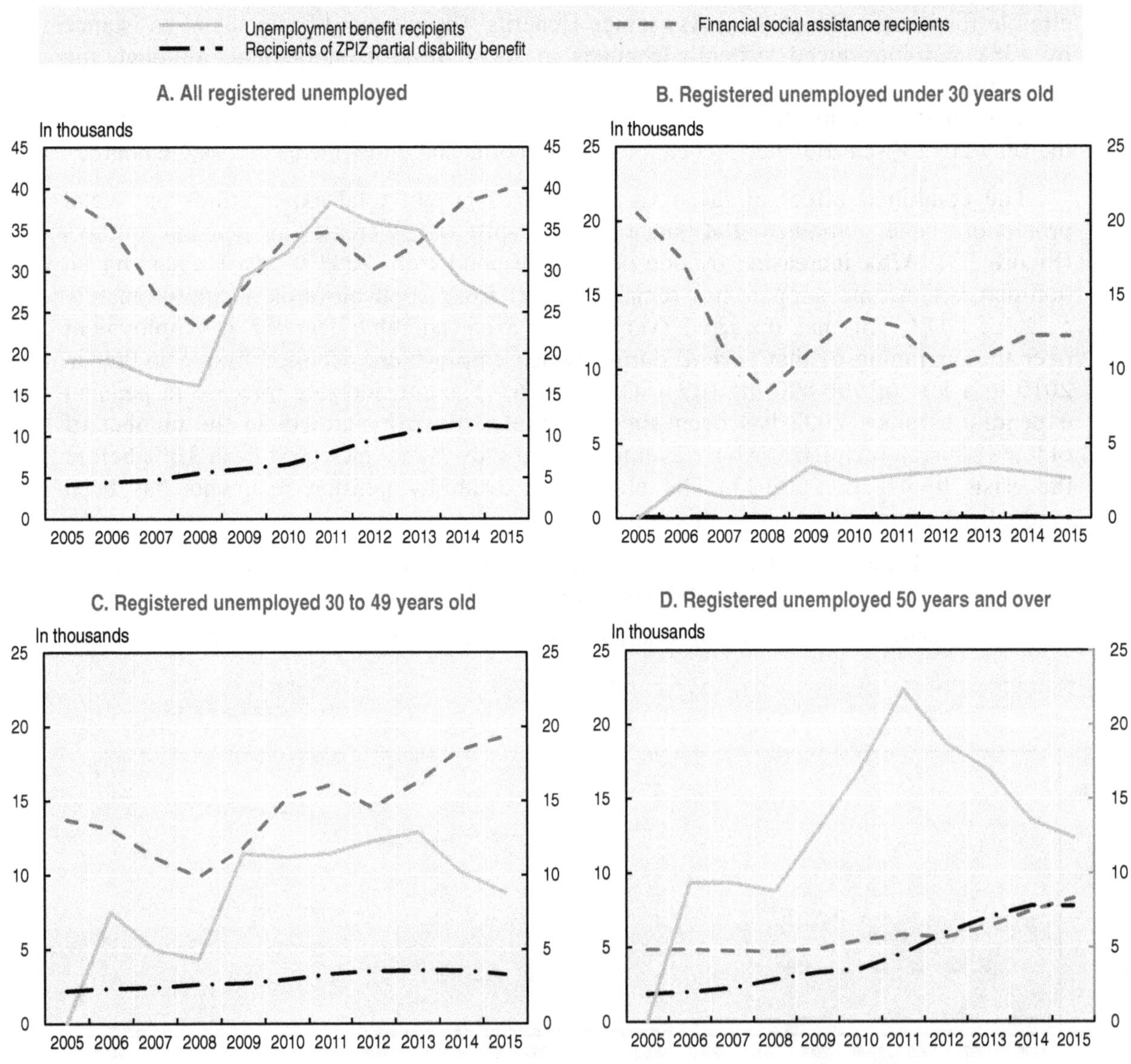

Source: Employment Service of Slovenia.

StatLink http://dx.doi.org/10.1787/888933415101

However, this decrease has been more than offset by an increase in the number of recipients of the other two forms of working-age income support. Among unemployed workers aged 15-29, this increase is almost exclusively due to increased rates of entitlement to social assistance. These are considerably higher than among older unemployed, reflecting the relative inaccessibility of unemployment benefits for the younger age group. Among the unemployed aged 50 or more, entitlement to partial disability benefits is far more common, with 21.2% of the unemployed receiving such benefits in 2015. By contrast, entitlement rates are much lower among workers aged 30-49 and 15-29, at 6.7% and 0.1%, respectively.

The latest developments imply that the labour market policy response through the Slovene benefit system needs to be broader than anticipated before the crisis; with systems other than unemployment benefits now playing a much larger and still increasing role for people of working age.

Unemployment benefit coverage and adequacy

Replacement rates can be high and payment duration long for some groups

Slovenia has an unemployment insurance system that is relatively generous for low-wage earners (see Box 3.1). The initial rate at which previous earnings are replaced is set fairly high, at 80% of previous earnings. However, because the maximum gross monthly amount is set at EUR 893 – equal to 60% of the average wage – a majority of benefit recipients receive a lower replacement rate. In fact, the maximum benefit level is so low that even after the replacement rate decreases in subsequent months of continued benefit receipt (after three and 12 months, respectively, to 60% and 50%), a large share of the unemployed continue to receive the same level of benefits.

For low-wage earners in Slovenia, the financial incentives to become employed while receiving unemployment benefits are relatively weak. For such individuals, the unemployment trap – which measures the proportion of any increase in earnings that is lost through increases in taxes paid and withdrawals of benefits – is quite high in an international comparison (see e.g. Kierzenkowski, 2013). For example, for a married couple with two children where only one spouse is employed, having the second spouse move from receiving social assistance to full-time, minimum-wage employment would result in 88% of the increased earnings being lost due to taxes and reduced benefits (Figure 3.5).[2] The vast majority of the unemployment trap is attributable to the withdrawal of the unemployment benefit. In many other countries, the withdrawal of other benefits or increased taxes and social contributions also contribute considerably to the unemployment trap. The relatively small role of these other components reflect both a system of taxes and benefits which are less progressive in Slovenia than in many other countries and the absence of in-work benefits.

Figure 3.5. **Unemployment benefit traps are fairly high in Slovenia for low-wage earners**

Marginal tax rates for a transition into full-time work at 67% of the average wage, for persons receiving unemployment benefits at the initial level, 2014

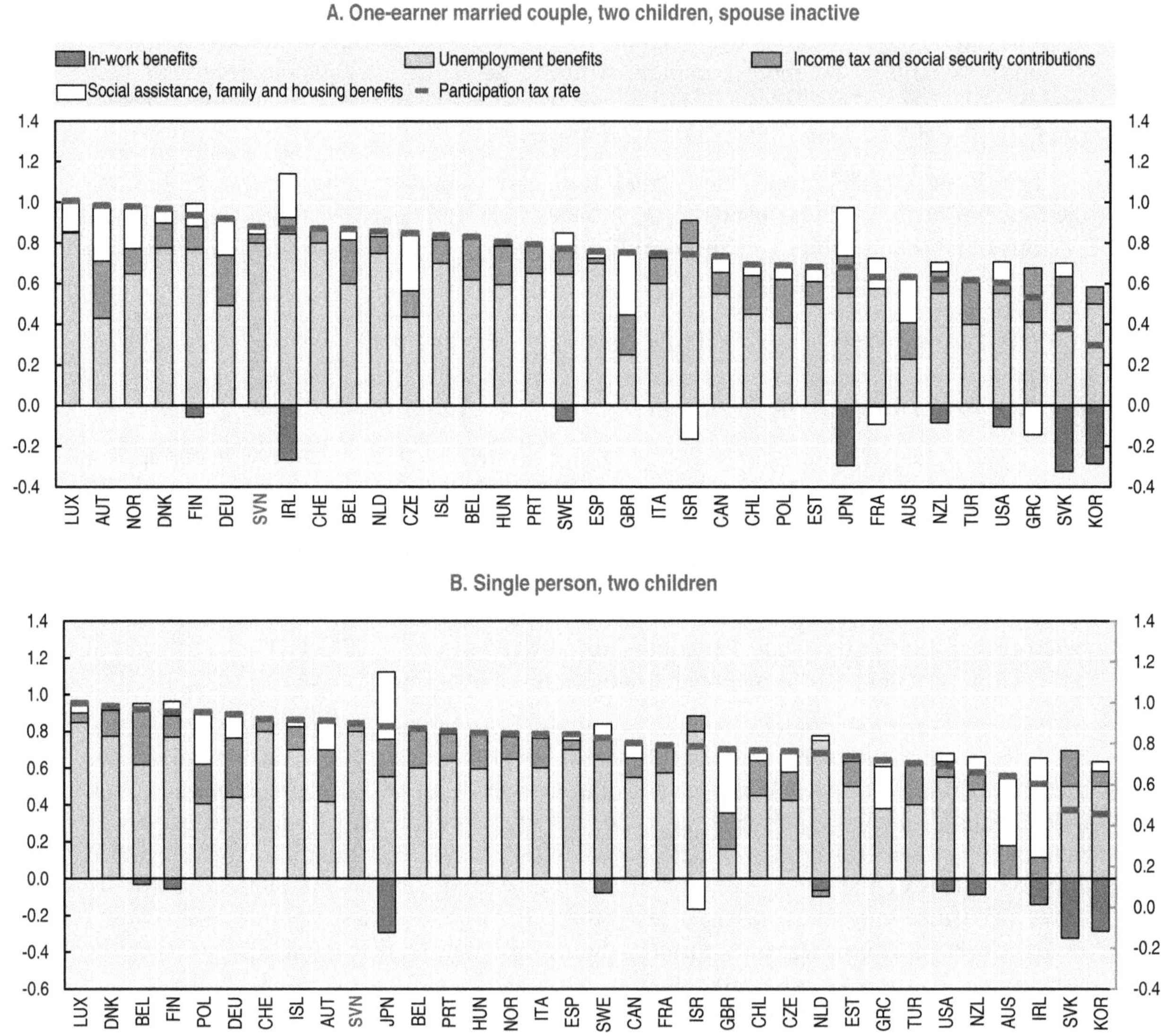

Note: Participation tax rates (otherwise known as effective tax rates) measure the extent to which taxes and benefits reduce the financial gain of moving into work. The estimates here relate to the situation of a person who has just become unemployed and receives unemployment benefits (following any waiting period) based on previous earnings equal to earnings in the new job. Social assistance "top-ups" and cash housing assistance are assumed to be available in both the in-work or out of work situation, depending on eligibility. Any benefits payable on moving into employment are assumed to be paid. The percentage of AW relates to the earnings from full-time employment of the individual moving into work. For married couples the percentage of AW relates to one spouse only; the second spouse is assumed to be inactive with no earnings in a one-earner couple. Calculations for families with children assume two children aged four and six and neither childcare benefits nor childcare costs are considered.

Source: OECD tax-benefits models (www.oecd.org/social/benefits-and-wages.htm).

StatLink http://dx.doi.org/10.1787/888933415112

Box 3.1. Main features of unemployment insurance in Slovenia

Conditions for unemployment insurance (UI) benefits: Involuntary unemployment, which includes no-fault layoffs from permanent and after fixed-term contracts. The minimum insurance period is nine months of contribution payments over the last 24 months (for workers under age 30, six months of contributions). Not eligible are individuals with student status who worked via a student temporary work agency.

The benefit level is calculated based on the average monthly earnings in the past nine months (five months for younger workers). The replacement rate is 80%, 60% and 50% for months 1-3, 4-12, and 13 or more, respectively, of benefit receipt. This is subject to a minimum gross monthly payment of EUR 350 and a maximum payment of EUR 892.50 (the latter was decreased from EUR 1 050 in May 2012).

	Length of potential benefit duration (months)	
Prior work period[a]	1998-2010	2011-present
6-8 months (and age under 30)		2[b]
9 months – 5 years		3[c]
1-5 years	3[d]	
5-15 years	6	6
15-25 years	9	9
over 25 years	12	12
over 25 years (and age 50-54 years)	18[e]	19
over 25 years (and age 55 + years)	24[e]	25[f]

Notes:

a) Period for which UI contributions have been paid (excluding any period of UI benefit receipt) since last benefit claim.

b) Since 12 April 2013.

c) Nine in last 24 months.

d) 12 months in the last 18 months.

e) The insurance period does not reset for beneficiaries older than 50 years with 25 years of paid contributions when claiming the benefit.

f) The insurance period does not reset for beneficiaries who are older than 55 years when claiming the benefit and with at least 30 years of paid contributions prior to 12 April 2013; increased to 57 years and 35 years of paid contributions, respectively, from 12 April 2013.

In addition, unemployed individuals close to retirement (57 years or having 35 years of paid contributions) are paid pension contributions for two years. During January 2011 to April 2013, this period was reduced to one year; the shorter one-year payment period is due to come into effect once again in March 2018.

Displaced individuals who register with the employment service during their advance notice period may take time off work to engage in job-search activities, during which time they are entitled to compensation. During the first month of unemployment, their benefit is reduced proportionally to the number of days they received such compensation.

Source: Employment Service of Slovenia.

International comparisons of the unemployment trap are subject to an important caveat regarding specific circumstances in Slovenia which weaken cross-country comparability. Employers in Slovenia are required by law to pay both a travel allowance intended to compensate individuals for their work commuting expenses as well as a daily meal allowance. As discussed in Chapter 2, these are not subject to taxation and amount to approximately 13% of the average wage bill (although they vary considerably, they are generally relatively more important for lower-wage earners). Broadly comparable international measures of unemployment traps would thus take into account that net wages in Slovenia are approximately 10% higher than reported in official statistics. Because unemployment benefit recipients do not receive a travel allowance (except for activities related to job-search) or a meal allowance, including this additional income reduces the unemployment trap in Slovenia by approximately ten percentage points.

In Slovenia, the benefit duration for receipt of unemployment benefit is a strongly increasing function of work experience and age. The potential benefit duration varies from two months for young workers with 6-8 months of prior employment to 25 months for most workers over age 55. For younger workers, the potential benefit duration is calculated based on cumulative prior employment since last receiving unemployment benefits. For workers older than 57 years, however, the duration is set to 25 months as soon as the density requirement (nine months of UI contributions during the previous 24 months) is fulfilled. These parameters mean that seasonal employment can be sufficient for older workers to re-establish UI eligibility and thus weaken their incentives to seek permanent employment.

The duration for which individuals are entitled to unemployment benefits varies much more in Slovenia than in other OECD countries with unemployment insurance – particularly because of the long potential benefit duration for older workers (Figure 3.6). In about half of the European OECD countries, benefit duration is limited to one year or less, regardless of age.

Figure 3.6. **Unemployment benefit duration in Slovenia strongly increases with work experience**

Maximum duration of unemployment insurance payment for an employee with a complete affiliation by age, EU countries, 2012

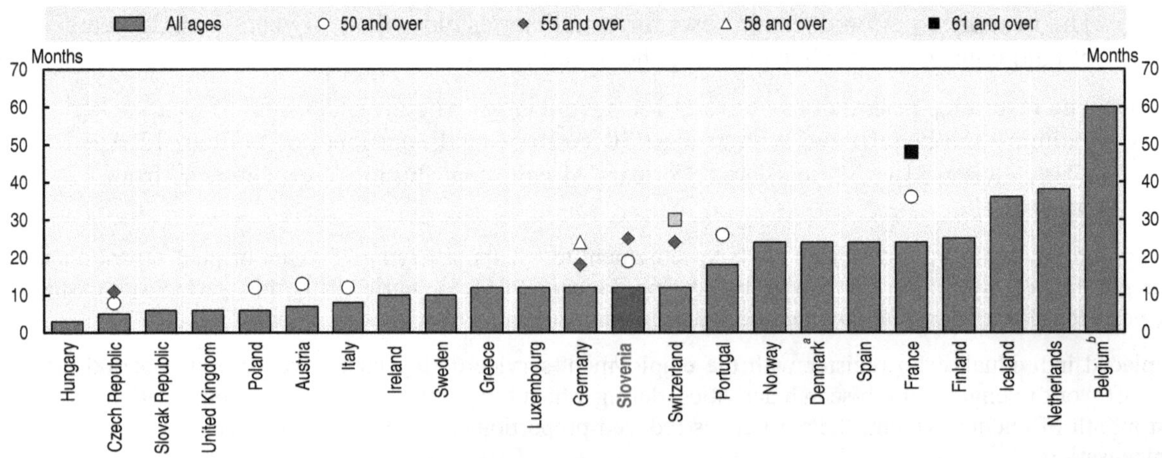

a) 18 months for an employee over 40 and 26 months for an employee over 45.

b) No time limit.

Source: OECD Tax and Benefits Systems: OECD Indicators, www.oecd.org/social/benefits-and-wages.htm.

StatLink http://dx.doi.org/10.1787/888933415123

Coverage of unemployment benefits is low in Slovenia, but many unemployed receive other income support payments

Individuals who become unemployed voluntarily are not eligible for unemployment benefits in Slovenia, as is the case in roughly one-third of OECD countries (Figure 3.7). As in other countries with similar provisions, there are a limited number of exceptions to this rule. For example, individuals who quit their job due the relocation of a spouse are eligible for benefits. In many countries where voluntary unemployment does not disqualify an individual for unemployment benefits, individuals may be eligible for benefits after a non-payment period which typically lasts several weeks.

Figure 3.7. **Slovenia has one of the strictest sanction regimes in the OECD for voluntary job quits**

Sanctions for voluntary job quits, scored from 0 (least strict) to 5 (most strict), 2014

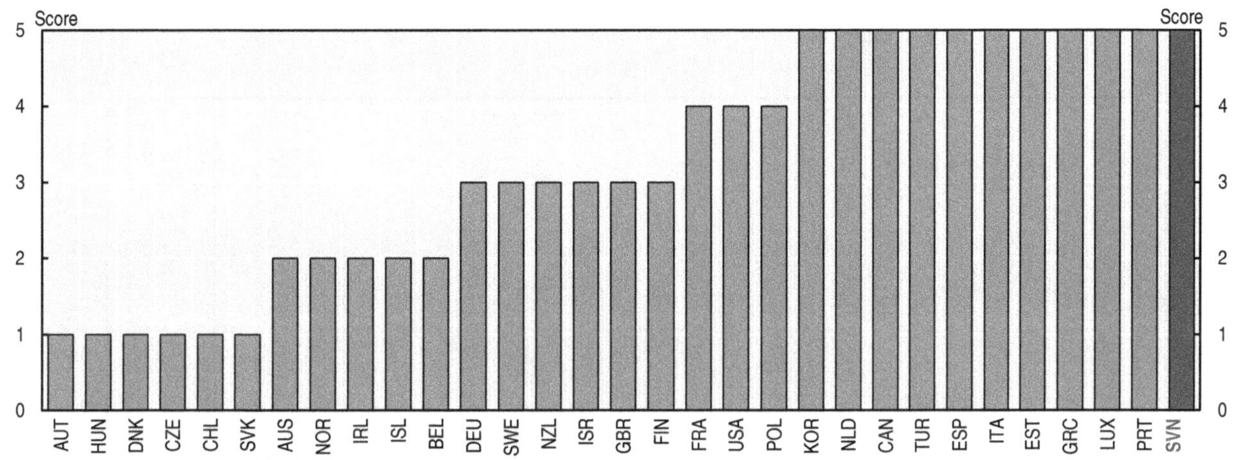

Note: Scores: 1 = sanction of 0-4 weeks (including benefit reductions); 2 = sanction of 5-9 weeks; 3 = sanction of 10-14 weeks; 4 = sanction of more than 14 weeks; 5 = ineligible for benefits.

Source: Author's calculations based on Langenbucher, K. (2015), "How demanding are eligibility criteria for unemployment benefits, quantitative indicators for OECD and EU countries", *OECD Social, Employment and Migration Working Papers*, No. 166, OECD Publishing, Paris, http://dx.doi.org/10.1787/5jrxtk1zw8f2-en.

StatLink http://dx.doi.org/10.1787/888933415138

Slovenia's exclusion of voluntary job quits from receiving unemployment benefits may not be quite as binding in practice as the international comparison may suggest. As workers are eligible for unemployment benefits at the conclusion of fixed-term contracts, a short, even one-day fixed-term contract following a voluntary separation is sufficient for establishing eligibility. In such cases, eligibility is assessed based on the entire prior employment period, and individuals are then eligible for unemployment benefits just as if their previous separation had been involuntary. In addition, there are indications that workers may collude with their employers to initiate layoffs which ostensibly occur for reasons of worker incompetence (which is distinct from negligence and entitles one to unemployment benefits), but are in fact done with the purpose of de facto early retirement via the unemployment system. The pattern of inflows into unemployment due to incompetence closely tracks the number of new old-age pension calculation requests, with spikes at the end of 2010 and 2012, which is highly consistent with such strategic behaviour (MDDSZ, 2016).

A relatively small share of the unemployed population in Slovenia receives unemployment benefits. In 2015, the ratio of benefit recipients to labour force survey unemployed stood at 0.24, considerably lower than in most other OECD countries (Figure 3.8). The low coverage rate is a result of a large share of long-term unemployed who have exhausted unemployment benefits and of the relative inaccessibility of UI among younger unemployed, including first-time jobseekers. However, as discussed in the following sections, a significant number of the unemployed population receives other forms of income support. Including these, the ratio of benefit recipients to labour force survey unemployment amounted to 0.76 in 2015.

Figure 3.8. **Relatively few unemployed receive unemployment benefits in Slovenia**

Ratio of the number of unemployment benefit recipients to the number of labour force survey unemployed, 2007 and latest available year

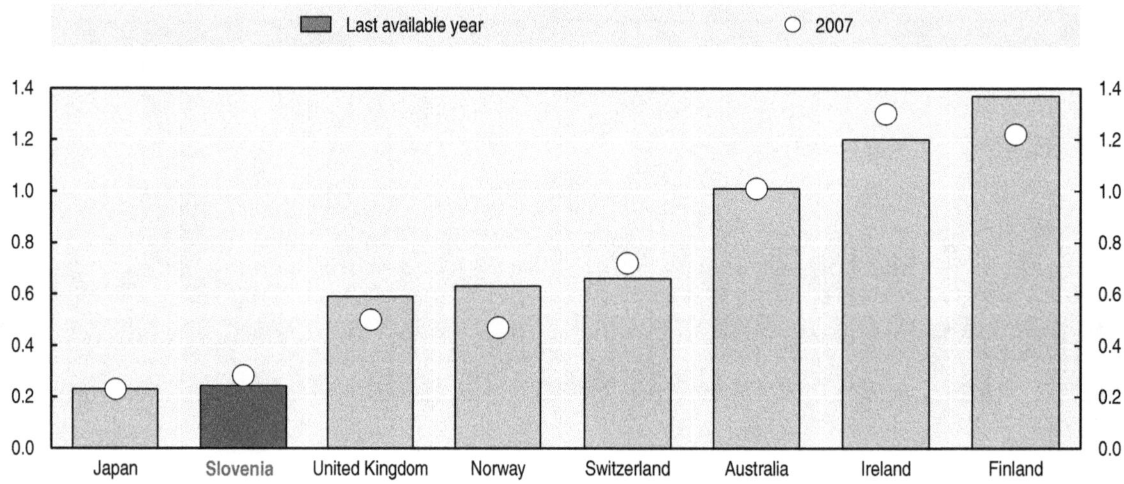

Source: OECD compilation based on labour force survey data.

StatLink http://dx.doi.org/10.1787/888933415141

Unemployment insurance reform in 2011 increased accessibility of benefits, although perhaps not primarily for the target groups

When the parameters of the current UI system were last subject to major legislative overhaul in 2011, one of the key goals was to increase benefit accessibility by shortening the length of previous employment required for eligibility. The 2011 unemployment insurance reform, the Labour Market Regulation Act, decreased the minimum employment period required for unemployment benefit eligibility to nine months in the preceding two years (previously, 12 months in the preceding 18 months) and introduced even lower required contributory periods for workers under age 30.

An analysis of the effects of the legislative changes by Dolenc et al. (2012) shows that in the year immediately following its enactment, the 2011 law had a relatively small effect on benefit accessibility. The share of UI benefits recipients among the unemployed increased by only one percentage point because of the new parameters, and only 2.5% of individuals who received unemployment benefits in 2011 would not have been eligible for benefits in 2010. While the total number of UI recipients increased considerably in 2011 and reached its highest level in the past ten years, the authors note that much of the increase is not attributable to the UI reform but rather the anticipated pension reform. More specifically, there was an unusual spike in UI claims amongst workers with over 25 years of work experience in December 2010, presumably due to individuals seeking more favourable early retirement conditions that required them to be registered as unemployed on December 31st, 2010 (note that the pension reform due to be enacted in 2011 was subsequently overturned in a referendum).

As a result of the 2011 unemployment insurance reform, the within-year variation in the number of unemployment benefit recipients has increased considerably during the course of any given year. The unemployment benefit caseload typically follows a seasonal pattern whereby it peaks in January, decreases during the course of the year and reaches a minimum in early fall. Since January 2011, the within-year ratio of maximum to minimum monthly recipients has increased from an average of 1.21 before enactment of the new law in 2011 to 1.36 thereafter.[3] This increase could plausibly be explained by the new eligibility requirements by which nine months of eligibility is sufficient to receive three months of unemployment benefits. If so, it could be the case that certain employers have now adjusted their staffing to offering nine months of seasonal work, with workers receiving unemployment benefits for the remainder of the year.

In addition to changing eligibility rules, the 2011 unemployment insurance reform increased benefit generosity, increasing the maximum benefit amount as well as the replacement rate in the first three months of benefit receipt. An analysis by Vodopivec et al. (2015) shows that the increase in the replacement rate for UI benefit recipients has decreased the rate at which individuals exited unemployment to employment during the period after the increase in generosity. They estimate that the decrease in exit rates was roughly commensurate with the 14% increase in benefits – that is, that the implied elasticity of exit to employment with respect to the replacement rate is close to unity. However, the effect was considerably smaller for displaced workers whose job losses were due to employer bankruptcy. Because bankruptcies indiscriminately affect all workers whereas individual lay-offs may target underperforming or incompetent workers (Galuscak et al., 2012), the discrepancy may be due to unobserved worker characteristics, such as work motivation and work ability.

Given the above result, the subsequent decrease in the maximum unemployment benefit amount in May 2012, from 68% to 58% of the average monthly gross wage, arguably increased the job-finding rate of UI recipients among higher-wage earners. Although this decrease was part of a broader set of fiscal consolidation measures that cut public expenditures across the board, the fact that it also had the effect of improving job-search incentives is a welcome side effect.

The unemployment insurance system serves as a bridge to early retirement

One important feature of Slovenia's UI system that facilitates the exit of older workers from the labour force is the payment of old-age pension contributions for unemployed individuals close to retirement. The ESS pays contributions for unemployed workers with (up to) two years of insurance remaining before becoming eligible for full retirement. Unemployed workers who are four years and one month from reaching full retirement can receive 25 months of unemployment benefits plus two years of paid pension contributions (during which they may also be eligible for means-tested social assistance). While such unemployed individuals are ostensibly required to engage in job search in a manner similar to the younger unemployed, in practice very few such individuals exit unemployment to employment (Dolenc et al., 2012).

Entering retirement via the unemployment insurance system has become increasingly common in recent years, with large spikes coinciding with anticipated pension reforms. Today, approximately 30% of all old-age pension recipients enter retirement in this manner: for example in 2014, 22.6% received unemployment benefits immediately prior to retirement, while 5.7% had exhausted their unemployment benefits and were receiving only paid old-age pension contributions (Figure 3.9).

Figure 3.9. **Almost one third of Slovene pensioners enter retirement through unemployment**

New pensioners by employment status immediately preceding retirement, 2005-14

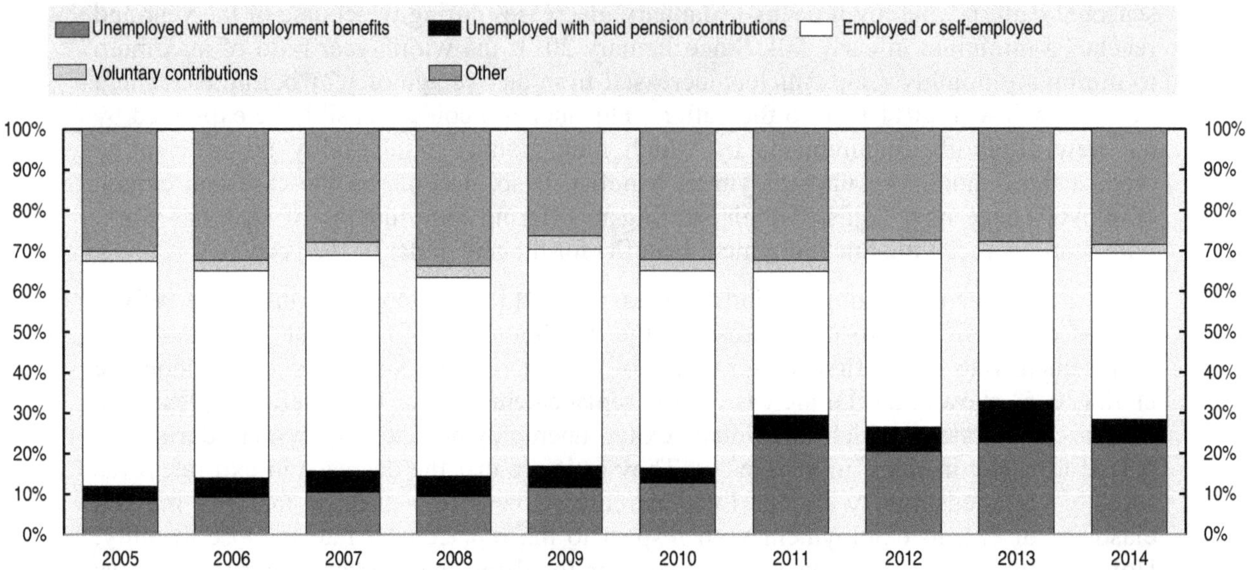

Note: Employed or self-employed also includes farmers and employed owners/shareholders. The category "Other" includes individuals without old-age pension contributions immediately prior to retirement.

Source: Pension and Invalidity Insurance Institute of Slovenia (ZPIZ).

StatLink http://dx.doi.org/10.1787/888933415151

The existing system of unemployment insurance suffers from underfunding and moral hazard problems

Despite Slovenia's high tax wedge on labour, the contributions allocated to unemployment insurance are grossly insufficient to fund the required pay-outs for unemployment benefits (COE, 2015). The unemployment insurance contribution rates total just 0.2% of pre-tax wages for permanent contracts and 0.44% of pre-tax wages for fixed-term contracts. Contributions from insured individuals and employers thus provide only 8% of the funds required for the payment of unemployment benefits, with the remainder being provided by the state budget. As such, the existing unemployment benefit system arguably has the characteristics of a social transfer system more than an insurance system.

In addition, there is evidence documenting the disincentive effects of the existing UI system for the reemployment rate of benefit recipients. Based on an analysis of individual unemployment spells, Vodopivec et al. (2015) document considerable spikes in exits from unemployment to employment among UI recipients after the exhaustion of benefits. Relative to the baseline of individuals not receiving unemployment benefit, the rates of exit to employment for individuals receiving unemployment benefit are less than half the rates for individuals not eligible for unemployment benefit in the two months preceding benefit exhaustion or reduction (Figure 3.10). Thereafter, the exit rates increase, particularly for those no longer receiving benefits. Such patterns are indicative of strong disincentive effects of unemployment benefits.

Figure 3.10. **Benefit exhaustion and reduction in Slovenia associated with increase in probability of exiting unemployment into employment**

Hazard rate of exiting unemployment into employment relative to baseline hazard rate of individuals not eligible for unemployment benefits, Slovenia, 2011

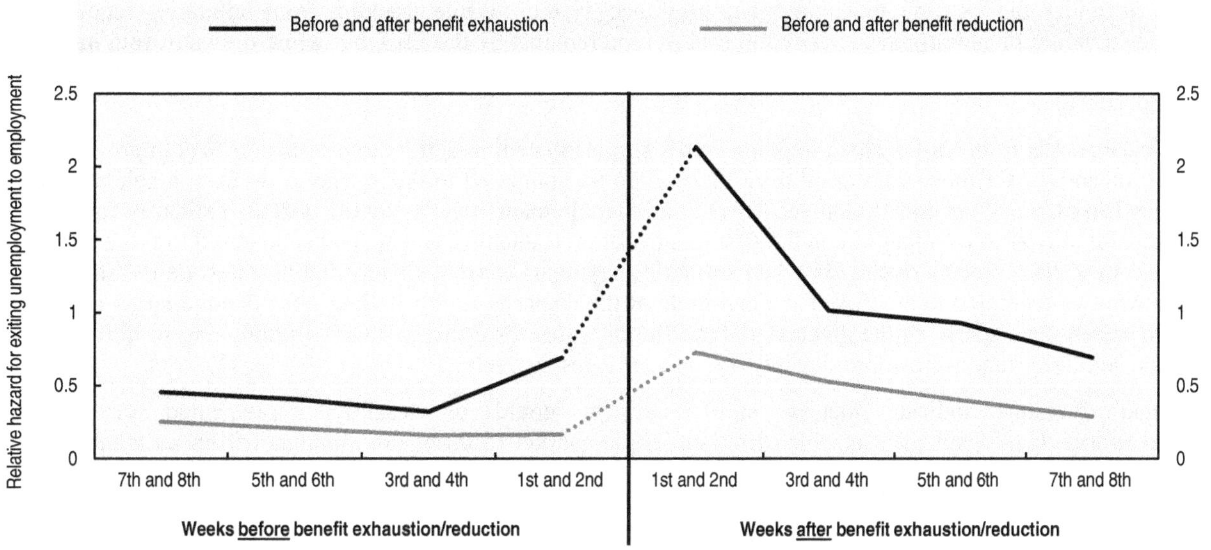

Source: Vodopivec et al. (2015), "The Effect of Unemployment Benefit Generosity on Unemployment Duration: Quasi-Experimental Evidence from Slovenia", *IZA Discussion Paper*, No. 9548, http://ssrn.com/abstract=2708361.

StatLink http://dx.doi.org/10.1787/888933415160

Another parameter of the existing unemployment benefit system that offers the potential for strategic behaviour is the possibility to voluntarily withdraw from and re-enter the unemployment registry, with the entitlement to unemployment benefits on hold during the intermittent period. Such voluntary deregistrations are possible, for example, for individuals allegedly moving abroad. This is considered as problematic by certain employment service providers among individuals engaging in informal employment or who otherwise sought to avoid participation in active labour market programmes. While the frequency of such strategic behaviour is unclear and may not be pervasive, the existence of such loopholes offers the potential for misuse.

To address the above described problems, Slovenia may consider complementing its existing unemployment insurance system with a system of Unemployment Insurance Savings Accounts (see Box 3.2). To jump-start such a hybrid system, it could rely on elements of the existing scheme, e.g. by allowing first-time unemployment benefit claimants to transfer a portion of the unused benefits to their individual accounts. By doing so, the benefits of the savings accounts system – improved incentives to take a job – could be activated rapidly while limiting the danger of strategic manipulation ("dive and run") by allowing just one such transfer in a lifetime.

Box 3.2. **Unemployment Insurance Savings Accounts**

To improve the job-search incentives of the unemployed while simultaneously decreasing the administrative burden of enforcing job-search requirements, Slovenia may consider introducing unemployment insurance savings accounts (UISAs). Under such a system, mandated unemployment insurance contributions are split between individual-level insurance savings accounts and a common, solidarity fund – with the latter, as in the existing system in Slovenia, co-financed by the government. In the event of a job loss, benefit recipients first draw from their savings accounts and, upon depletion, from the solidarity fund. Insufficient funds on individual accounts trigger payouts from the solidarity fund, and thus the benefit level and potential duration may stay the same as under the existing unemployment insurance system. While drawing from solidarity fund, benefit recipients would be monitored to verify job-search requirements by the ESS, but while drawing from individual accounts they would not be subject to monitoring. Upon retirement, positive account balances are transferred to the individual.

Empirical results from Chile, which implemented a similar system in 2002, indicate that UISAs improve the job-search incentives for those who draw from their UISA as compared to those who draw from a solidarity fund. Hartley Reyes, van Ours and Vodopivec (2011) find that claimants who are entitled to the solidarity fund have a significantly lower job-finding rate in the first months of their unemployment spells compared to those who were entitled to a UISA, but by month six when solidarity payments cease their job-finding rates are the same as for those who were entitled to a UISA. The magnitude of the disparity in job-finding rates is quite large: in the first month, when the disparity is the greatest, the job finding rates for prime-age men withdrawing from their UISA and the solidarity fund were approximately 4% and 21%, respectively.

Simulation results indicate that a similar system could be feasibly implemented in Slovenia. Based on individual-level data in which lifetime labour market histories are simulated from an administrative panel in Slovenia, Vodopivec (2010) shows that a UISA system could be a viable alternative to a modest UI system. Assuming a contribution rate of 3% of a person's wage and replacement rates similar to the ones currently in effect, over 55% of workers would never experience a negative balance over their working life and over three quarters of workers would retire with a positive balance that would be added to their old-age pension. It should be emphasised that the simulation results understate the viability of introducing UISAs in Slovenia because they do not account for the changes in behavior on the part of the unemployed – changes which the results from Chile show can be substantial.

Source: Reyes Hartley, G., J.C. van Ours and M. Vodopivec (2011), "Incentive effects of unemployment insurance savings accounts: Evidence from Chile", *Labour Economics*, Vol. 18/6, pp. 798-809; Vodopivec, M.. (2010), "How Viable are Unemployment Insurance Savings Accounts? Simulation Results for Slovenia", *Comparative Economic Studies*, Vol. 52/ 2, pp. 225-247.

Social assistance and incentives to participate in the labour market

Slovenia has a range of means-tested benefits but rules were harmonised

Slovenia's social assistance policy since the onset of the economic crisis has been driven by two competing factors. On the one hand, various governing coalitions have sought to increase social transfers and curtail increases in poverty rates, while on the other, they have been forced to reduce government expenditures in response to a rapid accumulation of public debt. During the initial phase of the crisis up until 2012, the generosity of social benefits was increased. Subsequent increases were moderated by the 2012 Fiscal Balance Act, which made limited adjustments in social transfers contingent on economic growth surpassing a threshold growth rate. Because economic growth in 2015 exceeded the 2.5% threshold, the level of benefits in 2016 have been adjusted considerably. In addition, enforcement of social benefit eligibility has been strengthened since 2012.

For individuals without dependent children, the basic form of social assistance in Slovenia is a means-tested cash transfer called Financial Social Assistance (FSA). Its level is linked to a basic minimum income which is adjusted to account for changes in prices, although its adjustment was also subject to the 2012 Fiscal Balance Act. In 2016, its level is set at EUR 289, which is the level of FSA received by a single unemployed individual with no dependants. While its level is typically subject to relatively minor biannual adjustments, there have been two considerable increases since the onset of the economic crisis at the end of 2008, when it amounted to EUR 222: in January 2012 it was increased by 12.7% and in January 2015 by 7.3%. In real terms, its level has thus increased by 21% since the end of 2008.

FSA is administered by the Centres for Social Work (CSW) and is initially granted for a period of three months. Subsequently, it can be granted for a maximum period of one year and can be prolonged an unlimited number of times if circumstances remain unchanged. Permanent assistance can be granted for those whose social status is not likely to improve and who fulfil other conditions, such as being above 63 years (women) or 65 years of age (men). In case of permanent incapacity for work, individuals may also qualify for FSA if they are not eligible for disability pensions.

Individuals receiving FSA are also eligible for additional means-tested cash transfers. Emergency Financial Social Assistance (EFSA) is granted on an ad hoc basis for exceptional circumstances to cover extraordinary and urgent expenses. The Supplementary Allowance (SA) is for individuals with permanent incapacity and intended to cover the additional costs of care. Up until 2012, SA was administered by the Pension and Disability Insurance Institute (ZPIZ), but it has since come under the responsibility of the CSW.

In contrast to income taxes, social benefits are calculated taking into account the family as a whole, including the spouse's income and property. For these purposes, social workers at the local CSW office have access to detailed information on income, property and savings; receipt of in-kind transfers (food, housing etc.); and any misconduct on the part of the beneficiary (e.g. failure to register with the Employment Service).The Exercise of Rights to Public Funds Act 2010, implemented in January 2012, made non-contributory social benefits more targeted by harmonising the criteria for means-tested payments.[4] Previously, criteria had varied across different types of benefits – for example, student scholarships were subject to criteria that included income but not wealth. In addition, it introduced the enforcement of a provision that part of the benefits previously received by the deceased have to be repaid from any inheritance received by next-of-kin in the event of the FSA recipient's death (Stropnik and Prevolnik Rupel, 2015).

Recipients of FSA are also eligible to receive a so-called activity allowance that is contingent on being employed or engaged in volunteer work. The monthly benefit amount is EUR 76 for individuals working part-time or at least two hours a month as a volunteer and EUR 152 for individuals working almost full-time.[5] The activity allowance thus provides strong incentives to engage in some volunteer work, but comparatively weak additional incentives for actually taking-up full-time work.

For individuals with dependent children, the most important social transfer is the child allowance. Child allowances are fairly high for low-income families, both in real terms and relative to other means-tested cash transfers (Stropnik and Prevolnik Rupel, 2015). Because child allowances are the first social transfer to which a family is entitled and because it is factored into calculating the level of subsequent means-tested benefits,

its receipt may preclude many families from qualifying for FSA. Among recipients of FSA in December 2015, 11 800 had children and thus qualified for the child allowance; this compares with 238 000 total child allowance beneficiaries (Trbanc et al., 2016).

As previously discussed, the number of social benefit recipients initially increased after the onset of the economic crisis, but decreased dramatically with the 2012 reforms (Table 3.1). Child allowances underwent the largest parametric changes (Stropnik and Prevolnik Rupel, 2015). The eligibility threshold, calculated based on household per capita income relative to the average net monthly wage, was lowered from 99% to 64%. Furthermore, child allowance was no longer payable for full-time student dependants over the age of 18. Another important factor leading to a decrease in the number of benefit recipients was the introduction of the above-mentioned partial repayment of social benefits in the event of the FSA recipient's death. This considerably decreased the number of SA recipients and moderately decreased the number of FSA recipients, due to the fact that the latter tend to be younger, with over 95% of recipients below the age of 65 (Trbanc et al., 2016).

Table 3.1. **Number of child and supplementary allowance recipients has decreased since the 2012 reforms**

Number of recipients and beneficiaries of means-tested benefits, Slovenia, 2008-14

Year	Child allowance - beneficiaries	Financial Social Assistance (FSA) - recipients	Extraordinary FSA - recipients	Supplementary allowance - recipients
2008	376 802	37 001	3 816	45 111
2009	378 348	42 012	5 245	46 492
2010	374 466	49 005	5 491	46 789
2011	367 525	47 393	4 872	46 749
2012	283 361	44 419	3 351	12 641
2013	237 576	46 107	4 309	9 201
2014	238 325	50 580	5 595	9 364

Source: Social Protection Institute of the Republic of Slovenia.

StatLink http://dx.doi.org/10.1787/888933415290

Inactivity traps in Slovenia are almost as high as unemployment traps

While not as high as those relating to unemployment, inactivity traps in Slovenia also remain fairly large (Figure 3.11). For example, for a one-earner married couple with two children, 79% of the increased earnings are lost due to taxes and reduced benefits when moving from receiving SFA to full-time, low-wage employment. As in most other OECD countries, the majority of the inactivity trap is attributable to the withdrawal of social assistance, family and housing benefits, and only a minor share results from increased income tax and social security contributions. To address the weak incentives to become employed, Slovenia may consider implementing a form of tax credit or wage subsidy that increases the income of an individual who becomes employed (see Box 3.3).

Figure 3.11. **Inactivity traps are fairly high in Slovenia**

Marginal tax rates for a transition into full-time work for persons without entitlement to unemployment insurance but entitled to social assistance if applicable, 2014

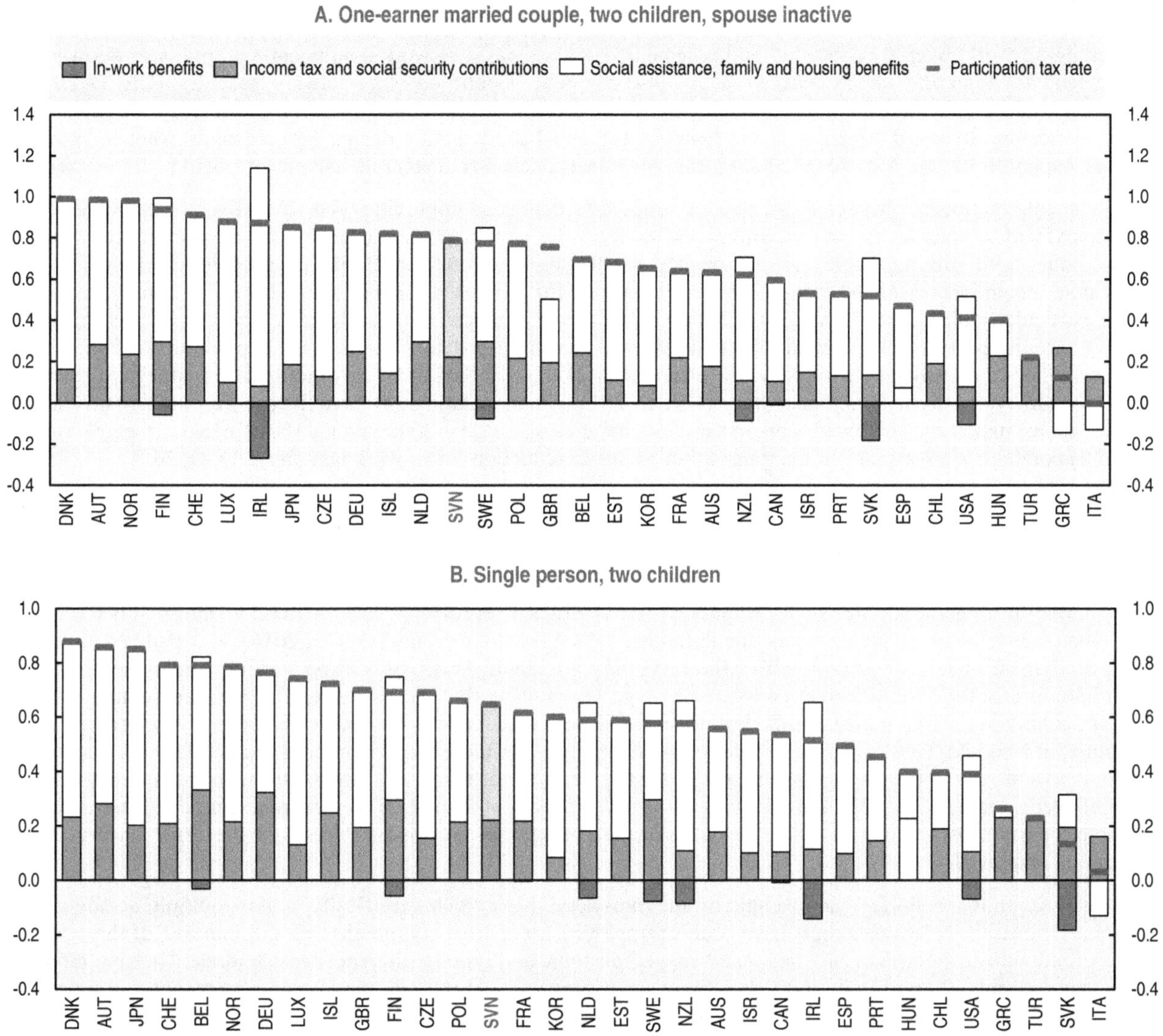

Note: Participation tax rates measure the extent to which taxes and benefits reduce the financial gain of moving into work. The estimates here relate to the situation of a person who is not entitled to unemployment benefits (e.g. because they entitlements have expired). Instead, social assistance and other means-tested benefits are assumed to be available subject to relevant income conditions. Where receipt of such assistance is subject to activity tests (such as active job-search or being "available" for work), these requirements are assumed to be met in the out of work situation. Cash housing benefits are calculated assuming private market rent, plus other charges, amounting to 20% of the full-time wage for all family types. Any benefits payable on moving into employment are assumed to be paid. The percentage of AW relates to the earnings from full-time employment of the individual moving into work. For married couples the percentage of AW relates to one spouse only; the second spouse is assumed to be inactive with no earnings in a one-earner couple. Calculations for families with children assume two children aged four and six and neither childcare benefits nor childcare costs are considered.

Source: OECD tax-benefits models (www.oecd.org/social/benefits-and-wages.htm).

StatLink http://dx.doi.org/10.1787/888933415178

Box 3.3. Employment-conditional transfers: Some lessons for Slovenia

Given that the interaction of various social benefits and income taxes can create strong financial disincentives to becoming employed, transfers to individuals tied to being employed can be an effective way to improve incentives for taking-up work. Such transfers can be implemented in two ways: as work-contingent tax credits or allowances implemented within the tax system, or as work-contingent benefit or wage-subsidy schemes (OECD, 2011). Regardless of how they are implemented, they are phased out at higher levels of income, and they encounter the equity-efficiency trade-off which is at the heart of tax and benefit policy design: governments want to provide income support for lower-income individuals, but this affects decisions to enter the labour force and hours worked.

Employment-conditional transfers involve a trade-off between improving the incentives for people not in employment to enter work, and incentives for some of the new entrants and people already employed to work fewer hours with earnings at levels that qualify for the in-work transfer. Rapid tapering of the transfer with individual income increases the marginal effective tax rate for those who remain entitled to it, but limits the fiscal costs, particularly if a country's wage distribution is highly compressed as in Slovenia. A lower taper rate limits the size of any increase in the marginal effective tax rate, but applies it to a larger total population. In either case workers who are already employed may, for example, work fewer hours or be less motivated to engage in training which would eventually lead to higher wage (OECD, 2011). Permanent in-work benefits can become a major factor in the labour market for employed workers: in the United Kingdom, by 2008 about 11% of people in employment faced a tax rate of 70% or more on marginal earnings due to reductions of in-work benefits (OECD, 2014).

For countries where the key problem is not to reduce in-work poverty but to strengthen work incentives, "into-work" benefits that are paid only temporarily following a transition into employment are an appealing option. Since in-work marginal tax rates are not increased, this approach may in the longer term reduce in-work poverty through higher earnings. In some countries, such transfers take the form of a lump-sum payment of the remaining UI benefit entitlement. In Bulgaria and the Slovak Republic, an individual is entitled to 50% of the remaining UI benefit and in Romania 30%; while in New Zealand the individual gets a fixed lump-sum (OECD, 2016). In Japan and Korea, a "re-employment bonus" of around half of the remaining UI benefit is conditional on starting employment with at least one-third of the UI entitlement period remaining. Recognising that the incentives for becoming employed can be particularly weak for parents with dependent children, some countries specifically target these groups. For example, in Belgium, lone parents who have been unemployed for more than six months are entitled to a maximum of EUR 918, or 2% of the average annual wage, for the first year after starting employment. In Ireland, individuals unemployed for over 12 months and receiving UI or unemployment assistance who become employed full-time are eligible for payments totaling EUR 387, or 1.2% of the average annual wage, per child, in the first 13 weeks after becoming employed.

Austria's Kombilohnbeihilfe is an example of an "into-work" policy that specifically targets multiple demographic groups. To qualify, individuals must have been unemployed for at least six months and fall into one of three target groups: individuals older than 50 years, handicapped persons, and those with dependent children. They are eligible for a wage subsidy of up to EUR 3600, or 9.3% of the average annual wage, if they become employed full-time; for those employed less than 35 hours per week, the benefit level is cut by half. The benefit is paid for at most one year. The system is administered by the PES and is financed from UI contributions; in 2012, beneficiaries received EUR 830 on average and represented 0.2% of total employment (Lechner and Wetzel, 2014). Tamler et al. (2011) argue that the measure had a positive effect on employment outcomes. Immediately after exhausting the benefit, 50% of individuals remained employed; after one year, the employment rate stood at 40%. On the other hand, there are indications that the subsidy has relatively large deadweight costs, as more than half of interviewed beneficiaries said they would have accepted the job regardless of the subsidy. In addition, 80% of those interviewed believed it facilitated employment but also gives them an incentive to accept a lower-paid job.

Source: Lechner, F. and P. Wetzel (2014), "Stimulating Job Demand: The Design of Effective Hiring Subsidies in Europe - Austria", European Employment Policy Observatory, March 2014; OECD (2011), *Taxation and Employment*, No. 21, OECD Publishing, http://dx.doi.org/10.1787/9789264120808-en; OECD (2014a), *Connecting People with Jobs: Activation Policies in the United Kingdom*, OECD Publishing, http://dx.doi.org/10.1787/9789264217188-en; Tamler, P., Löffler, R. and K. Schmid (2011), "Kombilohnbeihilfe. Eine Evaluation.", Arbeitsmarktservice Österreich; OECD (2016), *Taxing Wages*, OECD Publishing, Paris, http://dx.doi.org/10.1787/tax_wages-2016-en.

The statistics in Figure 3.11 are also subject to additional caveats due to circumstances specific to Slovenia. In addition to the travel and meal allowance previously discussed, childcare benefits in Slovenia are strongly progressive, with considerably lower subsidies for those entering employment. In addition, those on social assistance are afforded a variety of additional fringe benefits – including the above mentioned activity allowance – that can considerably skew the incentives to seek formal employment among FSA recipients. A 2016 Ministry of Finance report taking into account such circumstances calculates that the inactivity trap for a married couple with two children amounts to 88% when *both* parents move into minimum wage jobs if they live in close proximity to their workplace and are thus not eligible for travel allowances (MF, 2016). On the other hand, assuming the latter amount to roughly 10% of net wages, they calculate a 79% inactivity trap.

Social assistance receipt as a percentage of the population varies considerably by region in Slovenia, and, at over 8%, is particularly high in northeast Slovenia (Figure 3.12). While these are historically disadvantaged regions where there is arguably a greater need for social benefits (Banerjee and Jesenko, 2015), there is also a greater potential for false reporting of income due to the proximity to Austria. Accordingly, a 2015 Ministry of Labour report on preventing informal employment notes a "considerable increase in the number of anonymous tip-offs relating to employment and undeclared work of unemployed persons who are recipients of unemployment benefits or social assistance, mainly in Austria. Because there is no exchange of information of the relevant information between the Republic of Slovenia and the Republic of Austria, there was no possibility to take action against the unemployed individual" (MDDSZ, 2015).

Figure 3.12. **FSA benefit receipt is more frequent in north-eastern Slovenia**

FSA benefit receipt as a percentage of the respective population by municipality, 2011

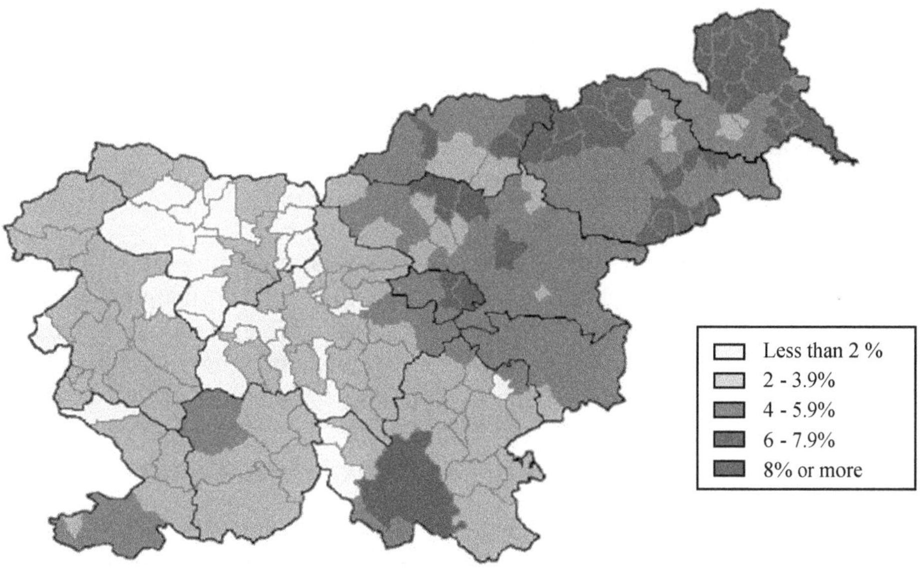

Source: Statistical Office of the Republic of Slovenia, MDDSZ, Surveying and Mapping Authority of the Republic of Slovenia.

StatLink http://dx.doi.org/10.1787/888933415184

Disability benefits increasingly used to lower effective retirement age

Slovenia has a parallel system of disability pensions and disability benefits, using a rather narrow definition of disability

The Slovene system of disability insurance is comprised of a system of disability pensions, including in-work transfers and benefits for jobseekers undergoing vocational rehabilitation, and a set of separate disability benefits provided based on physical impairment (see Box 3.4). In 2015, 85 700 people received disability pensions and an additional 45 200 received disability benefits (ZPIZ, 2016), equivalent to 4.2% and 2.2% of the Slovene population, respectively. Among individuals receiving disability benefits, approximately one-quarter were in the ESS unemployment registry and a small proportion received benefits while undergoing vocational rehabilitation. In total, about three in four disability benefit recipients thus had some work capacity.

The existing legislation, which with minor changes has been in effect since 2003, takes a fairly narrow view of disability. It considers an individual's ability to continue working based on their occupation, education and experience, as well as their physical and mental health limitations. Establishing what specifically should constitute an individual's occupation has proven difficult in practice, as it requires reconciling subjective and often detailed knowledge of various tasks which an individual may be required to perform in a given occupation with the individual's actual abilities or experience. In practice, the invalidity commissions which establish eligibility have thus taken an even narrower view, evaluating individuals mainly based on job requirements and hazards in their previous job position (MDDSZ, 2016).

For the future, the recent pension reform white paper (MDDSZ, 2016) sensibly recommends that the disability commissions should take a broader view on individual's disability that is not limited to their past employment. This would facilitate the activation of individuals who are capable of performing a wide variety of tasks, albeit in different types of job positions. Simplifying the criteria would also ensure a more consistent application of disability classifications. Given that student work has also been covered by disability insurance, a simplified set of criteria would also be sensible because much of the work performed by students is unrelated to their field of study and should not be considered their career.

In addition, Zaviršek (2014) mentions that the existing system suffers from a lack of flexibility inhibiting the labour market reintegration of people with disability. Working-age individuals who might otherwise consider re-entering employment may be hesitant to do so because they are unsure about whether they may permanently lose their disability benefits even if their new employment proves unsuitable and thus short-lived.

Box 3.4. The main characteristics of disability insurance in Slovenia

Disabled individuals are classified into three categories of disability by the Pension and Invalidity Insurance Institute of Slovenia (ZPIZ), based on remaining work capacity:

- Category I – individuals without capacity to perform organised productive work;
- Category II – individuals who have lost 50% or more of their capacity to work in their occupation;
- Category III – individuals fulfilling one of three conditions: no longer able to work full-time but with the capacity to work part-time; has lost less than 50% of the capacity to work in previous occupation; can work full-time in the normal occupation but no longer capable of working in the assigned job position.

Individuals are eligible for **disability pensions** based on their remaining work capacity and age, with the requirements for individuals to undergo vocation rehabilitation (and thus not be eligible for a disability pension) at a given level of disability becoming less stringent with increasing age. In addition to eligibility criteria related to the payment of insurance contributions, individuals must satisfy one of the following conditions:

- Category I – disability;
- Category II – disability for individuals who are over 55 years of age and are not capable of full-time work without rehabilitation;
- Category II – disability and over age 50 and not capable of even part-time work without rehabilitation.

In instances of work-related disabilities, individuals are eligible for disability pensions regardless of prior contributions; otherwise, individuals must also have a sufficient period of compulsory contributions in order to qualify: for example, for an individual over 30 with less than tertiary education, contributions must have been paid for one-third of the period between the age of 20 and the onset of the disability. In addition to disability pensions, means-tested supplements are available specifically for various types of incapacity.

Prior to being eligible for disability pensions, individuals may receive a variety of other benefits. The partial benefit is for individuals who can no longer work full-time (Category III); their income is topped up with the proportional disability pension based on the extent to which they work part-time. The disability benefit is for individuals who have completed occupational rehabilitation and can continue to work in their own occupation on a full-time basis, but not at the job position they have been assigned. Individuals receiving these benefits who are not employed are required to register as unemployed with the ESS.

The vocational rehabilitation benefit is paid to individuals undergoing vocational rehabilitation, which most commonly lasts one month but can last up to a year. The temporary benefit is paid to individuals who have completed vocational rehabilitation but have not yet been reassigned to a suitable job position. In contrast to the other disability benefits, the temporary benefit is paid by the employer. Recipients of the vocational rehabilitation and temporary benefits are not required to register as unemployed with the ESS; temporary benefits can be paid for no more than two years.

In addition, people may be entitled to a disability benefit for physical impairment based solely on their degree of physical impairment (and subject to age and contributory requirements); this is paid in addition to other benefits and is not means-tested.

Source: Pension and Invalidity Insurance Institute of Slovenia (ZPIZ).

Recent reform has failed to encourage the take up of vocational rehabilitation and unemployment with a partial disability benefit is on the rise

Despite recent attempts to strengthen incentives, vocational rehabilitation take-up remains low in Slovenia (Table 3.2). In 2015, only 145 individuals initiated vocation rehabilitation, in most cases lasting no more than one month (some undergo rehabilitation for up to 11 months). The 2012 pension reform increased benefits received during the rehabilitation process, from 100% to 130% of an individual's hypothetical disability pension, in order to provide incentives for a higher take-up; however, the average payment, while high compared to other disability transfers, averaged only EUR 482

Table 3.2. **Disability benefit and disability pension recipient counts have been gradually declining**

Disability benefit and disability pension recipients, Slovenia, 2006-15

	Vocational rehabilitation	Temporary benefit	Partial benefit	Benefit while waiting for reassignment[a]	Disability benefit	Total partial disability recipients	Disability pension recipients
2006	269	30	16 513	17 043	18 918	52 773	95 736
2007	285	63	17 254	16 481	19 390	53 473	94 511
2008	282	116	18 172	15 923	20 154	54 647	93 389
2009	285	188	15 271	15 142	20 156	51 042	92 123
2010	305	253	15 318	14 197	19 829	49 902	91 051
2011	336	322	15 407	13 133	19 378	48 576	90 219
2012	362	398	16 102	11 996	19 626	48 484	89 384
2013	351	473	15 733	10 860	19 535	46 952	88 361
2014	334	539	15 566	9 634	19 833	45 906	87 250
2015	312	609	15 771	8 664	19 834	45 190	85 749
Must register with ESS if unemployed?	n.a.	No	Yes	Yes	Yes		n.a.

Note: "Benefit while waiting for reassignment" includes recipients of benefits classified under pre-2003 legislation with no similar categories in subsequent legislation; other categories combine individuals classified under either legislation into similar categories. The temporary benefit is paid only to those who are still employed by their employer; thus, such recipients are not required to register as unemployed.

Source: Pension and Invalidity Insurance Institute of Slovenia (ZPIZ) 2015, Annual Report, 2016.

StatLink http://dx.doi.org/10.1787/888933415306

While the total number of partial disability recipients has been slowly decreasing during the past decade, the number of unemployed individuals receiving partial disability benefits has been on the rise recently – creating a bridge for early retirement as more stringent pension requirements become binding (Figure 3.13). While prior to the economic crisis the vast majority of unemployed partial disability benefit recipients were aged 45-54, the last few years have also seen a dramatic rise in the number of individuals aged 55-59 receiving such benefits. For both age groups, these partial disability benefits are in effect permanent: mandatory medical checks are foreseen every five years only for persons who have acquired a right to benefit on the ground of invalidity before the age of 45 (EC, 2013). The share of partial disability benefit recipients who have been unemployed for five years or more has been steadily increasing, reaching 45% of all such cases in 2015.

Figure 3.13. **Increase in unemployed partial disability benefit recipients in Slovenia has been driven by older workers and long-term unemployed**

Unemployed partial disability benefit receipt by age group and duration of unemployment, 2005-15

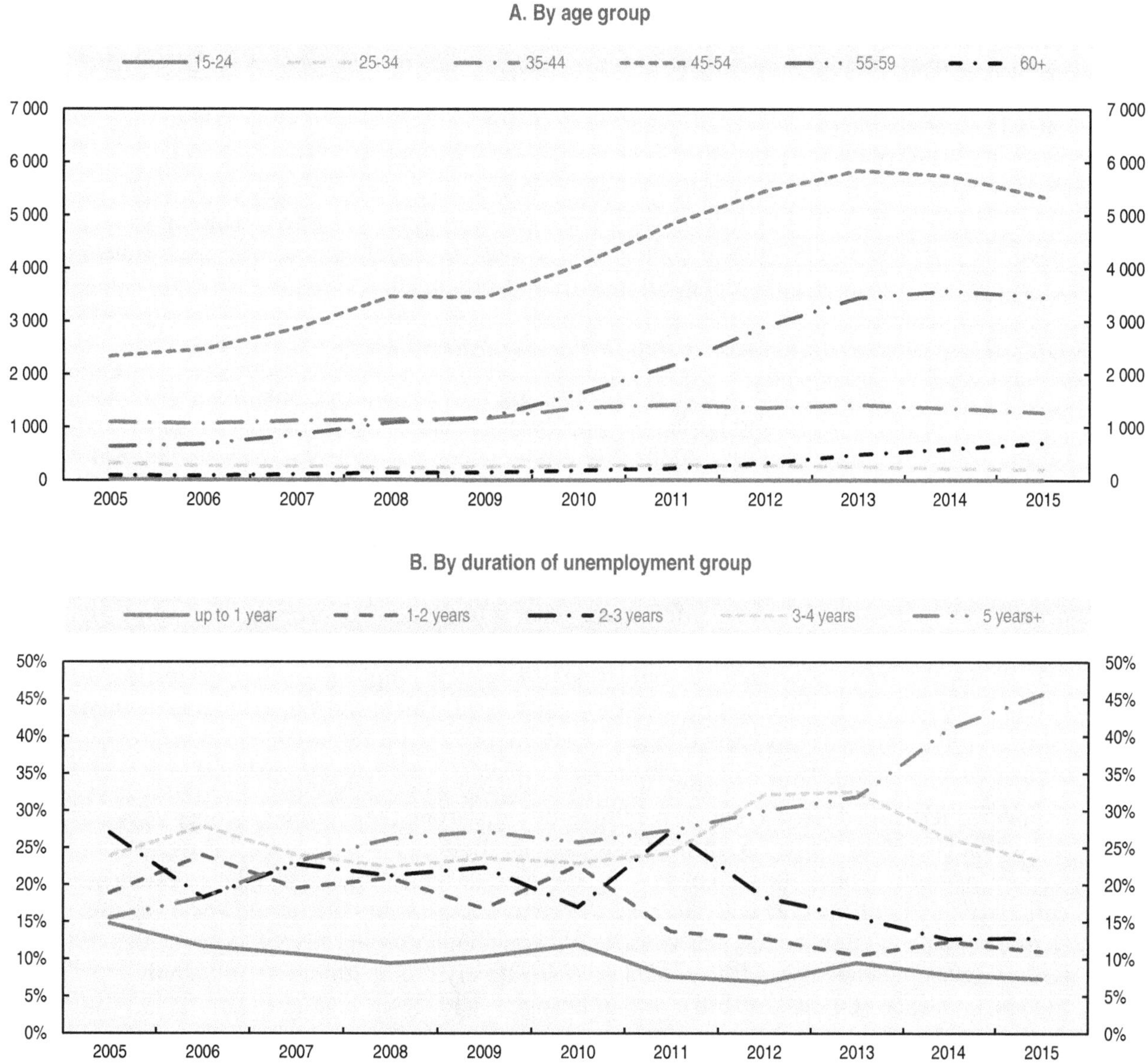

Note: Panel B refers to duration of unemployment which does not necessarily coincide with the duration of ZPIZ partial disability benefit receipt.

Source: Employment Service of Slovenia.

StatLink http://dx.doi.org/10.1787/888933415194

Pension reform will increase employment of older workers

One of the most significant challenges facing Slovenia is to increase the employment rate of its older workers. Employment rates among workers aged 60-64 are among the lowest in the OECD, while the Slovene population is projected to age more rapidly than most other OECD countries, leading to a considerable increase in the old-age dependency ratio in the future (OECD, 2015). Pension outlays have increased significantly since the 2009 recession, contributing to a growing public debt that threatens the long-term viability of the pension system. While the necessity for reform has been apparent for quite some time – prior to the financial crisis, the last pension reform with major changes was passed in 1999 – a proposed reform in 2010 was subsequently voted down in a popular referendum. However, given the undeniably unfavourable demographic trends and fiscal imperatives, a subsequent government was able to implement a major pension reform in 2013.

The 2013 pension reform was a step in the right direction

The 2013 reform introduced a number of significant changes that strengthen the incentives for older workers to remain in employment, particularly for women. When the reform comes into full effect by 2020, it will have increased the retirement age by four years for women (from 61 to 65) and two years for men (from 63 to 65). Early retirement will still be possible for those who entered regular employment at a young age, more specifically at age 60 for those with at least 40 years of qualifying contribution periods. This means a 2.33-year increase for women in the necessary qualifying contribution period and a two-year increase for men. The reform also decreased the scope of qualifying periods that serve to lower the effective retirement age: under the new legislation, the latter now includes only years of regular employment, maternity leave, compulsory military service and periods of regular employment (hence, excluding student work) for individuals 15-18 years of age.[6]

The 2013 pension reform also significantly tightened eligibility for those who completed tertiary education. Under the previous legislation, the required number of years for which contributions had been paid to establish eligibility was reduced for those with tertiary degrees. Under the parameters of the new scheme, these have been excluded entirely. This modification will increase the required contribution period for a sizable share of the population. Given that younger cohorts contain progressively larger shares of tertiary-level educated graduates and the relatively long duration of study for Slovene students (OECD, 2014b), these changes will have a significant effect on increasing the effective retirement age even after the parameters of the reform are fully in effect in 2020.[7] Combining this factor with the lower employment rates for younger workers due to unfavourable labour market conditions, current younger cohorts have relatively fewer years of insurance periods than their counterparts in previous years. For example, in 2002, workers aged 30-34 averaged around 11 years of insurance period, while in 2015, workers in this age group averaged just below 8 years – a difference of over three years (ZPIZ, 2016).

The 2013 reform also modified how an individual's pension base is determined. The new system takes into account the 24 consecutive years of insurance most favourable to the individual, rather than the best 18 years. The pension assessment base is defined relative to the average net wage in the year contributions were made, with a minimum pension base of 76.5% of the average net wage and a maximum that is four times the minimum base. Upon meeting the minimum qualifying condition of 15 years of contributions, the scheme pays 26% of the pension assessment base for men and 29% for women. The subsequent accrual rate is 1.25% per year and the resulting net replacement rate after 40 years of contributions is 57.25% for men and 60.25% for women.

In addition, individuals not satisfying the full retirement conditions are subject to a reduction in the pension by 0.3% per month of retirement before the statutory retirement age; conversely, deferred retirement results in a 1% increase per three months of additional employment, up to 12% (equivalent to three years of additional employment). In 2015, 20.7% of new retirees were entitled to bonuses due to deferred retirement, while 3.6% were subject to reductions for not fulfilling the retirement conditions. This compares favourably to previous years, when there were significantly less individuals with deferred retirement and more who were subject to reductions.

Incentives to remain in employment are weak for older workers

How do the financial incentives to continue working in Slovenia compare to other OECD countries? Figure 3.14 indicates that Slovenia has strong disincentives to remain in employment for those aged 60-64, with an additional year of working associated with a 4% decrease in net pension wealth.[8] Consistent with the above discussion of its changes, the recent pension reform has increased the incentives to remain in employment. However, the statistics refer to changes in net pension wealth for men, who were not as significantly impacted by the recent pension reform; the changes compared to 2008 would be much greater for women. At the same time, the figure accurately depicts the incentives for women to remain in employment when the new system comes into full effect in 2020 because the pension reform has largely equalised the retirement conditions for men and women.

In addition to continuing working and qualifying for bonuses due to deferred retirement, workers who are eligible for retirement can continue working under several different arrangements – although the take-up rate for these arrangements is fairly low. First, individuals eligible for retirement can continue working part-time and receive a proportional pension which is increased by 5% if they are less than 65 years of age. At the conclusion of such part-time employment, individuals have their pension recalculated to reflect the increased contribution period. In 2015, there were 800 such individuals in Slovenia, representing 0.1% of the 612 000 pensioners (ZPIZ, 2016). Secondly, people eligible for retirement can continue working full-time and receive 20% of their pension while they work. Upon exiting employment, they are then also eligible to have their pension recalculated to reflect the increased contribution period. In 2015, 3 076 individuals opted for such an arrangement, a considerable increase on the previous year but still relatively small as a share of total pensioners. Thirdly, individuals can receive a full pension and work via a so-called temporary and occasional work contract, which is subject to social security contributions and an additional 25% duty payable by the employer. In 2015, 4 997 individuals engaged in this type of part-time work, most of them under age 65. In total, 1.5% of pensioners also engaged in some form of formal employment (albeit mostly part-time).[9]

Figure 3.14. **Weak incentives in Slovenia to remain in employment past age 60**

Change in net pension wealth in OECD countries when continuing to work past age 60, 2008 and 2012

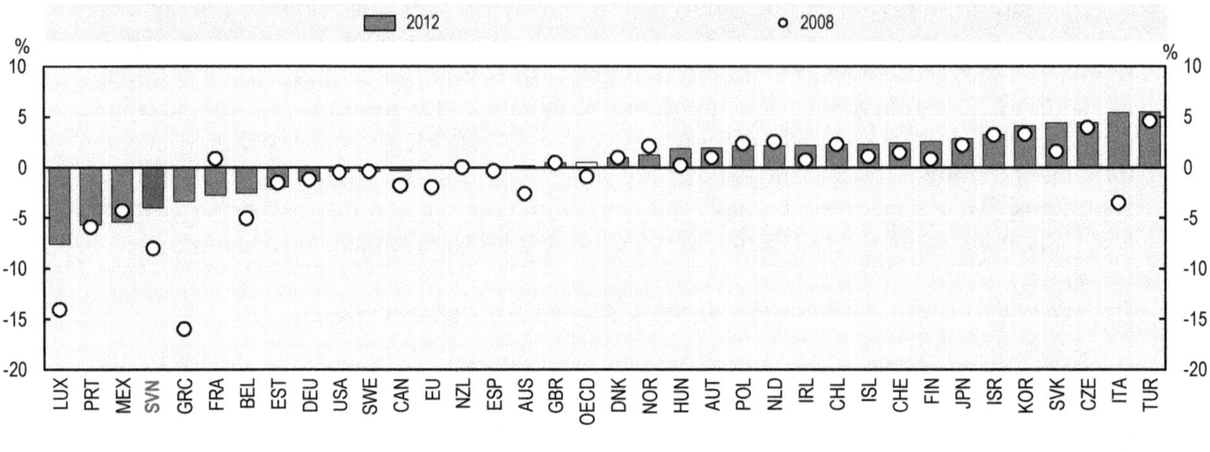

Note: The analysis labelled as 2012 is based on parameters and taxes for 2012, but long term legislated rules that were known at the time of publication are taken into account. In particular, the pension reform of 2013 for Slovenia is reflected in the calculations. The change in pension wealth is a measure of the incentive to remain in the workforce for an additional period. It measures the level of the pension promise from remaining in employment for an additional year. The calculation is the annual average increase in males' pension wealth when working from age 60 to 64. Net pension wealth is the present value of the flow of pension benefits, taking account of the taxes and social security contributions that retirees have to pay on their pensions. It is measured and expressed as a multiple of gross annual individual earnings in the respective country.

Source: OECD Pension Models (www.oecd.org/els/public-pensions).

StatLink http://dx.doi.org/10.1787/888933415208

The 2016 White Paper on pension reform contains useful proposals for reform

The White Paper proposes many sensible changes to the pension system, including especially the following (MDDSZ, 2016):

- Possibility to receive a full pension upon satisfying the requirements and continue working (paying same social security contributions as before), possibly with upper limits.
- Further increasing the retirement age (various scenarios are discussed, with different replacement rates, but generally proposing a two-year increase in the statutory retirement age and five years of additional working years).
- Levying equal social security contributions on all forms of labour.
- Compulsory matching of individual's contributions in supplementary schemes provided by employers or determined by sectoral collective agreements or introducing opt-out possibilities (i.e., that individuals would by default be enrolled in a supplementary scheme).
- Abolishing Category III of partial disability and introducing mandatory vocational rehabilitation for such individuals instead.
- Simplifying eligibility criteria, including terminology (currently, seven different phrases e.g. pension qualifying period) to emphasise years of paid contributions.

Key findings and recommendations

Despite recent reforms which increased the targeting of social benefits, there is additional scope for boosting work incentives in Slovenia. In addition, while the 2013 pension reform mandated gradual increases in retirement age, early retirement pathways continue to exist via the unemployment and disability insurance systems which threaten to undermine the goals of the pension reform.

Existing system of paid pension contributions and long unemployment benefit payment provides a bridge to retirement for unemployed older workers

Unemployed older workers in Slovenia are disproportionally low-skilled and thus disadvantaged in terms of their job-finding prospects, and the existing system provides weak financial incentives to become employed. Individuals can effectively retire via the unemployment insurance system up to four years and one month prior to reaching the regular conditions for retirement. Unsurprisingly given the relatively favourable parameters, the use of such a bridge to retirement has risen since the 2013 pension reform has increased the retirement age, with approximately 30% of individuals entering retirement via unemployment in recent years. Such developments threaten to negate the recent pension reform's goal of increasing the employment rate of older workers.

In order to increase the incentives for older workers to actively seek work, Slovenia should abolish the payment by the ESS of social security contributions for older workers close to retirement and consider decreasing the maximum potential benefit duration of unemployment benefits. In addition to reinforcing the obligation to actively seek work for such workers, which thus far has arguably not been actively enforced, such measures would also improve the motivation of older unemployed to participate in ALMPs, whose take-up rates are especially low (see Chapter 4). For those exhausting unemployment benefits, the existing system of means-tested social assistance should suffice as an income support mechanism for eligible individuals.

Increase unemployment insurance contributions to make the system better funded, disproportionally increasing contributions for fixed-term contracts

Under the existing system, being employed on a nine-month fixed term contract suffices to be eligible for three months of unemployment benefits. Certain seasonal industries appear to be exploiting the less stringent eligibility requirements by adjusting their staffing policies to this arrangement. Although employers' unemployment insurance contributions were increased in 2013 for fixed-term contracts, at 0.3% of pre-tax wages they remain grossly insufficient to cover the actual costs of providing unemployment benefits: over 90% of expenditures are covered from the general government budget. Public policy should force employers to internalise a much larger part of the cost of paying unemployment benefits and not shift it to the public budget.

Introduce temporary into-work benefits for newly employed low-paid workers to make work pay and decrease welfare dependency

Incentives to become employed full-time are weak for social transfer recipients, particularly for low-wage earners. While hiring subsidies do exist in Slovenia, they are currently directed at employers who are initially exempt from paying social contributions when hiring individuals from certain vulnerable groups. However, these subsidies do not directly affect the incentives for individuals to become employed. For FSA recipients, an existing cash transfer – the so-called "activity bonus" – is intended to stimulate activity, but it offers weak incentives for full-time work, especially compared to volunteer work or part-time work. Furthermore, because social benefits take into account household income while income taxes take into account individual income, the progressivity of the tax system does not directly address incentives to enter employment.

Introducing a temporary "into-work" benefit for low-skilled workers similar to what is currently done in Austria would significantly improve their incentives for becoming employed and, if carefully designed, would not impose significant fiscal costs. For example, long-term FSA recipients who become employed full-time could be eligible to receive a monthly benefit during their first year of employment. The benefit could be administered by the CSWs alongside existing benefits and slowly phased out at higher levels of income. The benefit could be further targeted by restricting eligibility to particularly vulnerable groups, such as older workers and younger women with children. Given that a relatively large share of workers in Slovenia receives wages close to the minimum wage, such additional restrictions on eligibility may be necessary to limit the number of benefit recipients who would have become employed even without the benefit.

Decrease taxation of labour in favour of increased taxation of wealth and property

The tax system in Slovenia relies heavily on labour taxes and social contributions, resulting in a high tax wedge which diminishes the incentives to work. Taxes on wealth, on the other hand, remain low: revenues from taxes on property in Slovenia were only 0.6% of GDP in 2013 (OECD, 2015), one-third the OECD average and considerably lower than in countries such as France (3.9%) or the United Kingdom (4.1%). In addition to decreasing unemployment and inactivity traps, decreasing the labour taxes would also reduce incentives for informal employment. Slovenia should also consider introducing a cap on social security contributions: at 14.5% of GDP, social contributions are among the highest in the OECD.

Explicitly link statutory and minimum retirement ages to life expectancy; calculate pension rights over lifetime contributions

The current system in which the statutory retirement age is fixed to a pre-determined level has required periodic increases as the fiscal unsustainability of the retirement parameters has become apparent. Given that Slovenia's population is set to age rapidly in the coming decades (OECD, 2015), the necessity of increasing the retirement age will likely continue in the future to ensure that the system remains viable. In addition to distracting public attention from other critical public policy debates, the present arrangement leads to increased uncertainty about important retirement parameters and diminishes the ability for individuals to make informed retirement decisions. At the same time, it may make sense to retain the possibility of retiring below the statutory minimum retirement age for those with enough years of contributions given the relatively large gap between life expectancy between high and low-educated elderly individuals, especially for men (OECD, 2014c). A further sensible reform would be to increase the pension basis from the current 24 years to an entire lifetime of contributions as is the case today in most OECD countries. This would increase the fiscal sustainability of the system and improve incentives to pay more than the minimum required contributions, which is a common practice among the self-employed.

Introduce mandatory vocational rehabilitation for employable individuals receiving partial disability benefits to foster employment of older workers

Recent years have seen a considerable increase in long-term unemployed individuals receiving disability benefits, particularly those with minor disabilities (Category III disabilities). The existing arrangement appears to serve as an alternative pathway to early retirement. The pension reform white paper (MDDSZ, 2016) sensibly recommends introducing mandatory vocational rehabilitation for such individuals, after which they are no longer eligible for disability benefits. In addition, Slovenia should consider phasing out the disability benefit for physical impairment, possibly increasing payments for means-tested or work-contingent benefits. In 2015, there were around 50 000 recipients of this benefit, amounting to EUR 31.6 million or one-fifth of total spending on disability benefits (ZPIZ, 2016). Privately-funded invalidity schemes can take the role of existing disability benefit for physical impairment.

Notes

1. The tax wedge is measured by the total taxes paid by employees and employers, minus family benefits received, divided by the total labour costs of the employer.
2. Specifically, the statistics refer to an individual earning 66% of the average wage, which closely corresponds to the minimum wage in Slovenia after including travel and meal allowances.
3. These statistics exclude the year of the greatest economic contraction, 2009, which saw an abnormal pattern due to the large inflows into unemployment. The increased cyclicality is in fact mostly apparent since 2013; the magnitude of the within-year variation in 2011 is comparable to that of 2010.
4. In fact, the combined effects of the reform were deemed too restrictive, and eligibility criteria were relaxed somewhat in 2014 (Trbanc et al., 2015).
5. The precise cut-off for the higher activity allowance is work for 128 hours per month, which corresponds to at least 80% employment. To be eligible for the volunteer allowance, individuals must sign an agreement with a volunteer organisation for at least 24 hours of annual volunteer work.
6. Generally, the decreases amount to eight months for compulsory military service and eight months per child. The reductions are subject to some restrictions, including at least 38 years of employment with paid contributions.
7. Although this effect will, in the long-term, be dampened by the 2015 introduction of social contributions for those working via student temporary employment agencies; a very common situation for Slovenes in tertiary education.
8. Note that the statistics for Slovenia in 2012 calculate incentives in the steady state, using the parameters that will be in effect in 2020.
9. In addition, pensioners may also work via civil-law contracts, although no statistics are available on the scale of such practices.

References

Banerjee, B. and M. Jesenko (2015), "Economic Growth and Regional Disparities in Slovenia", *Regional Studies*, Vol. 49/10, pp. 1722-1745.

COE – Council of Europe (2015), "10th Annual Report of the Republic of Slovenia on the Application of the European Code of Social Security," Strasbourg, https://rm.coe.int/CoERMPublicCommonSearchServices/DisplayDCTMContent?documentId=090000168059945f.

Dolenc, P. et al. (2012), "Empirical Analysis of the Effects of the Labor Market Regulation Act", Paper presented at the 22nd Statistical Days, Radenci, Slovenia, 12-13 November 2012.

EC – European Commission (2013), "Your social security rights in Slovenia", Mutual Information System on Social Protection, European Commission, Brussels, July.

Galuscak, K. et al. (2012), "The determination of wages of newly hired employees: Survey evidence on internal versus external factors", *Labour Economics*, Vol. 19/5, pp. 802-812.

Kierzenkowski, R. (2013), "Restructuring Welfare Spending in Slovenia", *OECD Economics Department Working Papers*, No. 1061, OECD Publishing, Paris, http://dx.doi.org/10.1787/5k44v50kwzxx-en.

Langenbucher, K. (2015), "How demanding are eligibility criteria for unemployment benefits, quantitative indicators for OECD and EU countries", *OECD Social, Employment and Migration Working Papers*, No. 166, OECD Publishing, Paris, http://dx.doi.org/10.1787/5jrxtk1zw8f2-en.

Lechner, F. and P. Wetzel (2014), "Stimulating Job Demand: The Design of Effective Hiring Subsidies in Europe - Austria", European Employment Policy Observatory, March.

MDDSZ - Ministry of Labour, Family, Social Affairs and Equal Opportunities (2015), "Poročilo o dejavnostih in učinkih preprečevanja dela in zaposlovanja na črno za leto 2014" [Report on activities relating to the prevention of informal employment in 2014], Ministry of Labour, Family, Social Affairs and Equal Opportunities, Ljubljana, May 2015.

MDDSZ (2016), *Bela knjiga o pokojninah* (White Paper on Pension System Development), Ljubljana, April, www.mddsz.gov.si/nc/si/medijsko_sredisce/novica/article/1939/7901/.

MF - Ministry of Finance (2016), "Končno poročilo o pregledu izdatkov s predlogi nabora možnih rešitev s finančnimi posledicami za leta 2017–2020 na področju socialne varnosti in pokojninskega varstva" [Final report on reviewing spending proposals with a range of possible solutions including financial implications for the 2017-2020 period in the area of social security and pensions], Ljubljana, March 2016.

OECD (2016), *Taxing Wages*, OECD Publishing, Paris, http://dx.doi.org/10.1787/tax_wages-2016-en.

OECD (2015), *Economic Surveys: Slovenia*, OECD Publishing, Paris, http://dx.doi.org/10.1787/eco_surveys-svn-2015-en.

OECD (2014a), *Connecting People with Jobs: Activation Policies in the United Kingdom*, OECD Publishing, http://dx.doi.org/10.1787/9789264217188-en.

OECD (2014b), *Education at a Glance: OECD Indicators*, OECD Publishing, Paris, http://dx.doi.org/10.1787/eag-2014-en.

OECD (2014c), *Health at a Glance: Europe*, OECD Publishing, Paris, http://dx.doi.org/10.1787/health_glance_eur-2014-en.

OECD (2011), *Taxation and Employment*, OECD Tax Policy Studies, No. 21, OECD Publishing, Paris, http://dx.doi.org/10.1787/9789264120808-en.

Reyes Hartley, G., J.C. van Ours and M. Vodopivec (2011), "Incentive effects of unemployment insurance savings accounts: Evidence from Chile", *Labour Economics*, Vol. 18/6, pp. 798-809.

Stropnik, N. and Prevolnik Rupel, V. (2015), "ESPN Thematic Report on Social Investment: Slovenia", European Social Policy Network, http://ec.europa.eu/social/BlobServlet?docId=13833&langId=en.

Tamler, P., R. Löffler and K. Schmid (2011), "Kombilohnbeihilfe. Eine Evaluation.", [*Kombilohnbeihilfe*. An Evaluation],Arbeitsmarktservice Österreich, Vienna.

Trbanc, M. et al. (2015), "Socialni položaj v Sloveniji 2013-2014 - Končno poročilo" [Social Situation in Slovenia 2013-2014 – Final Report], Social Protection Institute of the Republic of Slovenia, Ljubljana, February 2015.

Trbanc, M. et al. (2016), "Socialni položaj v Sloveniji 2014-2015 – Končno poročilo" [Social Situation in Slovenia 2014-2015 - Final Report], Social Protection Institute of the Republic of Slovenia, Ljubljana, February 2016.

Vodopivec, M. (2010), "How Viable Are Unemployment Insurance Savings Accounts? Simulation Results for Slovenia", *Comparative Economic Studies*, Vol. 52, No. 2, pp. 225-247, http://econpapers.repec.org/RePEc:pal:compes:v:52:y:2010:i:2:p:225-247.

Vodopivec, M. et al. (2015), "The Effect of Unemployment Benefit Generosity on Unemployment Duration: Quasi-Experimental Evidence from Slovenia", *IZA Discussion Paper*, No. 9548, http://ssrn.com/abstract=2708361.

Zaviršek, D. (2014), "Slovenia ANED country report on the European semester", Academic Network of European Disability experts, http://www.disability-europe.net/contenaned/media/ANED%202014%20-%20Task%205%20-%20SI%20-%20final.doc.

ZPIZ - Zavod za Pokojninsko in Invalidsko Zavarovanje (2016), "2015 Annual Report", Ljubljana.

Database references

OECD Income Distribution Database www.oecd.org/social/income-distribution-database.htm.

OECD Social Expenditure Database, www.oecd.org/social/expenditure.htm.

Tax and Benefit Systems: OECD Indicators Database, www.oecd.org/social/benefits-and-wages.htm.

SORS LFS Employment Database, http://pxweb.stat.si/pxweb/Database/Dem_soc/Dem_soc.asp.

Chapter 4

Investing in the employability of jobseekers in Slovenia

The Employment Service of Slovenia (ESS) is a well-functioning and modern public employment service with a strong focus on job placement. It has established a strong role as a job-broker by offering extensive recruitment services to employers. Just like employment services in many other OECD countries, it invested in user-friendly e-services with the aim to increase service availability and accessibility for both jobseekers and employers. The ESS has a large and diverse client base and only around a quarter of the unemployed are not registered with the ESS. Despite all those strengths, a number of challenges prevail, holding back re-employment for more people and at an earlier stage. Also, as the ESS does not administer the income-replacement benefits of all of its clients, the activation of jobseekers appears inconsistent in some circumstances. This chapter identifies a number of areas where consideration should be given to additional measures or adjustments to existing ones and a co-ordinated approach to activation by all actors involved.

The statistical data for Israel are supplied by and under the responsibility of the relevant Israeli authorities. The use of such data by the OECD is without prejudice to the status of the Golan Heights, East Jerusalem and Israeli settlements in the West Bank under the terms of international law.

Hit very hard by the Global Financial Crisis, Slovenia's unemployment rate still stood at 8.4% in Q4 2015, well above the 4.7% recorded in Q4 2007. All unemployed people in Slovenia can register with the Employment Service of Slovenia (ESS) (see Box 4.1) and only around a quarter of the unemployed are not registered with the ESS. But the client base of the ESS is very diverse: only one-fifth of ESS clients receive unemployment insurance (UI) benefit, which is also administered by the ESS; 35% receive means-tested social assistance, which is administered by the Centres for Social Work (CSW) (see Box 4.1); another 10% receive a partial disability benefit which is administered by the Pension and Disability Insurance Institute of Slovenia (ZPIZ); and the remaining 35% of jobseekers do not receive any cash benefit. This creates considerable policy co-ordination challenges. Overall, the ESS appears as a modern employment service with a strong focus on placement. But against the background of high unemployment it cannot help all clients to the same degree or the degree necessary.

This chapter discusses the role of the ESS as a job-broker who offers extensive recruitment services to employers in Slovenia. It analyses ESS interventions during the unemployment spell and suggests that the ESS misses an opportunity for early activation and needs to address frequent parking of harder-to-place jobseekers. The use of Active Labour Market Programmes (ALMPs) varies considerably over time and some groups of disadvantaged jobseekers have a low likelihood of being referred to such programmes. Considering the ESS performance management system also suggests that ensuring a rapid return to work may be more difficult for some clients, especially when responsibilities are shared with the CSW.

Box 4.1. **The Employment Service of Slovenia and the Centres for Social Work**

Employment Service of Slovenia

Slovenia's Public Employment Service (PES), the Employment Service of Slovenia (ESS), is a public agency directly reporting to the Ministry of Labour, Family, Social Affairs and Equal Opportunities (MDDSZ). It has an annual contract with the MDDSZ, which stipulates the ESS budget, tasks and personnel. Its operations are steered by a tripartite Board, which consists of 13 members, representing employers and trade unions (three members each), the government (six members) and the ESS workers' council. The ESS consists of the Ljubljana-based headquarters, 12 regional offices, 59 local offices and 11 Career Centres. The ESS combines the functions of job-brokerage, employment counselling, referrals to active measures, administration of unemployment insurance benefits, provision of life-long career guidance, and issuing work permits to foreign workers.

The ESS headquarters set the standards for the professional and operative implementation of all ESS procedures and runs a number of centralised functions (i.e. IT, analysis and statistics, legal, human resources, finance, and accounting departments). The ESS regional offices are responsible for employer outreach activities, co-operation with contracted providers and providing support to local offices within their region. The ESS local offices work directly with the clients and grant access to unemployment insurance, provide counselling and job-brokering, make referrals to active labour market programmes and liaise with the Centres for Social Work and other local institutions in their area. The 11 ESS Career Centres are either co-located with one of the ESS local offices or in a separate location. The remit of Career Centres is to offer career advice and, hence, they are open not only to ESS registered jobseekers, but also to other jobseekers, students, parents, and teachers. The centres offer a combination of self-service tools (e.g. access to the ESS vacancy database, information on vocational training, and detailed descriptions of occupations), basic personal career counselling and workshops (e.g. on job-search techniques). Around 40% of ESS registered jobseekers regularly use the Career Centres.

Box 4.1. **The Employment Service of Slovenia and the Centres for Social Work** *(cont.)*

Centres for Social Work

The remit of the municipal Centres for Social Work (CSW) is to provide material subsistence to families and children through administering a range of social assistance benefits (Financial Social Assistance, Emergency Financial Social Assistance, and Supplementary Allowance; see Chapter 3 for details). Different to the ESS, there is no central or regional structure for the CSW and all of the 62 CSW in Slovenia are managed on the local level, with each CSW reporting directly to the MDDSZ. Individuals requiring assistance must apply to the CSW in the area where they live. In contrast, individuals are free to decide which local ESS office to register with (e.g. they are free to choose one which is the area where they intend to look for work, for example).

The CSW offer information on applying for social assistance benefits, assist in completing the application forms and grant benefits to entitled households. In addition, the CSW provide personal counselling and support for families, including home visits. This includes identifying the basic dimensions of the clients' living circumstances and providing clients with support in addressing their problems (e.g. mental health problems, addiction, and social problems). With this remit the CSW will also have the central role for the implementation of *social activation*. Social activation is seen as a holistic approach to enabling individuals and families to resolve their problems and empower them to actively participate in society and integrate into the labour market. At the time of writing this report, the final approach to social activation, the actors involved and their responsibilities were not yet fully defined. But during meetings of the OECD team with various stakeholders it became clear that the current discussion focusses too much on measures and programmes to resolve social problems and too little on having labour market activation as the ultimate objective.

Source: EC (2014), "Blended service delivery for jobseekers, Peer Review Host Country Paper", ESS Central Office, Brussels, http://ec.europa.eu/social/main.jsp?langId=en&catId=22; and IRSSV – Social Protection Institute of the Republic of Slovenia (2015), "Podlage za pripravo in zagon programov socialne aktivacije" [Basis for the preparation and launch of social activation], Ljubljana, www.irssv.si/upload2/Porocilo%20socialna%20aktivacija_koncno.pdf.

The strong job-brokerage function of the ESS

Job brokerage is the process of matching jobseekers with employers who are seeking to fill vacancies either through facilitating job-to-job transitions or helping unemployed jobseekers into employment. A central function of any public employment service is to match jobseekers and employers. But the ESS operates in an environment where many vacancies are filled through other recruitment channels and it also recently lost its quasi-monopoly for the processing of all vacancies in the Slovene economy. The ESS has established a strong role as a job-broker by offering extensive recruitment services to employers. As the ESS involvement reduces the costs of the matching process for both jobseekers and employers, it could consider charging for these services in some circumstances. The ESS also closely co-operates with employers planning larger layoffs due to economic reasons. While the processes and interventions for displaced workers – i.e. workers who lost their jobs involuntarily due to economic reasons – affected by collective dismissals are well established, more support should be offered to workers affected by individual and small-scale dismissals. Furthermore, workers facing job loss should be given better incentives to engage in job search early on.

The position of the ESS as a job-broker

A comparison across European countries shows that the ESS has one of the highest market shares of European employment services with respect to involvement in recently concluded employment relationships: In 2012, the ESS was involved in one-fifth of such employment relationships against an European average of one-tenth (OECD, 2015a).[1]

Two drivers may explain this strong position: First, employers were legally required to notify any vacancy to the ESS until 2013 and, second, the ESS not only supports jobseekers in finding jobs, but also offers extensive recruitment services to employers.

Following a large drop in vacancies since the onset of the economic crisis the Slovene economy has started to recover and open vacancies have been on the rise again since 2013. In 2015, total vacancies even surpassed the pre-crisis peak of 2007. This is also reflected in the number of unemployed per open vacancy which is falling again but still above its pre-crisis trough (Figure 4.1).

Until 2012, all vacancies in Slovenia had to be reported to the ESS. Mandatory vacancy notifications were abolished for the private sector in April 2013 to remove bureaucratic barriers for employers (EC, 2011). The public sector and business entities owned by the state still have a notification obligation towards the ESS. Private employers still have an obligation to make all vacancies publicly available, with rare exceptions (Employment Relationships Act (ZDR-1), Article 24). One option to comply with this requirement is the publication of vacancies in the ESS database. Although the ESS has lost is past quasi-monopoly over vacancies, it still has not lost its attractiveness for many employers due to the extensive recruitment services it offers (see below).

Figure 4.1. **Overall vacancies in Slovenia are on the rise again**

Stock of vacancies in the economy (yearly average) and LFS unemployed per vacancy (ratio), 2001-15

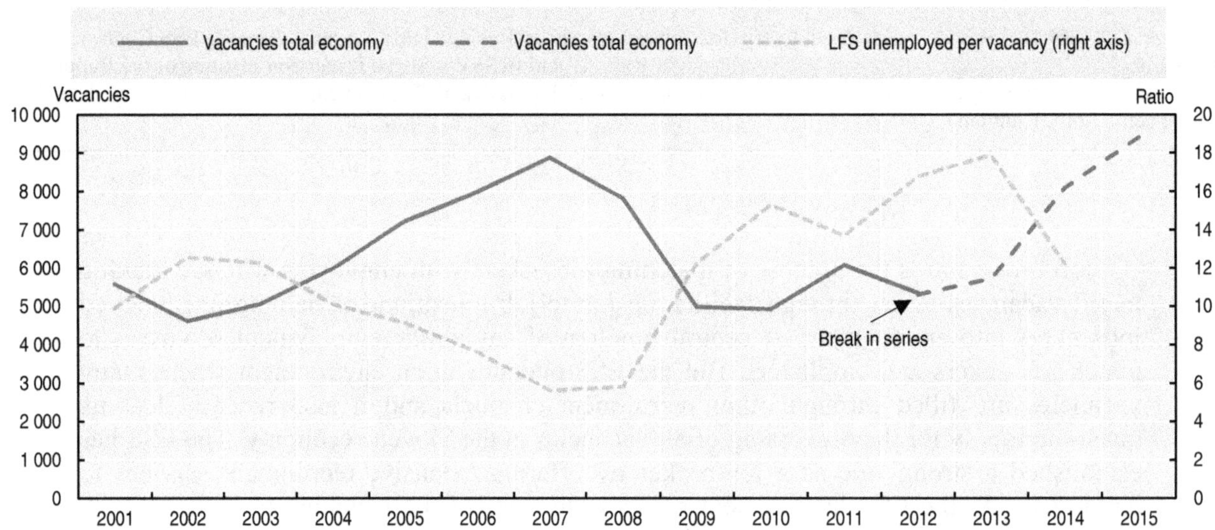

Note: The annual averages are calculated using quarterly data.

a) Between Q1 2001 and Q1 2013 the job vacancy data were taken from the Employment Service of Slovenia (ESS).

b) With the abolition of mandatory notification of vacancies to the ESS in April 2013, the Statistical Office of the Republic of Slovenia (SURS) no longer has complete coverage of all vacancies. The obligation to report vacancies to the ESS remains only for the public sector and for business entities owned by the state. Between Q2 2013 and Q4 2014 job vacancy data were forecasted, relying on an ESS survey conducted with employers with ten or more employees. For the conversion to the total population, shares from 2012 data were applied. Since Q1 2015, the SURS has been collecting vacancy data from the private sector with a sample survey. Public sector vacancy data continues to be supplied by the ESS.

Source: OECD *Employment Database*, www.oecd.org/employment/database, Statistical Office of the Republic of Slovenia and Employment Service of Slovenia yearly report.

StatLink http://dx.doi.org/10.1787/888933415210

Employer outreach services

The ESS has a strong emphasis on employer outreach services, reinforced in the Labour Market Regulation Act of 2010, which stipulates the ESS's role in enabling employers to carry effective business processes through timely and active mediation of suitable candidates. In order to fulfil this role, each local ESS office has specialised advisers for employers.[2] In addition, in 2015 the ESS established cross-regional outreach services for larger employers with large-scale recruitment needs in five of its regional offices. Services the ESS offers to all employers – regardless of size – include:

- The online vacancy database with electronic filing of vacancies and a CV data bank for jobseekers, where employers could search for suitable candidates.
- Support in advertising vacancies (e.g. drafting vacancies according to the employer's needs);
- Recruitment services: preselection of suitable jobseekers for vacancies;
- Organising speed-dating events for employers and pre-selected candidates on ESS premises and organisation of local and regional job fairs;
- Information and advice on training programmes and employment incentives;
- Information and advice on procedures related to employing workers;
- Issuing work permits for foreign employees and providing information and advice on employers' application process;
- Co-operation in cases of larger redundancies and in case of redundancies of disabled employees.

In addition to these service offers, the ESS also fosters relationships with employers through organising regular local and regional employer meetings and visiting employers with high recruitment potential – including both enterprises with an established customer relationship and those that have not used the PES services before. In 2014, the ESS visited over 3 000 employers, representing 2% of all active employers in Slovenia.[3] The ESS gathers feedback on its services through direct contacts with employers and also runs an annual employer satisfaction survey, covering the different aspects of its services to continuously improve their quality (EC, 2011 and 2014a).

Across the ESS services for employers, the recruitment service stands out as being more comprehensive than what many other PES in the OECD offer. For each vacancy advertised, employers have the option to choose whether they would like the ESS's active engagement in filling job vacancies. When ESS engagement is requested, ESS staff will sift jobseekers' profiles to identify suitable candidates and may also run pre-selection tests, before referring the most suitable candidates to the employer and organising the job interview. The number of candidates referred is usually low and depends on employer preferences (EC, 2011; Zakrajšek and Meke, 2011). ESS data from 2010 shows that the pre-selection activity of the ESS is far-reaching: for each vacancy with active mediation services on average only 1.5 jobseekers were contacted and potentially referred to the employer.[4] The interview outcomes are monitored through a feedback form for the ESS, which employers need to provide for each referred candidate.

The Finnish PES has also developed a specialised service for employers, which goes beyond basic services such as vacancy advertising and searching for potential jobseekers and which employers must pay for. The payable service includes tailored placement services, recruitment (selection and screening of jobseekers), outplacement, advice on company training and personnel hire (Duell et al., 2009). Also the Swiss PES has a strong emphasis on meeting employer's needs. The organisation of these services varies across cantons. Duell et al. (2010) cite the example of the canton of Basel-City, where one local employment office exclusively deals with employers and the acquisition of vacancies. In Switzerland, employers advertising a vacancy with the PES also have the option to request more intensive support from the PES, such as the pre-selection of candidates, but such services are free of charge.

In Slovenia, it can be argued that the ESS recruitment service takes over quite an extensive part of an employer's human resource function in the hiring process. Given that the service is free of charge, it is not surprising that it is a rather popular service among employers in Slovenia. In 2013, ESS active mediation services were used for 45 600 vacancies or 41% of all vacancies reported to the ESS (ESS, 2015b). The number of vacancies with active mediation services remained similarly high in 2014 and 2015.[5] Analysis of the mediation service shows that it is especially popular among micro (0-9 employees) and small (10-49 employees) employers. In 2013, of all vacancies for which ESS active mediation services were requested, 46% were posted by micro and 17% by small employers, while only 8% were posted by large employers (Stojak, 2014).[6] Mediation services are also used more often by employers recruiting workers with lower levels of education, those from the processing industry, catering, and building industry and those with their headquarters in the eastern regions (EC, 2011). While being a big benefit to employers, the ESS recruitment service is very resource intensive to deliver. In the light of high caseloads and imposed staff cuts the ESS therefore had to shift resources away from its services for employers. In addition, with the abolition of compulsory ESS vacancy registrations in 2013, the ESS now has to dedicate more resources to the acquisition of vacancies to keep up its market share (EC, 2014a).

With the ESS recruitment service saving employers a substantial part of their recruitment costs (e.g. in comparison to using private recruitment services), there is a case for the ESS to consider charging a service fee for its recruitment services. Such fees would enable the ESS to retain staff in this area to consistently deliver high-quality services and would also make the ESS accountable for the outcome of its services. The fees could be kept low (i.e. not on a cost-covering basis) not to put off employers from using the ESS services altogether and fees could, for example, be waivered if the employer hires a disadvantaged jobseeker.

Interventions for displaced workers

Displaced workers – i.e. workers who lost their jobs involuntarily due to economic reasons – are a major client group for the ESS. Already prior to the global financial crisis around 15% of newly ESS registered jobseekers were displaced workers. In 2009, the proportion increased to over 25%, gradually declining thereafter to just over 15% in 2015.

Regular and exceptional response measures following collective dismissals in Slovenia

Employers with imminent dismissals are obliged to notify the ESS about the redundancies and the planned redundancy process. The ESS then contacts employers to establish the number of redundant workers and their competencies. Especially in the case of collective dismissals,[7] the ESS informs workers about current vacancies with other employers, offers career advice and workshops on job-search methods. Up to three months before to the actual dismissal workers may also register with the ESS and can be enrolled in some active labour market programmes (see Box 4.7).

In case of large-scale redundancies special response measures may be introduced as has happened in response to the bankruptcy of the Mura textile company. In October 2009, Mura, Slovenia's largest textile manufacturer, filed for bankruptcy with over 2 000 workers (i.e. around 0.2% of all people in employment in Slovenia) facing redundancy. In response, the Ministry of Labour, Family, Social Affairs and Equal Opportunities (MDDSZ) established two labour funds (Labour Fund of Prekmurje and Regional Labour Fund Pomurje), with the aim of providing re-employment support for the displaced workers until June 2011. The total budget of the funds was around EUR 3.5 million, of which around two-thirds were financed by the European Globalisation Adjustment Fund. Support provided through the labour funds included job-search counselling, a range of different workshops (covering motivation, job-search assistance, etc.), job clubs and engaging with employers to establish re-employment opportunities. The ESS also received an extra grant from MDDSZ to offer additional places in its programmes supporting self-employment and on-the-job training.

Job-search assistance during the notice period is available, but take-up is low

During the notice period all dismissed employees – regardless of whether the dismissals was due to economic reasons or incompetence – are entitled to a minimum of two hours per week to search for employment. Employees are entitled to full wage compensation during this time. Employers must also enable employees to engage in a special job-search measure. Employees participating in this measure may be absent from work for at least one day per week to participate in ESS services and programmes. The employer is obliged to continue paying the employee during the days of absence at a reduced wage rate (70%), but can reclaim the expenses from the ESS. Workers taking up this offer who are entitled to unemployment insurance (UI) have their maximum benefit duration shortened by the number of days they participate in the measure. While the measure is a good starting point for preventing longer-term unemployment of displaced workers, take-up is low and the measure is "unpopular" with ESS staff due to its rather excessive administration.

The administration and design of the measure should be simplified and better incentives given to affected workers to increase take-up. Instead of making employees effectively pay for the measure, employers should be obliged to pay full wage compensation for the days to-be-dismissed employees engage in job search, without receiving reimbursement through the ESS.[8] Employees could also be given flexibility on how to use the job-search days – i.e. taking one day per week or taking several days in a row. A similar measure exists in Finland, were employees are entitled to paid employment leave during the notice period of 5-20 working days, depending on the length of the notice period (OECD, 2016). Also the Job Security Councils in Sweden are financed entirely through employer contributions (see Box 4.2). In addition, instead of leaving the choice of ESS registration to the dismissed workers, an ESS registration requirement should be introduced. Thereby the ESS could make employees aware of the measure and nudge more dismissed employees to engage in job search during the notice period. Furthermore, information obtained during the ESS registration process could be used by the ESS to identify dismissed workers who are likely to struggle with a quick labour market reintegration. Support measures like intensive counselling interviews and ALMPs could then be targeted specifically on those workers.

Interventions for displaced workers should be extended to cover individual and small-scale dismissals

Workers affected by individual or small-scale dismissal are also eligible to engage in job search during the notice period, but are not usually provided with special assistance as may be offered through the ESS in the case of collective dismissals. This is the case in many OECD countries, which tend to focus their targeted assistance to displaced workers affected by mass dismissals. Schemes aimed at individual or small-scale dismissals nevertheless exist for example in Canada (Québec), France and Sweden, where assistance is open to all displaced workers (Box 4.2).

Box 4.2. **Support schemes benefiting workers displaced individually or in small firms: The examples of Québec-Canada, France and Sweden**

The Continuous Entry Reclassification Assistance Committees in Québec

In Québec, workers affected by individual or small-scale dismissals can enrol in *Comités d'aide au reclassement à entrées continues* (CRECs). CRECs meet the needs of regions: i) facing multiple redundancies in small and medium-sized firms (therefore not reaching the 50-displaced workers threshold to qualify as a mass dismissal); and/or ii) that do not have enough PES staff to cope with the sudden influx of displaced workers in a local office. To ensure sufficient capacity is available, *Emploi-Québec* outsources these CRECs outplacement services to specialised external providers. The providers then develop a reclassification plan for each dismissed worker including a combination of tailored services to help workers find a job as quickly as possible. Displaced workers still requiring assistance once the CREC is dissolved are referred to the regular PES, *Emploi-Québec*.

The Job Security Councils in Sweden

In Sweden, once a permanent employee has been notified of the dismissal, both the employee and employer apply to a *Job Security Council* (JSC). The councils are based on collective agreements between social partners in a sector or occupational field (e.g. white-collar workers in the private sector) and are financed through employer contributions. The JSCs provide transition services such as individual counselling, career planning, job-search assistance and outplacement services. JSCs overall achieve very high placement rates, exemplifying the advantages of a systematic early intervention approach. On average, 80%-90% of dismissed workers find new jobs within 7-8 months, often without using any resources from the PES. The comparatively long notice period (a minimum of one month for newly employed workers up to six months after ten years of tenure) is thus used productively to help workers find a new job quickly, to take advantage of existing employer networks and to utilise workers' skills.

The Career Path Security Contract in France

In 2011, France implemented a tailored programme called *Contrat de sécurisation professionnelle* (CSP –Career Path Security Contract) to improve incentives for employer, affected employees and the PES to better facilitate the use of early transition services. Whatever their tenure, all workers dismissed for economic reason (individually or collectively) from a firm with less than 1 000 employees or from a firm filing for bankruptcy (regardless of size) are entitled to enter the programme. The programme lasts a maximum of 12 months and includes a range of measures such as job-search assistance, regular (weekly or monthly) intensive counselling with a dedicated caseworker specialised in supporting displaced workers, skills evaluation, access to training and follow-up support during the entire programme to improve re-employment prospects.

Box 4.2. Support schemes benefiting workers displaced individually or in small firms: The examples of Québec-Canada, France and Sweden *(cont.)*

The cost of the programme is shared between the PES, *Pôle emploi*, the employer and the employee, which facilitates co-operation between all actors. The employer must offer the CSP to any worker they plan to dismiss and is subject to a significant fine in case of non-compliance. Participating workers contribute to the financing through allocating part of their severance pay to *Pôle emploi*, waiving their notice period as well as their training rights acquired on the previous job. Due to the incentive structure, take-up of the programme is high: Participating workers receive a higher replacement income (80% of the previous gross wage) than other unemployment benefit recipients (between 57% and 75% of the previous gross wage) and are also entitled to a wage insurance if the new job pays less than 85% of the previous one. Due to the significantly higher replacement rate there is, however, the risk of a prolonged unemployment duration of programme participants.

Source: OECD (2015), *Back to Work: Canada – Improving the Re-employment Prospects of Displaced Workers*, OECD Publishing, http://dx.doi.org/10.1787/9789264233454-en; OECD (2015), *Back to Work: Sweden – Improving the Re-employment Prospects of Displaced Workers*, OECD Publishing, http://dx.doi.org/10.1787/9789264246812-en; Dares-Pôle emploi (2013), "L'accompagnement renforcé des demandeurs d'emploi : Évaluation du recours aux opérateurs privés par Pôle emploi de 2009 à 2011", *Synthèse.Éval'*, No. 03, January.

Scheduled interventions in the unemployment spell

The ESS has a large and diverse client base and only a quarter of the unemployed is not registered with the ESS; plausibly among those looking for regular employment the vast majority is registered. Owing to the diversity of clients and due to limited resources the ESS segments its clients. Generally a "work-first" approach is applied for more employable jobseekers. The intervention strategy for harder-to-place jobseekers has less of a "work-first" focus and interventions such as in-depth counselling are limited due to a lack of resources. The Slovene system misses an opportunity for early activation and suffers from parking harder-to-place clients and from a strict sanction regime.

Registration of benefit applications

All Slovenian residents who are unemployed may register with the ESS and use its services in their search for work. As has been shown in Chapter 3, the motivation to register with the ESS may differ for jobseekers, depending on their benefit entitlement. For claimants of UI, registration with the ESS is a prerequisite for UI eligibility. The ESS registration and the claim for UI can be done simultaneously. Jobseekers can register with any local ESS office of their choice regardless of residence, for example registering with an office located in the area where they intend to look for work (IRSSV, 2015). The registration as unemployed and the UI application have to be made within 30 days after the termination of employment in order to be eligible for UI and claimants can receive retrospective pay within this 30-day limit.[9] Even though it is generally easier to find a new job while still being in employment, the current rules offer little incentives for UI recipients to actively seek new employment before the current employment relationship ended or within the first 30 days of unemployment. This may be one of the reasons why the majority of OECD countries do not offer retrospective pay (OECD, 2015a). The absence of early activation may also explain why few displaced workers exercise their right to search for employment during the notice period and participate in programmes offered by the ESS during that period (see Box 4.7).

Slovenia should consider activating people at risk of losing their current job – either due to dismissal or due to the expiry of a fixed-term contract – while their current employment relationship still lasts. Such rules exist, for example, in Germany and Switzerland (see Box 4.3). One option would be to introduce job-search requirements already before the unemployment spell starts, as is done in Switzerland. A more far-reaching option would be to introduce mandatory ESS registration for people at risk of losing employment within, say, three days of having received notice from their employer[10] and for employees on fixed-term contracts, say, four weeks before the expiry of their current contract. Such requirements could be enforced through the introduction of lower-level sanctions (e.g. one week of foregone benefit entitlement as in Germany and Switzerland), which could be introduced together with other changes to the sanction regime as argued further below. Also the period for which retrospective pay can be claimed could be abolished. While early registration with the ESS is a means to identify individuals at risk of unemployment, it should not be equated with offering intensive services to everyone prior to unemployment. Instead, information gathered by default during the registration process should be used to identify workers who are likely to struggle with a quick reintegration into the labour market (e.g. long-tenured workers without any recent job-search experience).

Box 4.3. **Early activation to incentivise job-to-job transitions in Germany and Switzerland**

Around half of all OECD countries have waiting periods of three days up to a fortnight from the date of benefit entitlement (OECD, 2015a). Such rules are sometimes introduced as a cost-saving measure and also aim at encouraging people to search for new employment, while they are still in their current job. Waiting periods may, however, raise some equity concerns, as they disproportionately impact on low-income workers if they do not succeed to find employment during the notice period.

Early PES registration in Germany

Germany has no such waiting period, but instead requires all persons whose employment (or apprenticeship) relationship is about to end to register as a jobseeker with the PES three months before the end of the employment relationship. If there are less than three months between the end of the employment relationship and the notice thereof, the employee has to inform the PES within three days of having received notice. Employees who do not inform the PES in a timely manner (or without valid reason for failing to do so), receive a benefit sanction for one week – i.e. they do not receive benefit payments for one week and their total entitlement is shortened by one week. With this measure Germany aims to reduce unemployment duration or even prevent unemployment, as PES reintegration efforts can already take effect prior to unemployment.

Job-search requirements prior to PES registration in Switzerland

In Switzerland, unemployed jobseekers are required to register with the municipal offices as early as possible, ideally after the receipt of notice, but at the latest on their first day of unemployment. From the day of registration a five-day waiting period may apply, depending on the previous salary level. Following registration, the municipality forwards the registration to the local PES office within a week. While no sanctions apply for registering only on the first day of unemployment, jobseekers are, however, required start searching for work before unemployment starts. Jobseekers usually have the first intensive interview at the local PES office within 14 days of registration. At this interview they need to submit written proof of the vacancies they have already applied to before registering. Unemployment benefits may be suspended for one week, if the number of applications is judged to be insufficient.

Source: Duell, N. et al. (2010), "Activation Policies in Switzerland", *OECD Social, Employment and Migration Working Papers*, No. 112, OECD Publishing, http://dx.doi.org/10.1787/5km4hd7r28f6-en; OECD (2015), "Activation policies for more inclusive labour markets", in *OECD Employment Outlook 2015*, OECD Publishing, http://dx.doi.org/10.1787/empl_outlook-2015-7-en; and Sozialgesetzbuch Drittes Buch (SGB III), § 38 Rechte und Pflichten der Ausbildung- und Arbeitsuchenden, https://www.gesetze-im-internet.de/sgb_3/index.html.

Also for FSA claimants, registration with the ESS is a prerequisite for eligibility. However, ESS registration and the FSA claim cannot be done simultaneously, as FSA is not administered by the ESS, but by the CSW. FSA claimants therefore have to first register with the ESS and afterwards claim FSA at their local CSW. As Table 4.1 shows, the vast majority of new benefit claimants receive no cash benefits initially, as benefit entitlement is only established after registration with the ESS.[11] At the CSW caseworkers can check on the ESS computer system whether the registration as a jobseeker took place. This sequencing of events is generally enforced through CSW staff, but with the process being manual there is still room for error and discretion[12] on behalf of CSW staff. This merely manual interface between the ESS and CSW computer systems may be less of an issue during the initial FSA claim process, but creates problems for ongoing claims and the enforcement of work-search conditionality for FSA recipients. In some, but not all CSW, caseworkers may abstain from referring individuals with large perceived barriers to employment to the ESS. Instead they may discuss with the person directly and propose to enter an agreement on resolving social problems (with agreed activities and obligations) with the CSW as the basis for accepting the FSA claim (see Box 4.4).

Jobseeker characteristics and ESS segmentation

Throughout 2015 the caseload of jobseekers registered with the ESS continued to decline, with jobseekers remaining on the caseload now being more disadvantaged on average. There is some evidence of "parking", i.e. providing little services to clients who are perceived as being hard to place. While parking may have been an optimal strategy in times of high caseloads and low resources, it should now be reversed.

As the number of registered jobseekers declines, the remaining caseload becomes more disadvantaged on average

Following the peak in registered jobseekers in January 2014 at 129 840,[13] the number of registered jobseekers stood at just over 113 000 at the end of 2015. Around two-thirds of jobseekers received income-replacement benefits while one-third did not receive any cash benefit. The overall decline in jobseekers is driven by a decline of UI recipients and jobseekers without benefits, while FSA and partial disability benefit (ZPIZ) recipient numbers remained high over the same period (Figure 4.2, Panel A). With the caseload declining, jobseekers remaining on the ESS register are more disadvantaged on average. While numbers of short-term unemployed and jobseekers with less than two years on the register are on the decline, numbers of very-long term unemployed continue to rise (Figure 4.2, Panel B). This is also reflected in the assignment to ESS customer segments, with less jobseekers being classified as "directly employable" and more classified as "employable with intensive support" (Figure 4.2, Panel C).

Table 4.1 shows jobseekers for the categories of special interest for this report. Over half of UI recipients and 70% of ZPIZ recipients are over 50 years old. Younger and prime-age jobseekers are more likely to claim FSA or have no benefit entitlement, as they are less likely to meet the contribution conditions for UI. UI recipients appear to have shorter unemployment durations, while more than two-thirds of FSA claimants and over 90% of ZPIZ claimants are registered with the ESS for more than 12 months. This is partly driven by the fact that following the end of the UI entitlement, some previous UI recipients claim FSA. FSA and ZPIZ recipients tend to have lower levels of education than claimants of UI or jobseekers without benefit entitlement. One in three UI recipients and more than four in ten ZPIZ recipients are displaced workers, while much lower proportions of FSA recipients and jobseekers without benefit entitlement fall in the group of jobseekers who lost their job for economic reasons.

Table 4.1. **Jobseekers profiles in Slovenia vary across different benefit categories**

Number and percentages of registered jobseekers by type of benefit received, 31 December 2015

	All registered jobseekers	*Jobseekers by benefit receipt*			
		UI recipients	**FSA recipients**	**ZPIZ partial disability benefit recipients**	**No income-replacement benefits**
Newly reistered unemployed (on-flows)	97 210	33 000	3 030	620	60 560
(row percentages)		*34%*	*3%*	*1%*	*62%*
Total Stock	113 080	22 070	40 020	10 970	40 020
(row percentages)		*20%*	*35%*	*10%*	*35%*
Recorded inflow reason *(column percentages)*					
Expiry of fixed-term contract	44%	54%	42%	32%	45%
Displacement[a]	20%	33%	11%	43%	17%
Other[b]	15%	13%	15%	18%	14%
Unknown	20%	< 0.5%	32%	7%	24%
By age groups *(column percentages)*					
Youth (15-29 years)	24%	11%	30%	< 0.5%	31%
Prime age (30-49 years)	43%	34%	48%	30%	47%
Older unemployed (50 years and over)	33%	54%	21%	70%	22%
By duration *(column percentages)*					
Less than 12 months	49%	83%	32%	7%	58%
12-24 months	18%	15%	21%	11%	19%
More than 24 months	33%	2%	47%	82%	23%
By educational attainment[c] *(column*					
Less than upper secondary education	34%	29%	43%	49%	24%
Upper secondary education	49%	54%	46%	47%	50%
Tertiary education	17%	17%	11%	4%	25%
ESS segments[d] *(column percentages)*					
Directly employable	29%	39%	20%	1%	41%
Employable with additional activities	47%	43%	52%	36%	49%
Employable with in-depth support[e]	23%	18%	28%	64%	11%
Review groups by benefit receipt[f] *(row*					
Displaced workers[a]	22 990	32%	19%	21%	29%
Older unemployed (50 years and over)	37 190	32%	23%	21%	24%
Long-term unemployed (12 months or more)	58 180	7%	47%	17%	29%
Less than upper secondary education	38 560	17%	44%	14%	25%

Inflow and stock figures are rounded to the nearest 10.

a) The inflow reason is either i) termination of employment due to the bankruptcy or liquidation of the employer or ii) permanent redundancy due to economic reasons.

b) Includes the following inflow reasons: regular termination by agreement, worker incompetence, termination of operations (i.e. termination of the business as a sole proprietor, Cessation of self-employment), serious misconduct, ban due to inspection (e.g. prohibition of work carried out by a court or authority), expiry or interruption of Public Works, sentence over six months (e.g. extraordinary termination due to a conviction or imprisonment), separations due to employer not fulfilling obligations, false data at the conclusion of the employment relationship, unsuccessful probationary period (first six months of indefinite contract), termination with an offer of a new contract, unfair dismissal on the basis of the judgment of the Court, and transition between registries within the ESS.

c) Not included are jobseekers with unknown educational attainment, which represent less than 0.01% of the stock.

d) Not included are jobseekers not assigned to the one of the three segments (0.3% of the stock in 2015).

e) Includes jobseekers classified as temporarily unemployable (less than 0.01% of the stock).

f) This report has a special focus on displaced workers, older workers, long-term unemployed and low-skilled workers.

Source: Author's calculations based on data provided by the Employment Service of Slovenia.

StatLink http://dx.doi.org/10.1787/888933415316

Figure 4.2. **As the number of jobseekers in Slovenia declines, the remaining caseload is becoming more disadvantaged on average**

A. Registered ESS jobseekers by benefit claimed, end of year levels, 2005-15

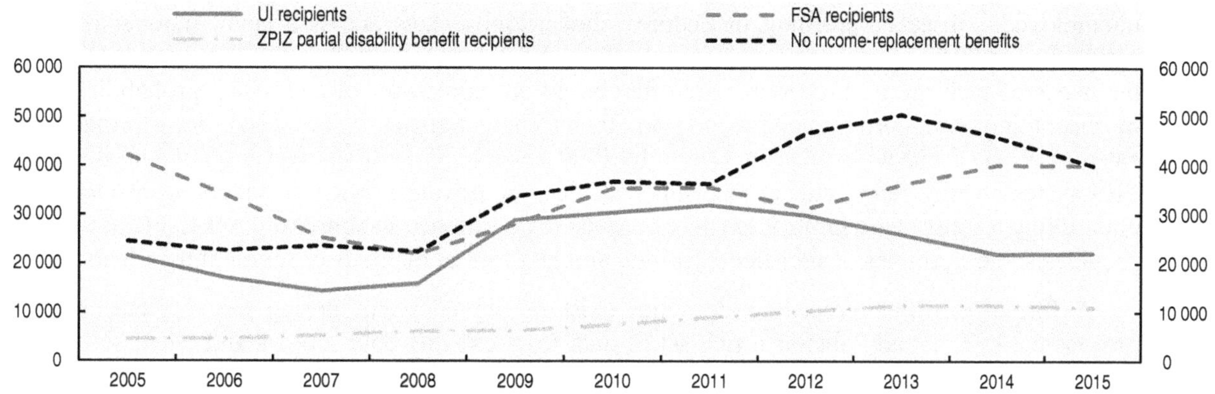

B. Registered ESS jobseekers by duration, end of year levels, 2005-15

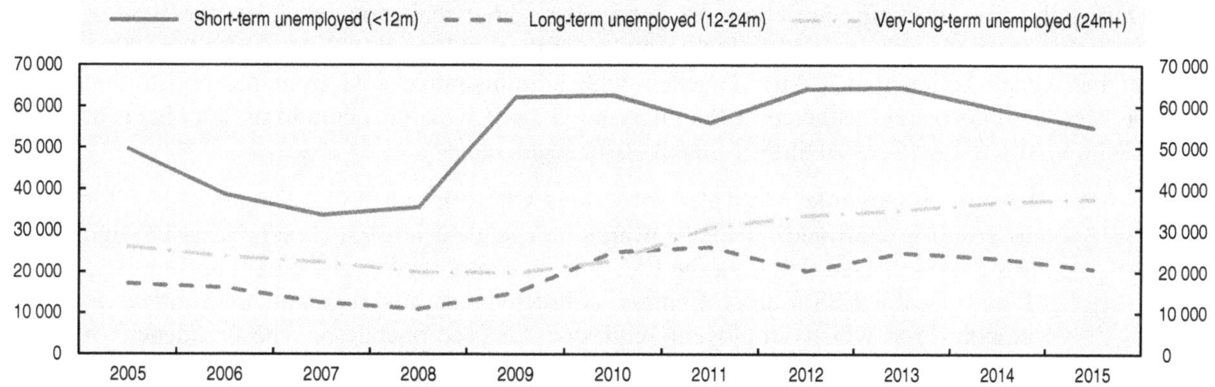

C. Registered ESS jobseekers by client segment[a], end of year levels, 2005-15

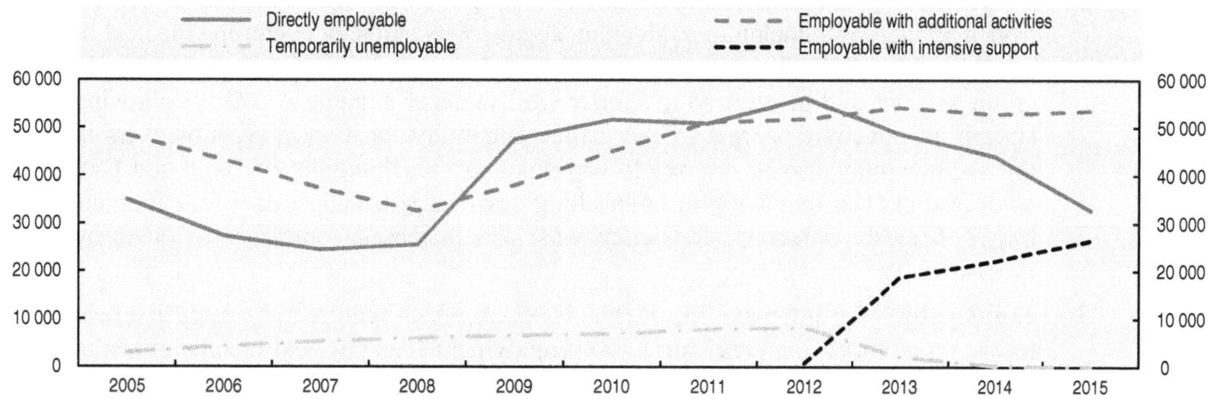

a) Excludes registered jobseekers with an unknown segment (in 2005, around 7% of jobseekers were not assigned to a segment; over time this share has dropped to less than 0.5% in 2015). Also excluded are registered jobseekers that are classified as permanently unemployable (in all years less than 0.05% of the stock). The category "employable with intensive support" was only created in 2012. Individuals in the category "temporarily unemployable" were either reclassified as "employable with intensive support" or removed from the unemployment register into a separate ESS register for temporarily unemployable individuals.

Source: Author's calculations based on data provided by the Employment Service of Slovenia.

StatLink http://dx.doi.org/10.1787/888933415228

The ESS divides jobseekers into three client segments, which determine client journeys

Public employment services need to concentrate their resources on jobseekers who have become long-term unemployed, or ideally those most at risk of becoming long-term unemployed. Jobseeker profiling procedures allocate jobseekers across a small number of categories, in order to manage scarce resources and deliver services that are appropriate for the needs of each group. Procedures are often based on regressions of claimants' probability of becoming long-term unemployed on their characteristics. The need for formal categorisation of clients is greatest where the PES caseload is particularly varied, where the PES systematically refers clients to distinct services or private service providers, or where counselling resources are limited and access needs to be rationed in some way. OECD (2015) provides some examples of statistical profiling and less formal methods of segmenting clients.

A formal profiling procedure does not exist in Slovenia, but during the registration process the ESS already obtains a rich set of data from existing data sources and client self-reports (including gender, age, citizenship, disability status, educational attainment, work experience, reason for termination of employment etc.). Once registered with the ESS, jobseekers usually have a first counselling interview with a caseworker within two weeks. During the first meeting counsellors ask jobseekers about their competencies, the type of work they are looking for and the help they expect to receive from the ESS in order to prepare an Individual Action Plan (IAP). Together with administrative data from the registration process, the information gathered in the interview is used by counsellors to assign clients at their own discretion to one of three different client segments:

1. **Directly employable**: Motivated jobseekers with relevant skills. The initial IAP for this group is short and directed towards independent job search supported through ESS e-services (see Box 4.5), the ESS contact centre (phone and email) and services offered by the ESS Career Centres. Jobseekers in this segment are referred to vacancies for which employers requested ESS co-operation. The frequency of counselling sessions is usually every four months, but in 2015 the interview frequency was increased significantly to monthly interviews.
2. **Employable with additional activities**: Jobseekers which require additional support from a counsellor to maintain motivation, acquire new skills, or overcome medical or other barriers. Jobseekers may receive in-depth career counselling, participate in group sessions and be referred to shorter workshops or suitable ALMPs. Following an upfront screening process to check their suitability for a vacancy, jobseekers in this segment may also be referred to vacancies for which employers requested ESS co-operation. The frequency of counselling sessions is usually every four months, but in 2015 the interview frequency was also increased somewhat to quarterly interviews.
3. **Employable with intensive support**: Jobseekers which require more intensive help to overcome more complex barriers to employment (e.g. physical or mental health problems, social problems, lack of skills). Basic interventions are similar to jobseekers in the second category. In addition, jobseekers in this segment may undergo a disability assessment under the Vocational Rehabilitation and Employment of Persons with Disabilities Act and be referred to vocational rehabilitation services. Jobseekers in this segment are given priority for vacancies advertised by employers that co-operate with the ESS in programmes targeted at disabled jobseekers. Counselling sessions are determined on individual needs with no fixed frequency.

The client segment can be changed during every counselling interview, based on a counsellor's ongoing assessment. A less strictly determined client journey for jobseekers in the segment "employable with intensive support" offers the ESS flexibility for this client group. Local offices can use this flexibility to adjust the frequency of interventions based on individual needs or as a function of capacity. More frequent counselling interviews in 2015 for claimants in the first two segments, however, are likely to have reduced the frequency of interventions for clients in the third segment, a strategy which is often referred to as "parking". In addition to reducing the intervention frequency for clients who were in the "employable with intensive support" segment already at the beginning of 2015, the ESS may have also "parked" additional clients – who were initially assigned to the other two segments – in this segment over the course of 2015. This is reflected in the further increase of the "employable with intensive support" segment in 2015 (Figure 4.2, Panel C), which cannot be explained by the development of other categories of harder-to-place client groups: the number of clients in this segment increased by around 4 300 between 2014 and 2015, but the number of very long-term unemployed (unemployment duration of 24 months or more) increased by only 770, and the number of older unemployed increased by only 450. The number of low-skilled workers even decreased by 1 990 over the same period.

"Parking" of some clients may have been an optimal strategy by the ESS in the past in order to use limited resources in the most efficient way. With the number of clients in the "directly employable" segment further declining, explicit or implicit parking should be reversed and more resources be put into harder-to-place clients in the future. With the segmentation and interventions strategy being largely discretionary, there is also a risk that many jobseekers are being parked as they are perceived to be less employable e.g. because of their age or their lower skill level. Ensuring better services for all jobseekers with limited resources could be better achieved by fixing customer journeys with respect to the frequency of counselling interviews and referrals to ALMPs (see below).

In addition to agreeing an IAP with the ESS, FSA recipients may also agree another action plan with their CSW. The two different action plans are, however, not usually co-ordinated. This may be confusing for jobseekers and is also a missed opportunity of ensuring that both institutions support the target of quick reintegration into the labour market. There is a formalised co-operation between the ESS and CSW since 2012 for FSA claimants and other registered unemployed with complex barriers to employment (e.g. mental health problems, addiction, and social problems). Such clients are referred to a joint ESS and CSW commission for the assessment of provisional non-employability (see Box 4.4). The Commission's task is to establish labour market barriers, decide which of the institutions is responsible for the client, and make suggestions for intervention. If the Commission finds that the individual is provisionally not employable, they are removed from the ESS unemployment register. An issue for the CSW is that they have to accept all claimants even though they may not have the means to intervene. Furthermore, without a remit for labour market activation, there is a risk that clients served only by the CSW do not have a clear pathway back to employment. The creation of the Commission coincided with a change in the segmentation of ESS clients. Since 2012, clients classified as "temporarily unemployable" are removed from the unemployment register and kept in a separate ESS register (Figure 4.2, Panel C). While most of this is a reclassification, the ESS was able to exclude some individuals with complex barriers to employment from the unemployment registry. For "temporarily unemployable" individuals an important issue will be the regular inspection of their situation and the timely re-entry into the unemployment register once their situation has improved.

Box 4.4. Assessing provisional non-employability

With its focus on providing immediate employment support, the ESS does not have the means and expertise to offer support to individuals with complex barriers to employment (e.g. mental health problems, addiction, and social problems). Providing such support is the remit of the CSW, which are responsible for providing support to individuals and families in difficult personal or social situations. Whether the barriers to employment warrant the suspension of labour market participation requirements is often a complex decision. For this reason the joint ESS and CSW Commissions for the assessment of provisional non-employability have been established in 2012. Referrals of registered unemployed to the Commissions are made by the ESS. The Commissions are organised on the local level and consist of at least three members (employment adviser, social worker and rehabilitation adviser plus additional experts depending on the individual's specific problems), which are jointly appointed by the manager of the local ESS and the manager of the responsible CSW. However, often the ESS and CSW advisers participating in the Commission have not dealt with the respective client before. The discussion of the Commission can result in two possible outcomes:

- **Provisional non-employability**: The local CSW is then the primary responsible institution and the individual is moved from the ESS unemployment register into the register of temporarily non-employable individuals. The person may be entitled to FSA, upon entering into an agreement on resolving social problems, but cannot continue claiming UI. If the situation improves to the CSW's satisfaction, the individual may be referred back to the ESS. Around 90% of individual cases discussed by the Commissions between January 2013 and May 2015 were assessed as provisionally not employable. The process for entering into agreements on resolving social problems as the basis for entitlement to FSA is, however, not standardised. Some CSW require all FSA claimants to first register with the ESS and will only sign agreements on resolving social problems following a Commission hearing. Other CSW may directly enter into an agreement on resolving social problems, without requiring an ESS registration. A clear risk of not involving the ESS in the process of resolving social problems is that future labour market activation is not part of a holistic approach to addressing the client's problems.
- **Continued unemployment status**: The individual remains in the ESS unemployment register, but is assigned to the local CSW where they must conclude an agreement on resolving social problems. Compliance with the agreement is mandatory and this requirement is also included in the individual action plan jobseekers agree with the ESS. Entitled individuals can continue to draw UI, if they comply with those requirements. Around 10% of jobseekers discussed by the Commissions between January 2013 and May 2015 remained on the ESS register.

In their conclusion, the Commission may also recommend referrals to active labour market programmes, vocational rehabilitation measures and the like. However, such recommendations are only meaningful if appropriate programmes are available, which may not always be the case. The Commission then only shifts responsibility from the ESS to the CSW, which are obliged to accept all referred individuals, without guaranteeing the support needed for the individual.

Source: IRSSV – Social Protection Institute of the Republic of Slovenia (2015), "Podlage za pripravo in zagon programov socialne aktivacije" [Basis for the preparation and launch of social activation], Ljubljana, www.irssv.si/upload2/Porocilo%20socialna%20aktivacija_koncno.pdf; ZUTD – Labour Market Regulation Act (2010, unofficial translation), Article 9 (Ability for work) and Article 117 (Procedure of establishing temporary unemployability of unemployed persons – General provisions), www.mddsz.gov.si/en/legislation/; and ZSVarPre – Social Assistance Act (2010), Article 35 [Agreement on resolving social problems] and Article 40 [Co-operation of the Employment Service of Slovenia with the Centres for Social Work in the treatment of specific groups of unemployed social assistance beneficiaries and other unemployed persons], www.uradni-list.si/1/content?id=99232.

Job-search requirements and assistance

In Slovenia, there are strict rules defining the availability of jobseekers and the suitability of job offers. Frequent monitoring of independent job search does usually not exist, but jobseekers have to report back on their efforts during counselling interviews at the ESS. High client-to-staff caseloads may, however, often hinder an individualised counselling approach. Options to address this in the future could be further increasing the number of staff working in front-line services and reconsidering client journeys for some jobseekers. In this respect e-services may be an important tool, especially as the ESS already has quite sophisticated e-services in place (Box 4.5).

Job-search and availability requirements in Slovenia leave some room for interpretation

In Slovenia, only around one-quarter of the unemployed – according to the Labour Force Survey (LFS) concept[14] – are not registered with the ESS, but plausibly among those looking for regular employment (e.g. not students looking for student work), the vast majority are. Since the onset of the economic downturn, unemployment increased for both registered and non-registered unemployed, but it fell earlier for the non-registered (Figure 4.3). The number of ESS registered individuals who are not LFS unemployed also increased during the downturn, albeit to a lesser extent than for registered unemployed. This resulted in a reduction in the ratio of registered ESS clients who are not LFS unemployed. Nevertheless, over the past five years still around two in five ESS clients were not unemployed in the sense of the LFS. While some of those ESS clients may be "employed" due to participation in ALMPs such as employment incentives or public works schemes, many may in fact be "inactive", as they do not actively seek work.

Figure 4.3. **Many registered jobseekers in Slovenia are not actively seeking work**

Unemployed by LFS status and ESS registration status (in 1000), 2006-2015, moving average

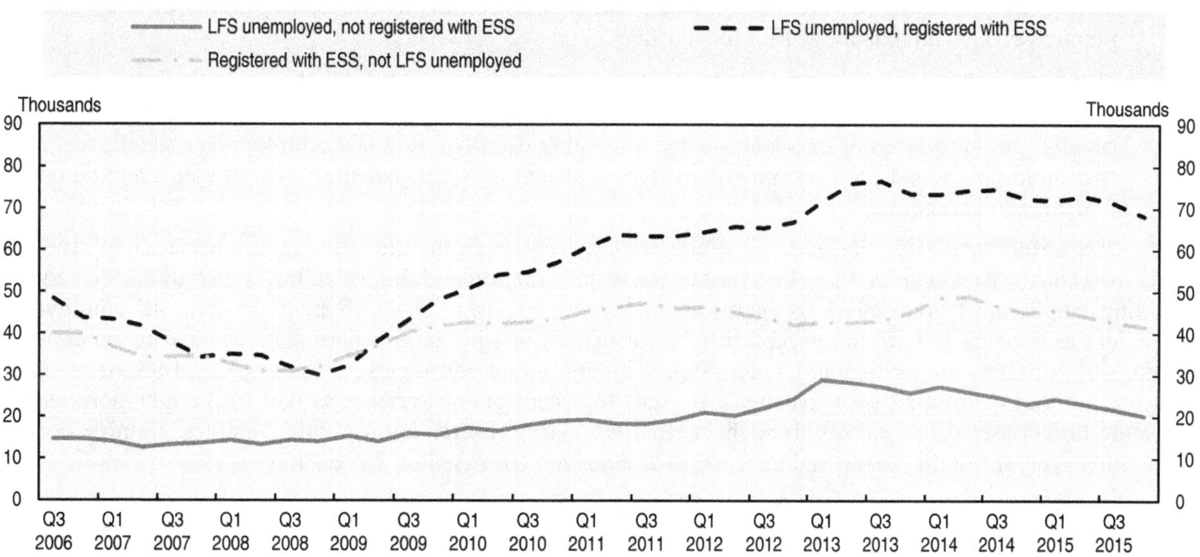

Source: Author's calculations based on data by the Statistical Office of the Republic of Slovenia.

StatLink http://dx.doi.org/10.1787/888933415235

Box 4.5. **E-services for "e-clients" provided by the Employment Service of Slovenia**

Technology is changing the way people interact with each other and the world around them. People expect to be able to access services online at a time which suits them with the expectation that online services offer additional benefits and are easier to use than non-digital equivalents. The PES is no exception and the ESS, just like other PES in many other OECD countries, invested in user-friendly e-services with the aim to increase service availability and accessibility.

In Slovenia, all registered jobseekers which create a customer account in the ESS online portal have access to the online vacancy database to search for vacancies and can also create an online CV to advertise themselves to employers. Furthermore, jobseekers have access to online guidance on job search like different self-assessment tools, tips on CV preparation and job interviews. The ESS online portal offers further functionality for jobseekers who sign an agreement during the first counselling interview with an employment counsellor to be served mostly or exclusively via the ESS online portal. Jobseekers become "e-clients" at their own request or because the ESS counsellors identified the person as capable of using the online portal. "E-clients" receive referrals to job vacancies from their ESS adviser through their online account and manage all documentation in their online account (e.g. updates of the IAP, documents relating to UI, invitations to job fairs). Also all contact with the employment counsellor is made on an e-coaching basis, i.e. via the online portal. For "e-clients" only the preparation of the first IAP, specialised or in-depth counselling and the agreement to be included in ALMPs require in-person attendance at a local office. A clear advantage of the online account is that ESS counsellors have a good overview of the jobseeker's job-search efforts. The counsellors also have the option to change the relationship with clients back to in-person attendance when the jobseeker does not actively use the online account (e.g. online portal is visited less than once in two weeks), does not respond to vacancy referrals or struggles with the online tool.

In 2014, there were 137 000 registered users of the ESS online portal, 60% of the registered caseload. In the same year, there were 21 600 "e-clients", representing around 10% of the caseload. The aim of the ESS is to increase the share of jobseekers who are "e-clients" and evidence from the United Kingdom and the Netherlands suggests that there is still room to increase the share of clients using e-services:

- United Kingdom: In 2014, 68% of unemployment benefit applications were completed online. Applications for Universal Credit, the new income-replacement benefit, can be made online only. Following the initial benefit application, jobseekers may be required to use the online vacancy database, with non-compliance potentially resulting in benefit sanctions. Other interventions, like the weekly or fortnightly job-search review meetings and less frequent in-depth counselling interviews, continue to require personal attendance at PES local offices.
- Netherlands: The aim of the Dutch PES is to mainly interact with jobseekers via digital services and only the most disadvantaged clients are entitled to receive more intensive support through individual coaching from the start of the claim. At the beginning of 2014, 95% of unemployment benefit recipients registered online and 85% use ongoing e-services such as managing their benefit claim and automatic matching to vacancies.

For the ESS further increasing the share of "e-clients" may require further advertising its e-services, but the ESS should also consider making the use of e-services mandatory for some. A higher online penetration also requires upskilling employment counsellors to enable them to be e-coaches. The ESS plans to train all employment counsellors as e-coaches, with the exception of local offices in Ljubljana, where staff decided to separate the functions of in-person counselling and e-coaching. With the rollout of online services ongoing, ESS management is also sometimes confronted with reluctance by staff to accept online services as part of the new normal. The ESS aims to address such concerns through internal marketing, presentations, staff meetings, training courses and by improving the online portal and its work-flow management based on feedback by staff.

Source: Department for Work and Pensions (2016), "Dashboard Jobseeker's Allowance: new claims", https://www.gov.uk/performance/jobseekers-allowance-new-claims; Employment Service of Slovenia (2015), "Letno poslovno poročilo 2014" [Annual Business Report 2014], Ljubljana, www.ess.gov.si/trg_dela/publicistika/letna_porocila; EC (2014), "Blended service delivery for jobseekers, Peer review host country paper", Employment Service of Slovenia Central Office, Slovenia; EC (2014), "Blended service delivery for jobseekers, Peer review host country paper", by U.W.V. Werkbedrijf, Brussels; and OECD (2014), *Connecting People with Jobs: Activation Policies in the United Kingdom*, OECD Publishing, Paris, http://dx.doi.org/10.1787/9789264217188-en.

Jobseekers enjoy some occupational protection in the first three months of unemployment, when they can only be offered jobs that comply with the type and level of their completed education (for first-time jobseekers or those re-entering the labour force after a break) or to the type and level of education required for the job held in the past 12 months ("appropriate" employment; Article 12, ZUTD, 2010). From four months of unemployment jobseekers must also accept job offers one level below their completed education respectively the education required for their previous job ("suitable" employment; Article 13, ZUTD, 2010). This protection is indefinite. Jobseekers do not have to accept *any* type of job they are capable of doing as in a number of other OECD countries that require the acceptance of all types of jobs from the start of the claim (e.g. Denmark, Ireland, and Poland) or after a certain duration of unemployment (e.g. Iceland, Germany, Switzerland, and United Kingdom; see Langenbucher, 2015).[15] Astonishingly, the same occupational protection also applies to FSA recipients.[16] In other OECD countries, recipients of means-test social assistance or unemployment benefit usually have to accept any type of job from the start of their claim (e.g. Australia, New Zealand, or recipients of unemployment assistance in Germany).

With respect to geographical mobility jobseekers in Slovenia must accept daily commuting times of up to three hours, unless they have children below age 15, in which case only two hours must be accepted. Similar requirements apply in the majority of OECD countries. Beyond the educational level and geographical protection, only health reasons are taken into account when determining whether a job offer is suitable for an unemployed person in Slovenia. Other OECD countries also often take family or personal reasons (e.g. caring responsibilities, spouse's work, lack of child care), working arrangements of the job (e.g. part-time, temporary contract), or moral or religious reasons into account. Jobseekers in Slovenia also must be available for regular work while participating in ALMPs, although employment counsellors could lift such requirements (Langenbucher, 2015). In this case, jobseekers are removed from the unemployment register, but data from the ESS suggests that this seldom ever happens.

Availability for work with respect to an earliest possible start date and accessibility of the client are not defined in Slovenia. According to the Labour Market Regulation Act, a jobseeker is assumed to engage in active job search, when she *"regularly follows advertised job vacancies (...) and duly applies for job vacancies (...); responds to the referrals of the Employment Service (...); attends job interviews at the request of the employer, Employment Service or other provider of measures; contacts the Employment Service within 15 days from the expiration of the period for performing the most recently agreed activity determined in the employment plan (...); and carries out all other activities agreed in the employment plan"*. (Article 11, ZUTD, 2010). This suggests that the labour market regulation allows for a relatively loose interpretation of seeking work (i.e. *"regularly"*) and non-active periods of up to a fortnight are acceptable. In connection with no frequent monitoring of independent job search (see below), a good proportion of registered jobseekers may in fact not actively seek for work and, hence, would not be classified as LFS unemployed.

The frequency of job-search monitoring is not very high

The ESS does not usually monitor independent job-search efforts on a frequent basis, like e.g. Australia and the United Kingdom do. In both countries these interventions may, however, often only involve a tick-box check of reported search efforts and a quick orientation towards possible job vacancies (OECD, 2012 and 2014). Jobseekers in Slovenia are expected to provide evidence of their job-search activities through copies of applications and through keeping a job-seeking diary during counselling interviews. For UI recipients the contact frequency changed in 2012, when fortnightly contact with the ESS (e.g. through attending a Career Centre or calling the Contact Centre) was made mandatory to address the high caseload and thus high UI expenditure. The measure was dropped again after one year. International evidence suggests that regular job-search monitoring can have a considerable impact on re-employment rates (see e.g. Borland and Tseng, 2007; Klepinger et al., 2002; and McVicar, 2008). Also the introduction of a fortnightly contact requirement in 2012 for UI recipients in Slovenia seems to have resulted in increased flows into employment and self-employment for UI recipients (Figure 4.4). As is shown below, it also resulted in a marked increase in sanctions for UI recipients (see Figure 4.6). For UI recipients the measure most probably resulted in net government saving. The shift of limited ESS resources towards UI recipients, however, came at the detriment of other jobseekers. In the same year employment off-flows decreased for FSA recipients and jobseekers without income-replacement benefits, resulting overall in a dip in employment off-flows and probably higher government expenditure for these groups. These issues should be evaluated through an impact evaluation and a cost-benefit analysis to show the full cost and benefits of the measure. The results could then guide the potential introduction of more regular job-search monitoring for all jobseekers regardless of benefit receipt.

Figure 4.4. **Fortnightly job-search review meetings in Slovenia in 2012 had a positive employment impact for unemployed insurance recipients**

Outflows to employment and self-employment, total number of registered jobseekers and benefit recipients, 2005-15

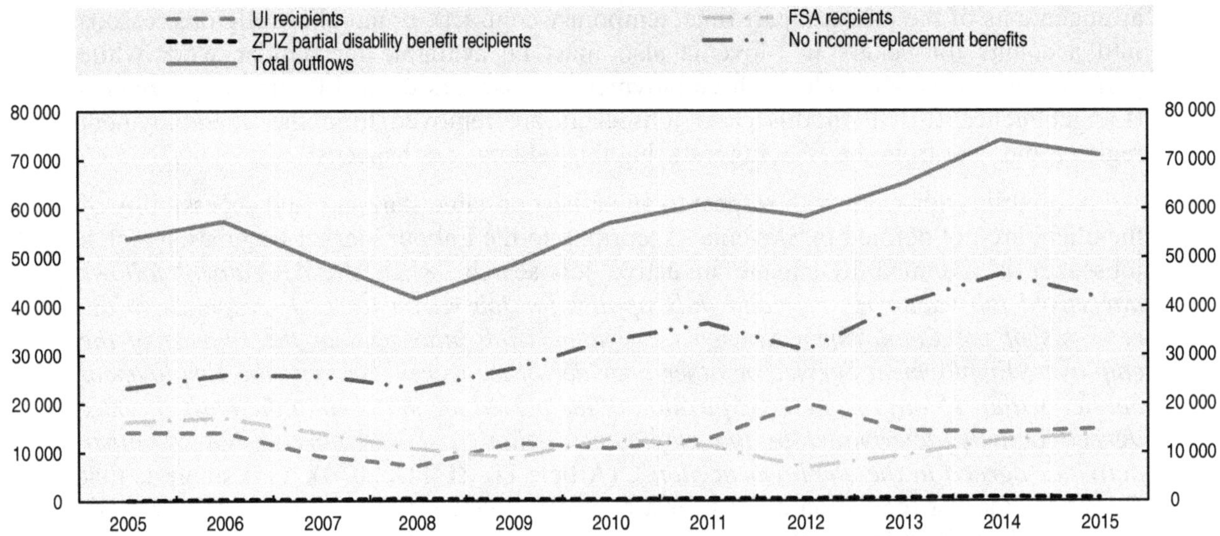

Source: Author's calculations based on data provided by the Employment Service of Slovenia.

StatLink http://dx.doi.org/10.1787/888933415240

Client-to-staff ratios are too high for individualised counselling

Jobseekers and counsellors jointly complete an IAP during their initial counselling interview which is then regularly updated during subsequent counselling sessions. The IAP sets out expectations on independent job search and any additional measures the jobseeker is expected to participate in, like e.g. workshops (see Box 4.6) and ALMPs. When employment counsellors identify more complex labour market barriers, they may send jobseekers for in-depth counselling to ESS advisers specialising in support for certain occupations, rehabilitation services or health support (e.g. doctors). In 2014, in-depth counselling interviews conducted by ESS staff represented around 6% of all interviews. The capacity of in-depth counselling seems low, given the high caseload of jobseekers with additional barriers to employment (compare with Table 4.1).

While mandatory interviews may have a positive employment impact through a threat effect, for the successful delivery of subsequent counselling services, the quality and individualisation of interviews is key (OECD, 2015a). The increased frequency of counselling interviews in 2015 for claimants in the "directly employable" (from every four months to monthly) and "employable with additional activities" (from every four months to quarterly) segments is likely to have facilitated more individualisation. The additional interviews are likely to have contributed to the further decline of jobseekers in the segment "directly employable" and jobseekers without benefits which represent half of the caseload in this segment (compare Figure 4.2 and Table 4.1). The increased interview frequency for jobseekers in the "employable with additional activities" segment may not have been sufficient to translate into a decline of the caseload in this category. Even though positive impacts for jobseekers in the first segment are likely, the impact may have been at the expense of jobseekers in the "employable with intensive support" segment due to overall ESS resource constraints. On average, the ESS client-to-staff ratio is high and has further increased during the recession. Whereas the average client-to-staff ratio was 325 in 2010, it increased to over 400 in 2013 due to an increasing caseload and parallel austerity-driven staff cuts. This is in stark contrast to other OECD countries which in response to the recession increased its PES front-line staff (e.g. by 50% between 2008 and 2012 in the United Kingdom; OECD, 2014a). In fact, these staff cuts may have exaggerated the rise in unemployment in Slovenia. Following a peak in 2013, client-to-staff ratios declined in 2014 to around 390 clients per front-line staff member. This was driven by the decline in unemployment and increased staff numbers as a result of new hires on fixed-term contracts[17]. Nevertheless, the average caseload still appears far too high to deliver any high-quality individualised service across all client segments.

Slovenia should consider hiring more ESS staff and reviewing the client journey and intervention frequency for different client groups. Hiring more caseworkers should be seen as an "invest to save" measure. Recent evidence from a German experiment suggests that reducing client-to-staff ratios enables more personalised services, which in turn has a positive impact on employment. In the experiment, 14 local PES offices hired additional caseworkers to lower the client-to-staff ratio to an average of 70:1 (from the usual 80:1 to 250:1) to improve the quality of placement services. Evaluations of the experiment showed that with the lower caseloads PES offices were able to intensify counselling, monitoring and sanction efforts as well as contacts with local firms, resulting in shorter unemployment benefit durations in the participating PES offices. The costs of hiring additional caseworkers were offset by decreased benefit expenditure already after a period of about ten months (Hainmueller et al., 2011; and Hofmann et al., 2012).

A review of client journeys for jobseekers in the different segments may help the ESS to "do more" with the existing resources. Fortnightly job-search review meetings for UI recipients in 2012 seemed to have had a positive impact on employment. The increased counselling interview frequency in 2015 may have resulted in a similar impact. An impact evaluation of both measures is key for a full cost-benefit appraisal. As both measures were targeted at more employable jobseekers, they may not serve as part of a strategy to "dig deeper into the caseload" and address the rise of more disadvantaged jobseekers and long-term unemployed more generally (see Figure 4.2). Against the background of an improving economic situation and more vacancies (see Figure 4.1), additional interventions for the "directly employable" segment should concentrate on increased monitoring of independent job-search efforts. Ideally this should be achieved using electronic tools (see Box 4.5) to free up staff capacity. The ESS could for example consider requiring all "directly employable" jobseekers to become "e-clients". In turn, jobseekers which are "employable with additional support" are likely to benefit from additional counselling sessions (e.g. every 6-8 weeks) to maintain their motivation and concentrate on their individual needs. Any free capacity should then be used to focus more on jobseekers "employable with intensive support". For some clients with complex barriers the ESS should also consider to bring in extra competence to deal with labour market barriers related to social and health problems.

Job-search assistance should be broadened through additional offers

Beyond job-search assistance provided by ESS counsellors, jobseekers can also be referred to career orientation workshops provided by external contractors since 2012. Concessions for these workshops are granted by the MDDSZ and registered jobseekers as well as workers at risk of displacement are eligible. The ESS refers individuals to the workshops and participation is mandatory and included in jobseekers' IAPs. Providers offer three different types of workshops:

- **Your career after age 50** is a three-day workshop targeted at jobseekers aged 50 and over. The aim of this workshop is to identify jobseeker's competencies and provide them with training on job-search techniques.
- **Effectively presenting yourself in the labour market** is a six-day workshop targeted at jobseekers who are without specific barriers to employment and who are able to navigate the labour market independently. The main aim of the workshop is to speed up the reintegration into the labour market.
- **In-depth counselling** is a workshop lasting around two months and targeted at long-term unemployed with some barriers to employment. The aim of the workshop is to increase jobseekers' motivation (i.e. their views on employment prospects) and empower them to navigate the labour market more independently.

Between 2012 and 2015, more than 56 000 jobseekers in Slovenia participated in the workshops, which cost around EUR 90 per participant. On average 14 individuals participated in the first two workshops and 18 in the third type of workshop. While no impact evaluation exists for the workshops, they are nevertheless considered successful, as re-employment rates increase following the completion of a workshop. The highest re-employment rates are noted for the second workshop, which on average includes jobseekers with lower labour market barriers than the other types of workshops.

Comparing workshop participant numbers with the claimant stock shows that around 11% of jobseekers in the "directly employable" and "employable with additional activities" ESS client segments have been referred to an "effectively presenting yourself in the labour market" workshop between 2013 and 2015. Over the same period, around 7% of the long-term unemployed and 4% of jobseekers aged 50 years and over have been referred to the "in-depth counselling" workshop and the workshop "your career after age 50". The lower referral rates are somewhat surprising, as older workers and long-term unemployed might particularly benefit from such workshops and also the deadweight of participation is likely to be lower for these groups (i.e. the likelihood of them finding employment also in the absence of the workshop). A recent comparative review of the PES-to-PES dialogue led by the European Commission found that IAPs together with targeted group activities are particularly helpful for the reintegration of older workers. Also the length of the workshops could be reconsidered. A three-day workshop for older workers is unlikely to enhance job-search skills and address issues such as social isolation and a lack of networking opportunities. The workshops for older workers should have at least the same length as the "effectively presenting yourself in the labour market" workshop. A further option would be to continue engaging with the participants of the workshop through a job club, which are options available to older workers in Denmark and the Netherlands (see Box 4.6).

Box 4.6. **"Job Clubs" for older workers in Denmark and the Netherlands**

Senior networks in Denmark

The "senior networks" consist of local, independent networks for seniors who are looking for jobs and other activities. The local networks are based on voluntary and active contributions from their members, and receive public financing. The Danish Government has allocated DKK 6.3 million per year for the period 2014-17. To be eligible for public support, the local network must have a co-operation agreement with at least one jobcentre, and at least 25 unemployed members over the age of 50. In some of the local networks a small fee is paid by the members to cover local social activities. The primary aim is to find jobs for seniors. Members are unemployed, above the age of 50, and searching for jobs. Early retired persons and pensioners are also included. "Help to self-help" is the basic concept of the network. Outreach activities to promote older workers are also among the priorities. The initiative is still of relatively small scale: In 2014, there were 24 sub-networks that provided jobs for 700 of their roughly 1 800 members.

The 55-plus networking meetings in the Netherlands

In the "55-plus networking meetings" 12-15 people meet a total of ten times, with meetings being facilitated by a dedicated work coach from the public employment service. The aims include supporting and inspiring each other, exchanging experiences, and sharing job networks. Tips and information about how to start one's own company are also on the agenda. Typical challenges in this age group are outdated knowledge about job-search and interview techniques; outdated job networks; and a lack of jobs in their occupations. While there is no formal evaluation of the measure, participants reported that they became more confident, gained more insight into their own competences, and became more capable of making their own choices. The rate of re-employment six months after the end of participation in the networking group was about 30% in 2012.

Source: EC (2012), "Peer PES paper – The Netherlands", Peer Review 'PES and older workers', by U.W.V. WERKbedrijf, Brussels, http://ec.europa.eu/social/main.jsp?langId=en&catId=22; OECD (2014), *Ageing and Employment Policies: Netherlands 2014: Working Better with Age*, OECD Publishing, http://dx.doi.org/10.1787/9789264208155-en; and OECD (2015), *Ageing and Employment Policies: Denmark 2015: Working Better with Age*, OECD Publishing, http://dx.doi.org/10.1787/9789264235335-en.

Benefit sanctions

Benefit sanctions are important for an effective activation regime, as sanctions can through a threat effect ensure that claimants remain available for work, actively seek work and comply with the requirements imposed by the law and enforced by the ESS. Slovenia should introduce lower-level sanctions to improve the effectiveness of its activation regime, as sanctions are currently very harsh and their application therefore appears inconsistent.

Slovenia has a very strict sanction regime

Unemployment benefit legislation in most OECD countries includes a benefit "sanction" concept, which may also be called a "deferment" or a temporary or permanent "stop" or "exclusion". Unemployment benefit recipients are typically subject to sanctions if they i) voluntarily quit their job, ii) refuse a suitable job offer, or iii) refuse or fail to participate in ALMPs and other PES interventions such as counselling interviews without a good reason. Slovenia has one of the strictest sanction regimes among OECD countries for refused job offers (Figure 4.5, Panel A) and refusals or failures to participate in ALMPs and other PES interventions (Figure 4.5, Panel B).

Figure 4.5. **Slovenia has one of the strictest unemployment benefit sanction regimes in the OECD**

Indicators on the strictness of sanctions, scored from 0 (least strict) to 5 (most strict)[a], 2014

a) Scores: 0 = no sanction applied; 0.5 = benefit reduction; 1 = sanction of 1 day to 4 weeks; 2 = sanction of 5-9 weeks; 3 = sanction of 10-14 weeks; 4 = sanction of more than 14 weeks; 4.5 = benefit entitlement suspended, but the individual has the possibility of restarting benefits after a short period in work (shorter than is required to generate a new benefit entitlement); 5 = Suspension of unemployment benefits.

Source: Author's calculations based on Langenbucher, K. (2015), "How demanding are eligibility criteria for unemployment benefits, quantitative indicators for OECD and EU countries", *OECD Social, Employment and Migration Working Papers*, No. 166, OECD Publishing, http://dx.doi.org/10.1787/5jrxtk1zw8f2-en.

StatLink http://dx.doi.org/10.1787/888933415259

Along with a large number of other OECD countries, jobseekers are not eligible for UI in Slovenia in case of resignation from their previous job (see Chapter 3).[18] Slovenia's sanction regime is also very strict for failures or breaches of obligations during the unemployment spell. In Slovenia, like e.g. in Portugal, Greece or the Slovak Republic, unemployment and related benefits are also terminated and remaining benefit entitlement lost, if the jobseeker refuses a suitable job offer or fails to participate in counselling interviews or ALMPs organised by the PES. In fact, in Slovenia, a breach of jobseeker obligations is not treated any differently to benefit fraud like giving false information or working while claiming a benefit. This is quite different to countries that impose short sanctions (of one month or less) or only a benefit reduction for a first refusal or failure. Around half of the countries with sanctions of a certain number of weeks have escalating sanction regimes and increase the length of the sanction for subsequent refusals. The remaining countries apply the same sanction for each failure. Among the countries with escalating sanctions, Belgium, Denmark, Finland and Italy terminate benefits for the second refusal of a job offer or failure to participate in an ALMP or other PES activities. In Denmark and Finland, benefit entitlement can still be restored once the person has worked in a regular job for a minimum period or (in Finland) participated in an ALMP (Langenbucher, 2015).

Sanctions in Slovenia have a far-reaching impact, as sanctioned jobseekers are excluded from the ESS register for six months and, hence, cannot any longer use any of the ESS services. Thereby sanctions are also a threat towards jobseekers who do not receive unemployment and related benefits. Sanctioned jobseekers who received benefits lose any remaining benefit entitlement and neither can claim FSA whilst excluded from the ESS register, nor continue to receive free health insurance. Such strictness is in stark contrast with countries where jobseekers in breach of their obligations receive a time-limited stop of their benefits, but may still use the PES services. Also in other countries, which terminate unemployment benefits like Slovenia, sanctions have not such a far-reaching impact. In Luxembourg, for example, sanctioned UI claimants may continue using PES services and those without UI entitlement may re-register with the PES after two months. In Latvia, deregistered jobseekers can only re-register after three months but can apply for the status "person seeking employment" and continue using some PES services (e.g. vacancy database, career counselling). In Greece, sanctioned jobseekers can re-register with the PES as a jobseeker without benefit entitlement. In most countries, sanctioned jobseekers without any other means of income can claim social assistance from their municipality.

Sanction rates vary across claimant categories

The sanction process starts with a compliance doubt raised against the jobseeker, usually by counsellors in local ESS offices. The case is then referred to specialised departments in the regional office for the processing of the sanction. While all breaches of obligation result in ESS deregistration, jobseekers can appeal for reinstatement. If the ESS upholds its decision, jobseekers can first appeal to the MDDSZ and then to the labour court. Interviews with ESS staff revealed a certain reluctance to initiate sanctions, as the sanction process is administratively burdensome and it is often difficult to prove that an individual did not apply for a particular vacancy or did not respond to a letter sent by the ESS. A breach of obligation may be easier to establish for clients using ESS e-services, as all job-search actions are recorded online. But users of e-services are still a minority of jobseekers (see Box 4.5). In 2014, 9% of sanctioned jobseekers appealed to the ESS against the initial sanction decision and for 45% the original sanction decision was not upheld (i.e. in favour of the appellant). This suggests that jobseekers usually only appeal if they have a good chance of success, e.g. because they have additional evidence in their favour. Appeals are initially reviewed at the ESS. Upheld decisions reviewed by the MDDSZ are seldom in favour of the appellant (less than 10% in 2014). Comparable data for Great Britain shows that, from 2012 to 2015, 24% of unemployment benefit recipients had their initial sanction decision reviewed by the PES and 59% of the reviews resulted in the original sanction not being upheld (i.e. in favour of the appellant). At the subsequent stage, which in Great Britain is a further reconsideration by the PES, 29% of all the decisions were in favour of the appellant. At the third stage, which is at court level, 22% of decisions were in favour of the appellant (DWP, 2016b).

Sanction rates are not low in Slovenia, but vary by type of benefit received and by region. On average, 6% of registered jobseekers were sanctioned and excluded from the ESS register over the course of 2015. Sanction rates were just slightly below the average for FSA claimants (around 5%) and almost double the average for jobseekers without income-replacement benefits (around 11%). In contrast, less than 1% of UI and ZPIZ live claims have been sanctioned and left the ESS register in 2015 (Figure 4.6).[19] Comparing sanction rates by region shows variation in the enforcement of sanctions, suggesting that the likelihood of being sanctioned depends on where jobseekers are registered. Sanction rates are much higher than the national average in the Koper and Kranj regional offices (8-9%), but only half the national average in the Murska Sobota regional office (3%).

Figure 4.6. **Unemployment benefit sanctions in Slovenia vary by benefit receipt**

Sanction decisions[a] as a percentage of annual live benefit claims[b], 2006-15

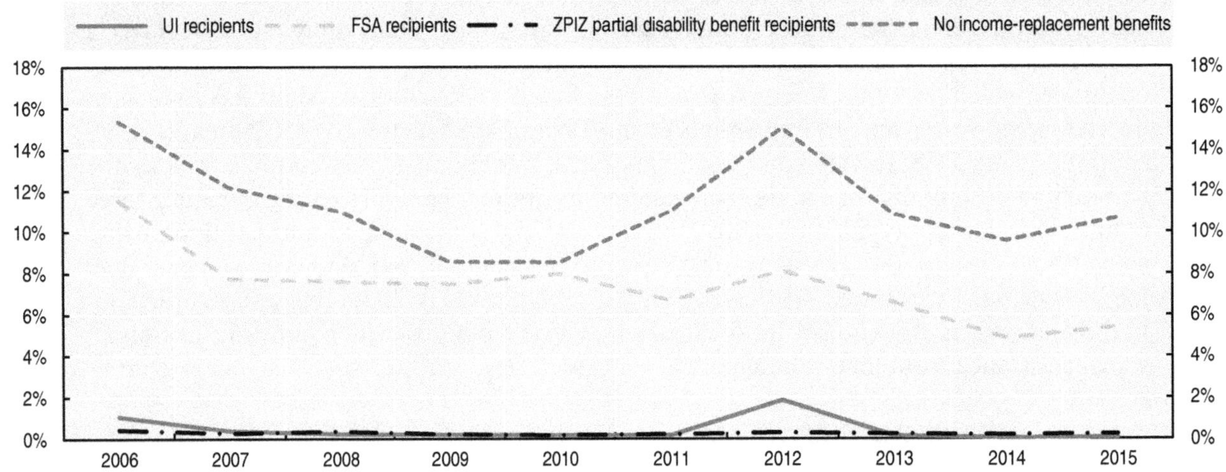

a) Sanction decision cover a breach of obligations due to refusals to take part in ALMPs, breaches of obligations relating to ALMP enrolment, not actively seeking employment, refusals to accept suitable employment and some other reasons (less than 0.5% of sanctions in 2015). Benefit fraud (e.g. giving false information, illegal employment) is not included.

b) Live claims in a given year add the claimant stock at the beginning of the year and total new registrations during the year.

Source: Author's calculations based on data provided by the Employment Service of Slovenia.

http://dx.doi.org/10.1787/888933415261

High sanction rates for jobseekers without benefits may be explained by lower incentives to comply with ESS obligations as they are not at risk of losing cash benefits. Similar considerations may apply for FSA recipients as the ESS registration and benefit receipt are not closely interlinked. When the ESS excludes non-compliant FSA claimants from its register it cannot stop their benefits as those are administered by the CSW. An automatic system to flag an ESS deregistration for CSW staff does not exist. CSW staff may therefore not discover the exclusion from the ESS register until they next see a FSA recipient, which could be three up to six months later. Hence, FSA recipients would need to report the ESS deregistration to the CSW themselves to avoid receiving unwarranted FSA payments, which they would need to repay later on. Even though the threat of repayment should be an incentive for FSA recipients to report themselves, it is unlikely that all FSA recipients are aware of this rule and some recipients may build up huge debts. In essence, the CSW may often need to write off debts, as needy households may not be able to repay their debt and legal procedures for the debt recovery can take a long time. Interviews with CSW offices also showed that some offices may not categorically stop their support for individuals without other means to survive following an ESS deregistration. Rather the CSW continues to work with the FSA claimant under an agreement on resolving social problems (IRSSV, 2015). Overall, as has been argued before, the division of responsibilities between the ESS and CSW and a lack of automated processes between the two institutions may result in an inconsistent and ineffective activation of FSA recipients.

Low sanction rates for UI and ZPIZ recipients may partly reflect high levels of compliance as the potential loss – benefits and ESS registration – is high. However, the low rates may also reflect a lack of job-search monitoring or enforcement. For example, sanction rates in Great Britain, with frequent monitoring and strict enforcement of job-search requirements, are much higher and a comparable statistic suggests that 18% of live claims received a sanction in 2013 (OECD, 2014a). In Slovenia, the year 2012 represents a peculiarity in the sanction statistics: Although sanction rates increased for all categories of jobseekers, the number of sanctions for UI recipients increased over 12-fold and the sanction rate reached almost 2% in that very year. This outcome was driven by increased enforcement of job-search obligations including fortnightly mandatory job-search reviews with UI recipients. The measure was subsequently dropped with a change in government, but shows that ESS processes impact hugely on compliance enforcement.

Sanctions are important for an effective activation regime and international evidence suggests that warnings about a possible sanction or the imposition of sanctions on UI or social assistance recipients can substantially shorten benefit claim durations and increase employment take-up by the sanctioned individuals. Nevertheless, some studies also suggest that the positive impact on exit rates and employment may come at the cost of lower quality of employment outcomes with respect to job duration, earnings, the occupational level or a higher incidence of part-time jobs. Some studies also explore the wider consequences of sanctions and provide evidence that there may be adverse consequences for child welfare, family welfare, and health.[20] Sanctions in Slovenia are strict and the application of sanctions inconsistent for different types of jobseekers and across regions. This may be driven by the high proof of burden and a cumbersome administrative process when imposing a sanction coupled with some reluctance by caseworkers to impose such harsh sanctions for a first breach of obligations. Slovenia should therefore facilitate the administrative process and consider introducing lower level sanctions in the form of a benefit reduction or suspension for a certain period, at least for a first breach of obligation, without excluding jobseekers from the ESS register. Compliance with the obligations should be made a precondition for the resumption of benefits. The sanction process of FSA recipients should be reconsidered as part of wider institutional changes relating to the administration of FSA.

The effectiveness of Active Labour Market Programmes

During longer unemployment periods, referrals to ALMPs can help improve employment prospects and keep up work habits through the regular attendance in programmes. Slovenia's expenditure on ALMPs ranks towards the lower end of OECD countries. Slovenia has established programmes in all ALMP categories – i.e. training, employment incentives, direct job creation and start-up incentives. But there is huge variation in spending on ALMPs and some disadvantaged jobseekers have a rather low likelihood of being referred to ALMPs. Impact evaluations of ALMPs are rare and should be extended to cover all major programmes for longer post-programme periods.

There is huge variation in the spending on active labour market programmes

The *OECD Database on Labour Market Programmes* provides data on patterns of labour market programme spending in OECD countries, where such data are available. At 0.28% of GDP, spending on active labour market programmes (ALMPs) in Slovenia was considerably below the OECD average of 0.43% of GDP.[21] Expenditure over the years varies a lot, as a result of huge variations in the MDDSZ budget available for ALMPs as well as European Social Fund (ESF) monies (see also Box 4.7): In 2013, EUR 60 million were available from the ESF, representing two-thirds of the ALMP expenditure in that year. In 2014, ESF funds dropped to EUR 47 million (53% of total ALMP expenditure) and for 2016 Slovenia expects around EUR 53 million from the ESF (57% of the planned ALMP expenditure). In response to the rising number of jobseekers in 2009, ALMP expenditure increased in 2009 and 2010 and entrant numbers nearly quadrupled between 2008 and 2009. Thereafter ALMP expenditure, however, dropped again in 2011 and 2012, albeit still rising numbers of jobseekers (Figure 4.7). Expenditure increased again in 2013 and 2014, but was exceptionally low in 2015, with both a low MDDSZ and no ESF funding for employment incentives. This is foreseen to change again in 2016.

Figure 4.7. **Spending on active labour market programmes in Slovenia is highly variable**

Participation in and expenditure on active labour market programmes[a], 2005-14

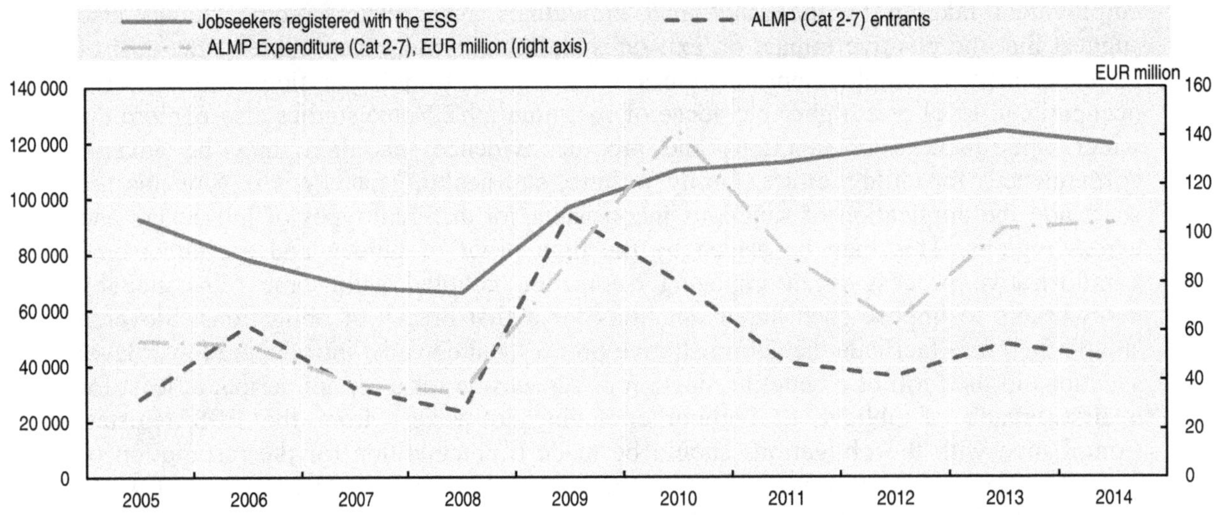

a) Entrant, participant and expenditure refer to all ALMPs in Categories 2 to 7, also those not shown in Table 4.2.

Source: European Commission (2015), "Labour Market Policy" (http://ec.europa.eu/eurostat/web/labourmarket/labour-market-policy/database).

StatLink http://dx.doi.org/10.1787/888933415272

Table 4.2 provides an overview of all major ALMPs in Slovenia between 2012 and 2015, including the programme's target group, duration, entrant numbers, expenditure in 2014 and 2015 and employment rates of participants finishing the respective programmes in 2012. Spending figures reflect total available funding from all sources (i.e. MDDSZ, ESF, Ministry of Education). In 2014, the ESF funded 47% of all active programmes run in Slovenia. A fifth of ESF funds were used to support start-up incentives, 36% to support employment incentives, and 44% to support training programmes. The MDDSZ has little funding sources available for these three categories and 83% of MDDSZ's ALMP expenditure in 2014 was used to fund direct job creation.[22]

Table 4.2 shows that in all years, expenditure is concentrated in a few programmes. Box 4.7 provides some details for the major programmes. Up to 2014 the most important ones were "development and training programmes" (institutional training), "on-the-job training", "employ.me" (employment incentive), "public works", and "subsidies for self-employment". The programmes "subsidies for self-employment" and "employ.me" have, however, ceased to exist after 2014. More expenditure is now concentrated in training programmes. ALMP spending per participant varies from less than EUR 1 000 for most of the larger institutional training programmes to EUR 4 600 up to EUR 9 000 for employment incentives, direct job creation and start-up incentives programmes. Analysis of post-programme employment rates shows that for all programmes employment rates grow over the 12 months following completion of the programme, apart from the "employ.me" (employment incentive) scheme and the "subsidy for self-employment". The findings for the latter two programmes are not surprising, given the rise in labour costs for previously subsidised employees in case of "employ.me" and unsuccessful self-employed in case of the "subsidy for self-employment".

Box 4.7. **Major active labour market programmes in Slovenia**

Training programmes

Slovenia recently put more emphasis on meeting employers' needs through getting employers involved in the development of programmes and using vacancy information to drive the provision of programmes. There has also been a shift towards offering more workplace training, which is seen as a relatively low-cost, but effective measure. While there were only around 2 000 entrants to workplace training in 2012, over 5 400 places were offered in 2015 and the programme continues to be offered in 2016 and 2017.

Workplace training

The Employment Service of Slovenia (ESS) runs two different workplace training programmes: **Work trial** and **on-the-job training**. The target group for the **work trial** is jobseekers who have been unemployed for at least three months. Until the end of 2015 the programme was targeted at those under age 30, but since 2016, it is targeted at those aged 30 years and more. Jobseekers referred to the work trial already have some recognised skills and competencies, but employers want to test their knowledge, skills and work habits during a one-month trial period. For each place on the programme the ESS usually proposes five candidates and the employer does the final selection. Employers may even propose a candidate. The cost for the ESS is relatively low, as the ESS only pays the participant's travel costs, the activity allowance (which is lower for recipients of Unemployment Insurance (UI)) and a small fee to the employer (EUR 201 per participant and month). Since 2016, the target groups for **on-the-job training** are i) low-skilled long-term unemployed who are older than 50 years and ii) young people. Jobseekers enrolled in this programme usually do not have any recognised knowledge, skills or competences and they need training with a mentor to gain the necessary skills and knowledge required for a job. The programme last one to three months, depending on the complexity of the training programme and the aptitude of the participant. As for the work trial the ESS usually proposes five candidates and the employer does the final selection. Also the ESS cost structure is similar, with only the fee for the employer being higher (EUR 370 for a two-month programme up to EUR 493 for a three-month programme). The long-term unemployed could particularly benefit from workplace training to obtain skills and demonstrate their abilities to employers. In 2015, only around a fifth of entrants to on-the-job training were long-term unemployed. The target group for the programme has therefore changed in 2016 to increase the number of long-term unemployed benefitting from the programme.

Institutional and integrated training

The programmes **preparation for national vocational qualifications (NVQ)** and **verification of NVQ** are usually linked, with participants preparing for three to six months for a NVQ and then doing the verification in one day. The aim of the programme is to increase jobseekers qualifications and acknowledge their skills through a qualification. The preparation courses can be part-time or full-time and both unemployed and displaced workers during the notice period can participate. The **development and training programmes** (institutional training) are also open to unemployed and displaced workers during the notice period, but participants usually have at least a general high school degree. The courses usually cover occupations for which labour shortages have been identified and are developed in close co-operation between employers and providers. The courses last between three days and six months and can contain both theoretical and practical training elements. Participant numbers more than halved between 2014 and 2015, as European Social Fund (ESF) monies were available for this first half of 2015 only. The programme **inclusion of unemployed persons into new and development projects** is class-room based training. The courses are offered through the Business Educational Centres, which are financed by the Ministry of Education. The ESS only pays for the participants' activity allowance and travel costs.

Box 4.7. Major active labour market programmes in Slovenia *(cont.)*

Institutional and integrated training

The programmes **preparation for national vocational qualifications (NVQ)** and **verification of NVQ** are usually linked, with participants preparing for three to six months for a NVQ and then doing the verification in one day. The aim of the programme is to increase jobseekers qualifications and acknowledge their skills through a qualification. The preparation courses can be part-time or full-time and both unemployed and displaced workers during the notice period can participate. The **development and training programmes** (institutional training) are also open to unemployed and displaced workers during the notice period, but participants usually have at least a general high school degree. The courses usually cover occupations for which labour shortages have been identified and are developed in close co-operation between employers and providers. The courses last between three days and six months and can contain both theoretical and practical training elements. Participant numbers more than halved between 2014 and 2015, as European Social Fund (ESF) monies were available for this first half of 2015 only. The programme **inclusion of unemployed persons into new and development projects** is class-room based training. The courses are offered through the Business Educational Centres, which are financed by the Ministry of Education. The ESS only pays for the participants' activity allowance and travel costs.

Employment incentives

The employment subsidy scheme **employ.me** aims to move different disadvantaged jobseekers into sustainable employment. The target groups have been changing over time and in 2014 included jobseekers over 50 years, jobseekers under 25 years, first-time jobseekers, university graduates under 30 years, and long-term unemployed. Employers are selected on the basis of a public tender and eligible employers receive a subsidy of EUR 5 000 for employment lasting at least one year. For participants under 30 years there was a similar programme called **the first challenge** were employers received EUR 7 250, if the employment lasted at least 15 months. The programme did not run in 2015, as there was no funding available, due to the end of the ESF co-funding. A new employment incentive programme – again co-financed with ESF monies – has now been created and will run for the rest of 2016 and 2017. The new programme will be targeted at jobseekers older than 30 years, in particular long-term unemployed, low-skilled individuals and other vulnerable groups.

Direct job creation

The largest direct job creation programme, called **public works**, offers employment in non-for-profit organisations. Other direct job creation programmes usually are one-off programmes to address a certain labour shortage (e.g. clearing up sleet and ice, helping with migration flows). The target group for public works are long-term unemployed and the programme is implemented and financed in co-operation with local communities. The monies provided by the central government depend on the economic growth and the unemployment rate in each local area and ranges from 55% to 95% (expenditure shown in Table 4.2 refers to ESS expenditure only). Participation in the programme usually lasts for one year, but may be extended to a maximum of two years. Participants are obliged to continue seeking for jobs in the open economy.

Start-up incentives

Between 2007 and 2013 the ESS ran an ALMP to promote self-employment consisting both of a seminar to provide assistance on becoming self-employed as well as a subsidy for those who became self-employed. The post-participation employment rates of these start-up incentives were high, with 67% of entrepreneurs who had been self-employed in 2012 being still self-employed in January 2015 (see also Table 4.2 and 4.3). The programme was not continued from 2014, due to a lack of funding and due to concerns that many of the programme leavers were in precarious situations earning very low income. An external evaluation of the programme is currently being carried out. The findings will guide the development of future start-up incentives on a smaller and more targeted basis.

Table 4.2. Overview of all major[a] active labour market programmes in Slovenia (2012-15): Participants and employment outcomes

Programme type/name	Target group	Programme duration	Entrant numbers				Total expenditure, EUR million		Expenditure per programme entrant, EUR		Employment rates of ALMP participants finishing in 2012		
			2012	2013	2014	2015	2014	2015	2014	2015	1 month	6 months	1 year
Training			**11 940**	**18 610**	**25 430**	**16 020**	**17.3**	**20.3**					
Integrated training													
Preparation for national vocational qualifications (NVQ)	Unemployed and dismissed workers during notice period	3-6 months	1 630	1 870	1 970	930	1.5	1.2	€780	€1,270	13.1	39.2	48.8
Institutional training													
Verification of national vocational qualifications (NVQ)	Unemployed and dismissed workers during notice period	1 day	1 350	1 720	1 630	1 340	0.4	0.3	€230	€190	19.4	42.6	52.2
Development and training programmes (institutional training)	Unemployed and dismissed workers during notice period	3 days to 6 months	4 880	7 240	12 540	5 640	3.5	4.5	€330 [b]	€440 [b]	14.2	30.4	39.7
Formal education	Unemployed	Usually 1 year (max. 3 years)	250	280	300	350	0.1	0.1	€440	€330	7.3	9.3	15.8
For the territory of Pokolpje (being active)	Unemployed (and employers)		850	750	280	420	0.2	0.4	€610	€840	9.3	18.3	25.8
Inclusion of unemployed persons into new and development projects	Unemployed	104 hours	820	2 020	1 250	1 020	0.2	0.1	€190	€140	6.7	17.9	26.7
Project learning for younger adults (PLYA)	Unemployed early school leavers (without completed education) up to 26 years	average duration 10 months	210	70	660	150	1.1	1.2	€2,000 [b]	€2,910 [b]	7.3	12.1	15.0
Employing first-time jobseeker university graduates	Unemployed under 30 years		-	-	-	770	-	4.5		€5,850			
Workplace training													
Work trial	Unemployed under 30 years who are unemployed for more than 3 months	1 month	-	-	1 700	1 130	0.8	1.2		€710 [c]			
On-the-job training	Unemployed who are unemployed for more than 3 months	1-3 months	1 960	4 670	5 120	4 290	9.5	6.9	€1,850	€1,610	32.7	52.3	59.1
Employment incentives			**4 420**	**4 870**	**4 100**	**40**	**29.1**	**0.2**					
Employ.me	Target groups include unemployed i) aged over 50 years; ii) youths under 25 years; iii) first job seekers; iv) under 30 years with completed university education; v) LTU etc.	12 months	1 770	3 960	3 170	0	18.5	0.2	€5,930 [c]		60.5	57.7	58.3
The first challenge	Unemployed under 30 years	15 months	2 650	240	480	40	3.2	<0.01	€6,690		72.1	75.0	76.6
50 plus programme	Unemployed aged 50 years and over		-	670	10	-	5.3 [d]		€7,780 [e]				
Employment of older unemployed			-	-	450	-	2.1		€4,630				
Direct job creation			**3 760**	**5 540**	**7 050**	**6 740**	**38.9**	**35.3**					
Public works	Long-term unemployed	12 (max. 24) months	3 760	5 540	6 860	6 260	38.9	33.2	€5,670	€5,300	13.6	16.3	17.8
Public works "Help with Migration Flows"						270		0.2		€760			
Public Works "Assistance in case of natural disasters"					200	210		1.9		€9,120			
Start-up incentives			**8 280**	**11 100**	**370**	**-**	**9.1**	**-**					
Self-employment assistance (seminar)	Unemployed		5 250	6 810	-	-	0.1	-	€51 [f]		35.4	85.8	86.8
Subsidies for self-employment	Unemployed		3 030	4 300	370	-	9.0	-	€4,590 [g]		84.8	80.1	78.2
Total			**28 400**	**40 120**	**36 950**	**22 800**	**94.3**	**55.9**					

Table 4.2. **Overview of all major[a] active labour market programmes in Slovenia (2012-15): Participants and employment outcomes** *(cont.)*

- Nil or less than half of the last digit used.

Entrant numbers and cost per participant rounded to the nearest 10.

a) Table 4.2 shows all ALMPs that were running in 2015. It also shows some selected programmes that were not any longer running in 2015. Not shown are a number of smaller programmes running in the years 2012 to 2014 (and before). Among them are "Employment to clean up after ice devastation of 2014" (direct job creation; entrants in 2014: 200); "Promoting social inclusion and equal opportunities in the labour market" (direct job creation; entrant numbers 2011 to 2014: 300); "Opportunity for me" (direct job creation; entrant numbers 2012 to 2013: 70); "Subsidised employment (providing home help and personal assistance)" (direct job creation; entrant numbers 2008 to 2012: 1 190); "Training for lifelong success" (training programme; entrant numbers 2008 to 2012: 1 920); "On-the-job training for Mura employees (bankrupt clothing manufacturer)" (training programme; entrant numbers in 2011 to 2012: 220); and "Promoting employment of FSA recipients" (employment incentive; entrant numbers 2008 to 2013: 730).

b) The expenditure per programme entrant is a two-year average (2012/2014 and 2014/2015), as some of the expenditure may be incurred in the year following the programme entry.

c) Average expenditure for all programme entrants in 2014 and 2015.

d) Shows the expenditure for 2013 and 2014 combined.

e) Average expenditure for all programme entrants in 2013 and 2014.

f) The programme "Self-employment assistance (seminar)" ran from 2008 to 2013. The expenditure shown is the average for all programme participants who entered the programme between 2008 and 2013.

g) The programme "subsidies for self-employment" ran from 2011 to 2014. The expenditure shown is the average for all programme participants who entered the programme between 2011 and 2014.

Source: Author's calculations based on data provided by the Employment Service of Slovenia.

StatLink http://dx.doi.org/10.1787/888933415322

Some disadvantaged jobseekers have a low likelihood of being referred to ALMPs

The Labour Market Regulation Act stipulates that recipients of UI and other social security benefits, persons from vulnerable groups in the labour market, and unemployed persons who have not yet participated in any ALMP should be given priority for referrals to ALMPs. Based on the act, the government adopts a plan for implementing ALMPs in a budgetary period. The plan details the purpose and objectives of ALMPs, volume and sources of funds, priority target groups, service providers, and methods for assessing the ALMPs.[23] In 2015, the priority target groups included disadvantaged jobseekers with an unemployment duration of more than six months, young people (15-24 years), low-skilled (less than secondary education or vocational qualification), first-time jobseekers who have been unemployed for at least two years, older workers (50 or more years), lone parents, and ethnic minorities (IRSSV, 2015). Several of these groups are target groups for this OECD report. Table 4.3 provides more detailed information on entrant numbers and employment outcomes for jobseeker categories in focus of this report (older workers, long-term unemployed and low-skilled workers) and by type of benefit received.

Not all jobseekers have an equal likelihood of being referred to ALMPs as Table 4.3 shows.[24] In 2012, younger and prime-age jobseekers had likelihood of referral above the country average, whereas the chance of being referred was far below average for older workers and those with low educational attainment. In contrast to the priorities stated in the ALMP plan, the same pattern is observed in 2015. Long-term unemployed have an average likelihood of being referred. FSA recipients and jobseekers without income replacement benefits have a higher likelihood of being referred to ALMPs than UI and ZPIZ recipients, which suggests that some jobseekers are only referred to ALMPs once their UI entitlement has expired.

The low likelihood of being referred to ALMPs for some disadvantaged jobseekers could be addressed by introducing standardised customer journeys for different client segments, which stipulate the referral to ALMPs after a certain period on the caseload. Ideally such segmentation would be based on statistical profiling. In the absence of such tools, referrals could be made depending on jobseeker characteristics and also the availability of ALMP resources. For example, younger and older jobseekers could be referred after, say six or nine months on the register, while the largest group – prime-age jobseekers – would be referred only after 12 months.

The ESS collects very rich data and regularly tracks post-participation outcomes for all ALMP participants over many months. The availability of such data is exceptional, as many other countries across the OECD do not have such data available on a regular basis. Table 4.3 also shows employment rates of previous programme participants 12 months following completion of the programme. It must be highlighted that post-participation employment rates are gross effects and cannot be used to judge a programme's impact in terms of additional employment outcomes achieved, as opposed to mere deadweight (i.e. employment outcomes that would also have occurred in the absence of the programme). Nevertheless, the data reveal that some programmes may be more suitable than others for different categories of jobseekers:

Table 4.3. **Programme participation and employment outcomes vary in Slovenia by target group**

Entrant numbers and employment outcomes of selected active labour market programmes, 2012[a]

	Active labour market programme (ALMP) entrants by ... *(numbers)*											
		Age			Category			Benefit receipt				
LMP name	Total	15-29 years	30-54 years	55 or more years	Long-term unemployed	Low educational attainment	Displaced workers	UI recipients	FSA recipients	ZPIZ partial disability benefit recipients	No income-replacement benefits
Training												
Integrated training												
Preparation for national vocational qualifications (NVQ)	1 630	500	10 990	40	600	400	240	380	400	30	820
Instituional training												
Verification of national vocational qualifications (NVQ)	1 350	390	920	40	580	290	230	260	330	30	730
Development and training programmes (institutional training)	4 880	1 450	3 290	150	1 640	880	540	1 310	840	70	2 660
Formal education	250	150	90	-	130	200	20	10	140	-	100
For the territory of Pokolpje (being active)	850	310	520	20	380	220	70	220	190	30	410
Inclusion of unemployed persons into new and development projects	820	180	540	110	430	190	150	230	180	100	310
Project learning for younger adults (PLYA)	200	210	0	0	50	180	-	-	100	0	110
Workplace training												
On-the-job training	1 780	680	1 070	30	780	200	250	180	440	30	1 140
Employment incentives												
Employ.me	1 770	210	1 240	330	1 430	280	600	230	210	70	1 270
The first challenge	2 650	2 620	30	0	520	260	110	70	340	-	2 230
Direct job creation												
Public works	3 760	1 040	2 210	510	2 330	650	390	640	970	230	1 920
Start-up incentives												
Self-employment assistance (seminar)	5 250	1 070	3 980	200	1 720	450	910	1 140	620	40	3 450
Subsidies for self-employment	3 030	780	2 160	100	1 190	262	640	250	200	10	2 560
Total	28 230	9 570	17 140	1 520	11 770	4 450	4 140	4 920	4 960	650	17 700
Memorandum item: Benefit claims												
Jobseeker stock at the beginning of 2012	112 750	27 130	63 810	21 820	56 660	40 700	31 000	31 870	35 630	8 960	36 300
On-flows during 2012	106 860	37 240	56 870	12 740	20 190	30 560	24 740	35 660	9 500 [b]	1 660 [b]	60 040
Live claims	219 610	64 370	120 680	34 560	76 850	71 260	55 740	67 530	45 130	10 620	96 340
	Proportion of individuals employed one year after finishing the ALMP *(percent)*											
Training												
Integrated training												
Preparation for national vocational qualifications (NVQ)	**48.8**	49.4	48.5	48.7	34.6	38.0	48.5	68.1	37.9	43.3	45.4
Instituional training												
Verification of national vocational qualifications (NVQ)	**52.2**	54.5	51.3	51.2	42.9	44.8	55.2	68.2	45.5	48.4	49.7
Development and training programmes (institutional training)	**39.7**	43.8	38.8	21.5	27.7	25.8	40.8	53.3	28.1	29.2	37.0
Formal education	**15.8**	10.6	24.5		14.6	9.7	33.3	30.0	7.2		26.0
For the territory of Pokolpje (being active)	**25.8**	29.4	24.3	6.3	16.0	14.3	23.3	37.8	12.2		27.5
Inclusion of unemployed persons into new and development projects	**26.7**	41.5	23.8	17.1	17.0	13.8	24.0	37.9	21.1	4.0	29.3
Project learning for younger adults (PLYA)	**15.0**	15.0			10.9	14.8			10.5		16.0
Workplace training												
On-the-job training	**59.1**	60.0	58.3	67.6	53.9	57.1	66.0	73.3	47.2	56.0	61.6
Employment incentives												
Employ.me	**58.3**	64.4	65.2	28.5	56.5	53.6	61.7	59.4	55.3	65.7	58.2
The first challenge	**76.6**	76.6	70.0		69.1	68.0	85.8	87.1	63.4		78.2
Direct job creation												
Public works	**17.8**	25.3	17.1	5.7	16.9	10.6	18.6	17.9	17.7	8.7	18.9
Start-up incentives												
Self-employment assistance (seminar)	**86.8**	88.3	87.0	74.9	81.4	75.9	87.6	91.2	71.0	75.6	88.3
Subsidies for self-employment	**78.2**	79.7	79.0	48.4	72.7	64.5	80.5	86.1	52.0	100.0	79.4

a) Entries into programmes that continued to exist at least until 2014. This represents 97% of all programme entries in 2012.

b) Inflow statistics may be misleading, as jobseekers usually must first register with the ESS before applying for benefit. Inflow statistics are therefore biased downwards. The figures shown therefore show claimant stock figures with a duration of up to one month.

Source: Authors calculations based on data provided by the Employment Service of Slovenia.

StatLink http://dx.doi.org/10.1787/888933415337

- A comparison by **benefit receipt** shows that UI recipients consistently have better than average post-programme employment outcomes. Employment rates are around average for jobseekers without income-replacement benefits and below average for FSA and ZPIZ recipients. The difference is less marked for "employ.me" and "public works", potentially reflecting that – regardless of benefit receipt – only more disadvantaged jobseekers are referred to these programmes. The average post-programme employment rate is similar for "on-the-job training" and "employ.me". FSA recipients, however, have better outcomes for the employment incentive "employ.me". This may indicate that a 1-3 month employment trial is often not enough for employers to retain FSA recipients beyond the trial. In contrast, the 12 months employment subsidy available through "employ.me" may help to increase the worker's productivity enough to make post-programme employment attractive for employers.
- Outcome rates by age show that not all programmes are suitable for **older jobseekers**. Their 12-months employment rates are around average for the training programme "preparation for national vocational qualifications (NVQ)" (and the related verification of NVQ) and even above average for "on-the-job training". This finding is in line with best practices highlighted in a recent PES-to-PES dialogue review by the European Commission, which highlighted that training measures targeted at employer's needs or in combination with work practice were found effective in Estonia, Poland and Germany (EC, 2012b). While these results seem positive, participation of older workers in these programmes is nevertheless low: Only 2-3% of participants in these programmes were 55 years or older in 2012 (see Table 4.3) and 2015 (not shown in table). Outcomes are only around two-thirds of the average for the training programme "inclusion of unemployed persons into new and development projects" and "subsidies for self-employment". The programmes "development and training programmes", "employ.me" and "public works" show even worse results.
- A comparison by **unemployment duration** shows that long-term unemployed more generally have below-average post-programme employment outcomes. Outcomes are more favourable and close to average outcomes for two schemes: "on-the-job training" and the "subsidy for self-employment".[25]
- **Low-skilled workers** also generally fare worse than average in terms of the likelihood of being referred to programmes. Some types of programmes may be more suitable for them than others. Their post-programme employment rates are closer to the average for "on-the-job training" than for classroom-based training programmes (e.g. "development and training programmes" and "inclusion of unemployed persons into new and development projects").
- **Displaced workers** have a lower than average likelihood of being referred to ALMPs, but for most programmes they have better than average outcomes. Their outcome rates are especially high for programmes operated directly at an employer like "on-the-job training" and employment incentives. While usually no special programmes for displaced workers exist, the ESS may offer additional support in the case of collective dismissals.

These comparisons of employment outcomes show that not all programmes seem to be suitable for all jobseekers. However, quantitative impact evaluations are needed to make a judgement on whether these programmes should be continued or expanded and if so, for which jobseeker categories. Qualitative evaluations could help to assess how programmes can be improved and may also help to understand why some programmes are more successful for some jobseekers than others.

Positive employment impacts are found for only a few programmes

Evaluation of ALMPs is crucial to ensure effective and efficient spending of public resources. Evaluations cover various aspects of the implementation of new policies and programmes and give insights into what effects the policies and programmes had, for whom and why. More generally, evaluations allow for a continuous improvement of policies and programmes or the termination of unsuccessful ones, and thereby demonstrate accountability and justify government expenditure on ALMPs.

An important recent study of the impact of training programmes and employment subsidies on labour market outcomes was conducted by Kavkler et al. (2012). The study evaluated the short-term impact of various programmes on the probability of finding and retaining a job during the period 2009-11. The analysis is based on ESS unemployment registry data and uses programme participation and propensity score matching to generate control groups.[26] Evaluating a broad range of programmes, it finds positive effects for the "verification of national vocational qualifications (NVQ)", whereas the "preparation for national vocational qualifications (NVQ)" did not show statistically significant positive results. They also find positive effects for the "work trial" programme that was running until 2011, which is however different to the current "work trial" or "on-the-job training" programmes (see Box 4.7) and offered an employment bonus for continued employment of the individual following the completion of the programme.[27] Hence, the results are likely to be biased because of the employment bonus.

On the other hand, Kavkler et al. (2012) find negative effects for the institutional training programmes "development and training programmes" and "formal education". Those observed negative effects should be interpreted with caution, however: the authors note that the short time frame available for the analysis precludes a definitive assessment of its effects, which could potentially be more long-term. Furthermore, a large share of individuals (43%) enrolled in the "formal education" programme did not successfully complete it: of those who were unsuccessful, approximately one quarter dropped out prematurely and a further one quarter did not complete it due to legitimate medical reasons. They also find negative effects for the previous version of "on-the-job training". Although similar to the "work trial" programme, the "on-the-job training" was intended for a broader pool of individuals and did include a lump-sum subsidy for continued employment, as the previous version of the "work trial" did. For employment subsidies ("employ.me" and a number of smaller programmes) Kavkler et al. (2012) find mixed or statistically insignificant results. In certain cases, their findings suggest employers exploit the subsidies for reducing labour costs, but fail to provide permanent jobs.

Given these mixed results, it would be advisable to extend the analysis by covering a longer post-programme period and by extending the analysis to more recent programme years. Both should be feasible, given the rich data available from the ESS. Larger programmes which are available for a wide range of jobseeker categories should be analysed for different jobseeker categories to confirm the notion that some programmes may be more suited for some types of jobseekers than others. On the basis of such results, it is then possible to calculate non-intervention rates – i.e. deadweight rates – and the additional employment impact resulting from the programmes. Even when programmes have an additional employment impact, the savings generated from the programmes may not exceed the total expenditure on the programme. For the full appraisal of programmes it is therefore also necessary to conduct a full cost-benefit analysis, which lists all benefits and costs incurred by participants and by the government.[28]

Managing performance to ensure a rapid return to work for all jobseekers

The ESS is managed through performance targets as is now common practice in successful public employment services around the OECD. Not all of the ESS targets may support the wider goals of reducing unemployment and they should therefore be reviewed to ensure they are achievable but challenging and do not give wrong incentives. As has been shown before, over a third of ESS clients claim their (FSA) benefit from the CSW. Current inconsistencies in the activation of FSA recipients are therefore problematic and better outcomes could be achieved through an improved institutional set-up.

ESS performance management

Ideally, performance indicators are available for inputs and final outcomes, and show the relationships between them. This is necessary to give policy makers and senior managers insight into the relative performance of different parts of the organisation and about what appears to be working. The performance targets for the ESS are developed by the ESS headquarters in close co-operation with regional offices and the MDDSZ. The national targets are then further broken down into regional targets, taking the labour market context in each region into account. Each headline performance target has a number of indicators for measuring progress against each of the targets. These indicators also allow for monitoring at the central, regional and local level. Performance against the targets is published on a monthly basis on the ESS intranet and can be accessed by all staff. The data are then used to discuss performance and identify good practices with staff in regional and local offices on a monthly basis. Good practices, which may be transferable to other regional or local offices, are then shared in meetings at the regional or central offices level (EC, 2013). In 2016, the ESS has five overarching performance targets (ESS, 2016):

1. **Reducing the number of long-term unemployed**: This should be achieved by reducing the number of long-term unemployed jobseekers from 59 700 in 2015 to 56 000 by the end of 2016 and to 40 000 by 2020. The number of long-term unemployed in ALMPs should be increased from 48% to at least 50% by the end of 2016. The share of long-term unemployed in all off-flows to employment increase from 24% to 27%.

2. **Earlier activation of younger, older and low-skilled jobseekers**: This should be achieved by reducing the average duration on the ESS register by one month for jobseekers under age 30 (from 11.5 to 10.5 months) and over age 50 (from 37.1 to 36.1 months) and for low-skilled jobseekers (from 33.3 to 32.3 months).

3. Increasing the effectiveness of mediation in employment (indicators not shown).

4. **Increasing the efficiency of ALMPs**: Increased efficiency is measured through post-programme employment rates six months after the completion of education and training programmes. The rate should increase from 43.6% in 2015 to 44.5% in 2016 for the around 11 000 planned entrants in 2016.

5. Establish the ESS as a central institution for lifelong career guidance (indicators not shown).

Not all of the 2016 ESS targets may support the wider goals of reducing (long-term) unemployment and some of them may even by dysfunctional. While the first target may support the prevention of long-term unemployment, it does, however, provide little incentive to reduce the large stock of already long- and very-long-term unemployed. The impact of the second indicator on reducing (long-term) unemployment is not obvious and may be achieved without ESS staff making any effort to do so. With a decline in unemployment being driven primarily by a reduction of the short-term unemployed, the proportion of long-term unemployed jobseekers referred to ALMPs should automatically increase. If ALMPs have indeed a positive impact on reducing long-term unemployment, the proportion of long-term unemployed referred to ALMPs should be much higher. However, instead of making this a PES target, referrals to ALMPs should be part of a standardised customer journey, as has been argued before. ALMP referrals would then not be seen as an outcome target, but as an intervention delivery target to monitor what proportion of customers were referred on time.

While it is the aim of all ALMP sponsors to increase ALMP efficiency, the fourth target for ALMPs may actually result in decreasing their efficiency. More generally, ALMP efficiency targets should be set for the ALMP providers differentiated by client group and not ESS staff. Setting a target for gross employment rates[29] may simply result in "cream-skimming", where ESS staff chooses participants who are easier to help.[30] This is unlikely to be prevented by the indicator on increasing the proportion of long-term unemployed in ALMPs, as the increase in the proportion is low. Increasing the efficiency of ALMPs requires an in-depth knowledge of the additional employment impact, which cannot be assessed without programme evaluation. Introducing incentive-based payment structures for external ALMP providers may provide the necessary incentive to increase efficiency, but such payments are no guarantee for increased efficiency and payment structures need to be well designed.

The indicator levels for the second target highlight how much low-skilled and older unemployed have been parked by the ESS, with average unemployment durations being close to or exceeding three years. The target nevertheless does not appear to be very challenging and may be achieved without any push by EES staff to activate jobseekers earlier on, if unemployment continues to fall. The target is meant to be achieved by focusing on a set of measures, which are however vague – e.g. intensification of services and activities, individualisation of treatment (ESS, 2016) – and not measureable. The promise that the target groups will benefit from support through counsellors specialised in supporting these target groups should be quantified through the frequency of those counselling interviews. For UI recipients there is also a stated goal to monitor jobseekers' IAPs and agreed activities closely to increase flows into employment (ESS, 2016). While this may result in increased support and, hence, flows into employment, it may be at the detriment of FSA and ZPIZ recipients and jobseekers without income-replacement benefits as has happened before in 2012 (see above). The ESS should have a target to prevent long-term unemployment for all jobseekers and this should be quantifiable.

Overall, the ESS targets should be reviewed to ensure that they are achievable but challenging and do not give wrong incentives to play the system just to meet the targets. Even though the 2016 ESS targets are all measurable, the relationship between inputs and outputs is often not clear and some of the input measures would in fact make better performance targets. A good example is the Swiss performance measurement system, which uses four performance indicators, which aim to incentivise i) quick reintegration into the labour market, ii) prevention of long-term unemployment, iii) prevention of benefit exhaustion, and iv) prevention of repeat claims. Local office performance is then evaluated on a regression-adjusted basis using a rich set of jobseeker characteristics and survey information on local labour market performance (Duell et al. 2010).

Over a third of registered jobseekers are clients of two institutions – ESS and CSW

UI recipients receive active and passive support through one public institution – the ESS. In contrast, jobseekers claiming FSA are required to deal with two institutions: Claims for the income-replacement benefit (FSA) – the passive side – have to be made at the CSW, whereas job broking and referrals to active measures – the active side – are provided by the ESS. While the ESS and CSW co-operate in different ways there are many inconsistencies, which potentially result in difficulties in the effective activation of FSA recipients. Merging the two institutions, fully or partially, or introducing a more formalised co-operation between them should seriously be considered.

Co-operation between the ESS and the CSW is not formalised

The institutional organisation of the ESS and the CSW is completely different. The ESS is a top-down managed public agency with national, regional and local offices. In contrast, the CSW currently have no such national and regional structure and work independently on the local level in each of Slovenia's municipalities, with the overall supervision being the responsibility of the MDDSZ. This difference in CSW and ESS management structures often makes co-operation between the two institutions difficult. Things have, however, already improved over the last decade and the ESS and the CSW now co-operate more closely on a formal as well as an informal level (IRSSV, 2015). The most important formalised co-operation is the joint ESS and CSW commission for the assessment of provisional non-employability. However, while CSW and ESS work closely together when clients are referred to this commission, such clients present a minority of ESS registered jobseekers (see Box 4.4). In 2015, around 40 000 jobseekers – over a third of all registered jobseekers – were FSA recipients and for the vast majority of them employability is undisputed. For these jobseekers difficulties in their consistent activation arise in a number of areas, as highlighted throughout the chapter:

- The approach to activating FSA recipients varies by location, as due to their local structure, there are no standardised procedures and guidelines, which all 62 CSW follow. For example, not all CSW insist on a prior ESS registration before processing the claims of employable FSA recipients.
- The co-operation between local ESS offices and the CSW may sometimes be impeded by the fact that FSA recipients must register with the CSW located in their area of residence, whereas they are free to select an ESS office of their choice (see Box 4.1). Hence, local ESS offices may have to deal with a number of CSW offices and vice versa.
- In addition to agreeing an IAP with the ESS, FSA recipients may sometimes also receive additional action plans from the CSW, which are, however, usually not co-ordinated with the ESS. Even when co-ordination is not the primary issue, both institutions may often lack the capacity to sufficiently help claimants in need of in-depth support.
- The procedures of the joint ESS and CSW commissions for the assessment of provisional non-employability may differ from one location to another, resulting in variation in the client groups covered and in assessment outcomes. While the commission may recommend further interventions, appropriate measures may not

always be available. The commission then only shifts responsibility from the ESS to the CSW, without guaranteeing support for the individual or identifying a clear path back into employment (see Box 4.4).

- The absence of clear enforcement procedures in case of FSA recipients' non-compliance with job-search obligations. However, even with better procedures, CSW caseworkers may be reluctant to impose sanctions for breaches of obligation established by the ESS, as the sanctions are harsh and may cause hardship for the individuals and families involved.

These issues may also be exaggerated by the fact that the overall aims of the two institutions are not closely aligned. While the CSW are mainly directed at dealing with people in crisis situations and solving major social problems of their clients, the ESS aims to improve the employability of its clients and aims at a quick reintegration into the labour market (IRSSV, 2015). The CSW also have no performance management system currently in place and, hence, are not given the duty or any incentives to ensure that nationally-financed government expenditure on FSA is kept low. Beyond a performance management system, unified procedures and guidelines are also missing for many CSW areas of work. Many decisions in the CSW are therefore taken on a case-by-case basis.

The way forward: Merging institutions or formalising the co-operation?

The *OECD Jobs Study* (OECD, 1994) recommended integration of the three main functions of the broadly defined PES: job broking, benefit administration and referral to active measures. In principle, such integration helps to ensure that:

- The placement objective of a rapid return to work is supported by benefit sanctions in cases of non-co-operation.
- The benefit administration's objective of enforcing eligibility criteria is implemented through job-search monitoring and referrals to job vacancies and ALMPs by the placement service.
- Training services and job-creation projects accept referrals of clients who are disadvantaged, poorly motivated or otherwise at risk of long-term unemployment. This may not be the case when they are autonomous bodies that can select their own participants.

In several OECD countries service delivery reforms have been designed to facilitate access to services and co-ordination between them through "one stop", "single counter" or "single gateway" access to related employment, benefit and other social services (OECD, 2013). It is convenient for clients to access services through a single point and this also helps to reduce duplication of intake processes, facilitate information-sharing, target interventions to suit individual needs and local circumstances, and co-ordinate service delivery. However, the co-location of the offices of different organisations at local level with a common reception desk is not the same as integration at the management level. Full-scale service integration is more easily secured in unitary and highly centralised countries like for example the United Kingdom (OECD, 2014a). In many countries, such an option is not feasible constitutionally or sought after politically and policy makers have devised various ways of requiring or encouraging different agencies and levels of government to co-ordinate and sometimes co-locate service delivery (OECD, 2013).

For Slovenia, different options for improving the stance on activation for FSA recipients should be considered, ranging from a full or partial merger, to integrated IT systems and a more formalised co-operation between the CSW and the ESS. Regardless of a more far-reaching reorganisation in the medium term, an urgent first step towards a more consistent activation of FSA recipients is the development of a performance management system for the CSW. Necessary steps include:

- Taking stock of the CSW client stock (employable versus not immediately employable clients) and the CSW key activities and outputs with respect to both social and labour market activation.
- Developing standardised procedures and guidelines for all major work processes in the CSW, based on best practices identified.
- Based on the first two steps, developing a set of indicators to assess performance of each local CSW towards timely and consistent activation.

A far-reaching option would be a merger of the ESS and the CSW thereby creating one single institution responsible for most of the income-replacement benefits and the activation of the working-age population. Nevertheless, even that would not be a full integration for all recipients of income-replacement benefits, as the benefits of ZPIZ recipients (10% of all registered jobseekers in 2015) are still managed by another institution. A full merger of all institutions responsible for income-replacement benefits was achieved in the United Kingdom in 2002, when two separate agencies responsible for employment services (and unemployment benefits) and income-replacement benefits (apart from unemployment benefits) were merged into one agency (OECD, 2014a). Such a merger would achieve the full integration of job broking, benefit administration and referral to active measures for employable FSA recipients. At the same time, it would also help brining not immediately employable FSA recipients within the remit of the same institution, helping to establish a clearer path back into the labour market for individuals who are provisionally not employable.

Another option would be a partial merger covering ESS-registered FSA recipients only. The administration of benefits of ESS registered FSA recipients would then become the responsibility of the ESS. It seems, however, inefficient to have two different institutions manage the same benefit for different client groups. Furthermore, it would not ensure an integrated approach to social and labour market activation with many clients then lacking access to one or the other.

A less far-reaching option would be a more formalised co-operation between the ESS and the CSW with standardised processes and procedures. The current differences in the institutional framework are an obstacle to a closer co-operation. A current plan by the MDDSZ foresees to create a regional office structure for the CSW. A new regional structure could be used to formalise relations between regional ESS and CSW offices. One option would be to make the new regional CSW offices responsible for the administration of FSA (and other social assistance benefits), while local CSW offices are responsible for frontline services only (e.g. counselling, social work services, referrals to programmes such as drug treatment). The CSW local offices could then concentrate on serving more disadvantaged clients, while ESS-registered FSA recipients would usually receive frontline services from the ESS only (unless they require any of the CSW front-line services in addition). Also the processing of FSA benefit claims could be made online, with support in local CSW offices only available for those who need help with filing a claim. The regional CSW offices would have responsibility to support the ESS through ensuring a timely and consistent activation of FSA recipients.

Without linking IT systems closer co-operation may, however, be difficult to implement. Linked IT systems would enable both institutions to get better statistical feedback on joint clients, thereby supporting standardised processes and procedures. Among other things this includes requiring an ESS registration prior to processing FSA claims, follow-up in case of non-compliance, co-ordinated action plans to address social issues and activation simultaneously. Important for the effective co-operation will be a regional structure for the CSW that aligns with the regional structure of the ESS, with co-location perhaps also facilitating co-operation. This does not seem to be given in the current plan for the regional CSW offices, which foresees the creation of 15 regional offices,[31] whereas the ESS only has 12 regional offices.

Key findings and recommendations

The ESS appears as a modern PES with a strong focus on job placement. The acquisition of vacancies in Slovenia has become more difficult since the abolition of mandatory notification of vacancies, but the ESS still plays an important role for many employers and offers extensive recruitment services for all employers who wish doing so. Online services for employers and jobseekers are well advanced and the ESS has the aim of increasing the use of these e-services. The ESS has a large and diverse client base and only around one-quarter of the unemployed (according to LFS criteria) are not registered with the ESS, but plausibly among those looking for regular employment the vast majority is. Despite all those strengths, a number of challenges prevail for Slovenia, holding back re-employment for more jobseekers, especially disadvantaged groups of jobseekers, and at an earlier stage.

Jobseekers should be activated earlier

Even though it is generally easier to find a new job while still being in employment, the current rules offer little incentives for UI recipients to actively seek new employment before the current employment relationship has ended or within the first 30 days of unemployment. Slovenia should consider activating people at risk of losing their current job – either due to dismissal or due to the expiry of a fixed-term contract – while their current employment relationship still lasts. Possible options include introducing mandatory ESS registration for people at risk of losing employment or job-search requirements already before benefit entitlement starts. Such new rules could then be enforced through the introduction of lower-level sanctions (e.g. one week of foregone benefit entitlement).

Also the offers available to displaced workers could be improved and extended to cover more of them. A job-search assistance measure exists for workers made redundant but take-up is low, especially in case of individual and small-scale dismissals. Take-up could be increased through dropping the rule on shortening the UI benefit payment duration by the number of days workers participate in the measure and making employers pay full wage compensation for the time employees to be dismissed participate in the measure. An early ESS registration requirement would make more workers aware of the measure. It would also help the ESS to target dismissed workers who are likely to benefit most from early intervention.

Harder-to-place clients are at risk of being "parked"

More frequent counselling interviews for claimants with few labour market barriers are likely to have reduced the frequency of interventions for clients which require more in-depth support, and thus contributed to "parking" of harder-to-place jobseekers. Parking of some client groups may have been a reasonable strategy by the ESS in times of limited resources and weak labour demand. With more and more employable clients moving into employment, parking harder-to-place clients on the caseload should be stopped. Parking of clients by the ESS is also reflected in the use of ALMPs: Not all jobseekers have the same likelihood of being referred to ALMPs and some groups with a stated priority for ALMP referrals (especially older workers and those with low educational attainment) have in fact a lower than average likelihood of being referred. The lower likelihood of counselling sessions and referrals to ALMPs for disadvantaged jobseekers could be addressed by introducing standardised customer journeys for different client segments, which stipulate the counselling frequency and referral to ALMPs after a certain period on benefit. Some increase in ALMP referrals for older and low-skilled unemployed may be seen in the following year, as more programmes are now targeted on them.

Reviewing client journeys may help do more with less or with the same

Recent short-term measures focusing on job-search monitoring and more frequent counselling sessions seemed to have had a remarkably positive impact on employment for some jobseekers, but better impact evaluations would be needed to support this claim. Recently tightened measures were, however, targeted at more employable jobseekers and, hence, may not serve as part of a strategy to "dig deeper into the client caseload". The ESS could free up resources by increased monitoring of independent job-search efforts for the most employable jobseekers. This should be achieved through making the use of electronic tools mandatory for this group of jobseekers to free up staff capacity. Capacity gains could be used to provide additional counselling to less employable jobseekers.

Hiring more caseworkers: Invest to save?

International evidence suggests that reducing client-to-staff ratios enables more personalised services (e.g. for jobseeker counselling or vacancy acquisition), which in turn has a positive impact on reemployment. A recent experiment from Germany shows that the hiring of additional PES staff was offset by decreased benefit expenditure after a period of about ten months. Hence, hiring additional staff may pay for itself through reducing the ESS caseload faster.

Sanctions are an important component of an effective activation regime

Sanctions are important for an effective activation regime and international evidence suggests that warnings about a possible sanction or the imposition of sanctions can substantially shorten benefit claim durations and increase employment take-up by the sanctioned individuals. Sanctions in Slovenia are among the strictest in the OECD and the application of sanctions appears inconsistent for different types of jobseekers and across regions. This may be driven by the high proof of burden and a cumbersome administrative process coupled with some reluctance by caseworkers to impose harsh sanctions. Slovenia should facilitate the administrative process and consider introducing lower-level sanctions in the form of a benefit reduction or suspension for a certain period for a first breach of obligation, without immediately excluding jobseekers from the ESS register. Compliance with the obligations should be made a precondition for the resumption of benefits.

ALMPs should be rigorously and systematically evaluated

Existing impact evaluations of ALMPs in Slovenia should be extended to provide a fuller picture of the employment impact of past and current programmes. On the basis of such results, in a second step, a cost-benefit analysis should also be conducted, which considers all benefits and costs incurred by participants and by the government. Programmes should then only be continued if they have a positive impact for both jobseekers and the society as a whole.

Activation of FSA recipients is not effective with the current institutional structure

Jobseekers claiming FSA are required to deal with two institutions: Claims for the income-replacement benefit have to be made at the CSW, whereas job broking and referrals to active measures are provided by the ESS. With this separation, consistent activation is not possible due to non-formalised and non-standardised activation processes and procedures and because the CSW tend to have a stronger focus on social integration rather than integration into the labour market. Two different options to better activate employable FSA recipients are discussed in this report: i) a full or partial merger of the CSW with the ESS and ii) a more formalised co-operation between the CSW and the ESS. The latter could also be used as a first step towards a merger in the long run.

Notes

1. One fifth may still be considered a low proportion of PES involvement in recently concluded employment matches. This is partly explained by the fact that individuals moving from non-employment into employment, as well as those changing jobs, are included in this market share estimate. Unemployed people seeking new jobs are much more likely to approach the PES as part of their job search than the employed, who usually prefer other routes (e.g. newspapers, asking friends or relatives, trade unions, or applying directly to employers).

2. In very small local offices (with up to three employees) the ESS has no specialised employer advisers and staff in these offices advises jobseekers as well as employers (EC, 2011).

3. The exact figure is 3 318, taken from ESS (2015b). The total number of employers in 2014 was 186 433.

4. In 2010, there were 58 100 vacancies for which employers had requested active mediation services. Around 85 000 jobseekers were contacted by the ESS in relation to these vacancies, of which some then were referred to the employers.

5. Employers asked for ESS active mediation services for 44 400 vacancies in 2014 ESS (2015b) and 44 800 in 2015 (data for 2015 provided by the ESS).

6. 15% of vacancies were mediated for medium-size employers (50 249 employees). For 15% of vacancies no information on the employer size was available. Numbers may not add due to rounding.

7. Collective dismissals in Slovenia cover redundancies within 30 days of i) at least 10 workers at an employer with 20-99 employees; ii) at least 10% of workers at an employer with 100-299 employees; or iii) at least 30 workers at an employer with 300 or more employees.

8. In essence, this is an extension of the current minimum of two hours of job search paid by employers to then eight hours of paid job search (for full-time employees).

9. If an unemployed person claims UI after the 30 day time limit, their benefit entitlement is shortened by the number of days between the 31st day after the termination of employment and the day of filing the application.

10. The notice period is 15 days for employees with up to one year of service with the employer in the event of an ordinary cancellation of the employment contract by the employer for a business reason or reasons of incompetence. After one year of service with the current employer the notice period increases to 30 days and further up to 80 days for employees with long tenure. The notice period is 15 days in the event of a cancellation through the employer for reasons of misconduct (Employment Relationships Act (ZDR-1), 2013, Article 94 (Minimum notice period), http://www.mddsz.gov.si/en/legislation/).

11. Comparing stock and flow ESS jobseeker figures by benefit claimed shows movements between the different recipient categories over the course of an unemployment spell. Inflow numbers for FSA recipients appear low. This is as many FSA recipients register with the ESS before receiving FSA. Also the ZPIZ statistics show that around 10% of the partial disability benefit stock was on no or on another benefit before claiming disability benefit. UI claimants on the other hand often remain unemployed beyond the

expiry of their UI entitlement and subsequently claim FSA or remain as jobseekers without benefits.

12. Most, but not all, CSW insist on the ESS registration before processing a claim for FSA.

13. Source: ESS monthly information; January 2014; http://www.ess.gov.si/_files/5517/MI0114.pdf.

14. According to the International Labour Organisation (ILO) definition of unemployment the "unemployed" comprise all persons above a specified age who during the reference period were without work (i.e. were not in paid employment or self-employment); currently available for work (i.e. were available for paid employment or self-employment during the reference period); and seeking work (i.e. had taken specific steps in a specified reference period to seek paid employment or self-employment). The labour force surveys implemented in most OECD countries use a recent past week (i.e. a fixed week each month or the week preceding the survey week) as the reference period for assessment of "without work" status. The reference period for assessment of "currently available" status in EU countries is a two-week (forward looking) period after the reference week. The reference period for "seeking work" status is the previous four weeks (including the survey reference week). Ongoing registration at an employment service without specific actions, or reading newspaper advertisements, etc. without answering them, is not usually treated as active job search.

15. It is assumed that all countries require suitable jobs to have wages and working conditions consistent with legal requirements (including minimum wages and administrative extensions of collective agreements), that certain types of work (e.g. prostitution) are not considered suitable work and that the unemployed should not be forced to join or leave a trade union or other organisation in order to take up suitable work.

16. Article 42 of the Social Assistance Act (ZSVarPre, 2010) stipulates that FSA recipients who received benefits for at least nine months in the past 12 months must accept any job offered to them or referred to them by the ESS. Failure to accept a job offer would result in the exclusion from the ESS register on the basis of Article 129 of the Labour Market Regulation Act (ZUTD, 2010). Article 129, however, stipulates that the exclusion from the register results only from a refusal of appropriate or suitable employment. Thus, the implementation of Article 42 of ZSVarPre could be legally challenged.

17. Client-to-staff ratios are calculated as stock of registered jobseekers at the end of the year (110 020 in 2010, 124 020 in 2013, and 119 460 in 2014) divided by the number of ESS front-line staff. Figures for front-line staff are not published, but based on interviews with the ESS management, and estimated to be around one-third of total staff. The ESS total staff was 1 016 in 2010, 903 in 2013, and 924 in 2014.

18. Jobseekers may, however, claim FSA. Individuals entitled to ZPIZ disability benefits and who terminate the employment relationship by own will or through own fault have their benefit rate reduced by 30%.

19. Sanction rates a calculated as the number of outflows of the ESS register due to a breach of obligation over the course of a year, divided by the live claims in a given year. Live claims are calculated by adding the claimant stock at the beginning of the year and total new registrations during the year.

20. See OECD (2015) for an overview of studies.

21. Not included is expenditure on PES and administration. If PES and administration is included, the expenditure on all active measures in Slovenia was 0.37% of GDP in 2013, against an OECD average of 0.56% of GDP. The OECD averages are unweighted averages. In 2013, no data was available for France, Greece, Israel, Korea, New Zealand, Poland, Spain, and the United Kingdom.

22. In addition, the Ministry of Education of Slovenia financed around 0.3% of the training programmes (Category 2) budget.

23. Labour Market Regulation Act, Article 35 and 36, http://www.mddsz.gov.si/en/legislation/.

24. The likelihood of being referred is calculated as the total number of entrants over the course of 2012, divided by the sum of the caseload at the beginning of the year and the total inflows over the course of the year.

25. Close to average outcomes for the employ.me scheme and public works mainly reflect a weighting-effect as the majority of jobseekers referred to these programmes are long-term unemployed.

26. Kavkler et al. (2012) rely exclusively on the ESS unemployment registry data and, hence, do not account for individuals who opt out of the unemployment registry before becoming employed.

27. The subsidy amounted to EUR 7 500 for employing an individual for at least 18 months following the successful completion of the programme.

28. The main benefit of a programme is its impact on participants' future earnings and the main cost is government expenditure on programme implementation and administration. In the calculation of participants' earnings, employer pension and social insurance contributions are added to gross earnings and the direct costs of working, such as child care and commuting costs borne by the employee are subtracted. Income taxes, payroll taxes, indirect taxes, reduced benefit payments, incentive payments or reimbursements of work expenses are all treated as transfers, with a positive or negative financial benefit to the participant being matched by a positive or negative financial cost for government finances so that there is no impact on reported net benefits for society as a whole. It should, however, be highlighted, that many potential costs and benefits are typically not taken into account because they are hard to quantify or cannot simply be inferred from market prices (OECD, 2015a). Fujiwara (2010) discusses the incorporation of several types of "wider social impacts", including work costs and leisure time, externalities and multiplier effects, and health and crime impacts in the cost-benefit analysis process..

29. Gross employment rates are the sum of deadweight (which also occur in absence of a programme) and additional (which can be attributed to the programme) employment.

30. Cream-skimming is a problem associated with employment and training programmes, where providers have some influence over choosing participants who use their services. They might then "cream-skim" participants who are likely to be easier to help. The risk of the current ESS targets is that ESS staff may implicitly or explicitly collude with providers through referring easy-to-help jobseekers.

31. Source: MDDSZ (2015), "Reorganizacija CSD: Predstavitev izhodišč" (Reorganisation of the CSW: The starting point, PowerPoint presentation by the MDDSZ).

References

Borland, J. and Y.P. Tseng (2007), "Does a Minimum Job Search Requirement Reduce Time on Unemployment Payments? Evidence from the Jobseeker Diary in Australia", *Industrial and Labor Relations Review*, Vol. 60, No. 3, April.

Dares-Pôle emploi (2013), "L'accompagnement renforcé des demandeurs d'emploi : Évaluation du recours aux opérateurs privés par Pôle emploi de 2009 à 2011", *Synthèse.Éval'*, No. 03, January.

Duell, N. et al. (2010), "Activation Policies in Switzerland", *OECD Social, Employment and Migration Working Papers*, No. 112, OECD Publishing, Paris, http://dx.doi.org/10.1787/5km4hd7r28f6-en.

Duell, N., D. Grubb and S. Singh (2009), "Activation Policies in Finland", *OECD Social, Employment and Migration Working Papers*, No. 98, OECD Publishing, Paris, http://dx.doi.org/10.1787/220568650308.

DWP – Department for Work and Pensions (2016a), "Dashboard Jobseeker's Allowance: new claims", https://www.gov.uk/performance/jobseekers-allowance-new-claims (accessed on 19.04.2016).

DWP (2016b), "Jobseeker's Allowance and Employment and Support Allowance sanctions: decisions made to December 2015", https://www.gov.uk/government/collections/jobseekers-allowance-sanctions.

EC – European Commission (2014a), "PES recruitment services for employers", by M. Dietz, H. Bähr, and C. Osiander, Brussels, http://ec.europa.eu/social/BlobServlet?docId=11569&langId=en.

EC (2014b), "Blended service delivery for jobseekers, Peer Review Host Country Paper", Employment Service of Slovenia Central Office, Brussels, http://ec.europa.eu/social/main.jsp?langId=en&catId=22.

EC (2014c), "Blended Service Delivery for Jobseekers, Peer Review Host Country Paper", by U.W.V. Werkbedrijf, Brussels, http://ec.europa.eu/social/main.jsp?langId=en&catId=22.

EC (2013), "Peer Review on Performance Management in Public Employment Services, Peer PES Paper", Employment Service of Slovenia, Brussels, http://ec.europa.eu/social/main.jsp?langId=en&catId=22.

EC (2012a), "Peer PES paper – The Netherlands", Peer Review 'PES and older workers'", U.W.V. WERKbedrijf, Brussels, http://ec.europa.eu/social/main.jsp?langId=en&catId=22.

EC (2012b), "PES and older workers: comparative paper", by Matthias Knuth, Brussels, http://ec.europa.eu/social/main.jsp?langId=en&catId=22.

EC (2011), "Effective Services for Employers, Slovenia Peer Country Paper", Employment Service of Slovenia, Brussels, http://ec.europa.eu/social/main.jsp?langId=en&catId=22.

ESS – Employment Service of Slovenia (2016), "Poslovni načrt za leto 2016" [Business Plan for 2016], Ljubljana, http://www.ess.gov.si/trg_dela/publicistika/letna_porocila.

ESS (2015a), "Letno poslovno poročilo 2014" [Annual Business Report 2014], Ljubljana, http://www.ess.gov.si/trg_dela/publicistika/letna_porocila.

ESS (2015b), "Letno Poročilo 2014" [Annual Report 2014], Ljubljana, http://www.ess.gov.si/trg_dela/publicistika/letna_porocila.

Fujiwara, D. (2010), "The Department for Work and Pensions social cost-benefit analysis framework: Methodologies for estimating and incorporating the wider social and economic impacts of work in cost-benefit analysis of employment programmes", *DWP Working Paper*, No. 86.

Hainmueller, J. et al. (2011), "Do Lower Caseloads Improve the Effectiveness of Active Labor Market Policies? New Evidence from German Employment Offices", *LASER Discussion Papers*, No. 52, University of Erlangen-Nuremberg, Germany, www.iab.de/897/section.aspx/Publikation/k110919j03.

Hofmann, B. et al. (2012), "Wirkung und Wirkungsmechanismen zusätzlicher Vermittlungskräfte auf die Arbeitslosigkeitsdauer – Analysen auf Basis eines Modellprojektes" [The Effect of Additional Job Placement Officers on Unemployment Duration – Lessons from a Pilot Project], *Zeitschrift für Evaluation*, Vol. 11, No. 1, pp. 7-38.

IRSSV – Social Protection Institute of the Republic of Slovenia (2015), "Podlage za pripravo in zagon programov socialne aktivacije" [Basis for the preparation and launch of social activation], Ljubljana, www.irssv.si/upload2/Porocilo%20socialna%20aktivacija_koncno.pdf.

Kavkler, A., Volčjak, R., & Mencinger, J. (2012), "Rezultati ciljnega raziskovalnega projekta št. V5 1045 'Vrednotenje največjih programov aktivne politike zaposlovanja, vključno z ukrepi proti gospodarski in finančni krizi'"[Results of the Targeted Research Project No. V5-1045 'Evaluation of the largest ALMP programs, including Measures Undertaken in Response to the Economic and Financial crisis], EIPF, Ekonomski inštitut, 2012.

Klepinger, D., T. Johnson and J. Joesch (2002), "Effects of Unemployment Insurance Work-Search Requirements: The Maryland Experiment", *Industrial and Labor Relations Review*, No. 56, pp. 3-22.

Langenbucher, K. (2015), "How demanding are eligibility criteria for unemployment benefits, quantitative indicators for OECD and EU countries", *OECD Social, Employment and Migration Working Papers*, No. 166, OECD Publishing, Paris, http://dx.doi.org/10.1787/5jrxtk1zw8f2-en.

McVicar, D. (2008), "Job Search Monitoring Intensity, Unemployment Exit and Job Entry: Quasi-Experimental Evidence from the UK", *Labour Economics*, Vol. 15, No. 6, pp. 1451-1468.

MDDSŽ – Ministry of Labour, Family, Social Affairs and Equal Opportunities (2015), "Reorganizacija CSD: Predstavitev izhodišč" [Reorganisation of the CSW: The starting point, PowerPoint presentation by the MDDSZ].

OECD (2016), *Back to Work: Finland – Improving the Re-employment Prospects of Displaced Workers*, OECD Publishing, Paris, forthcoming.

OECD (2015a), "Activation policies for more inclusive labour markets", in *OECD Employment Outlook 2015*, OECD Publishing, Paris, http://dx.doi.org/10.1787/empl_outlook-2015-7-en.

OECD (2015b), *Back to Work: Canada – Improving the Re-employment Prospects of Displaced Workers*, OECD Publishing, Paris, http://dx.doi.org/10.1787/9789264233454-en.

OECD (2015c), *Back to Work: Sweden – Improving the Re-employment Prospects of Displaced Workers*, OECD Publishing, Paris, http://dx.doi.org/10.1787/9789264246812-en.

OECD (2015d), *Ageing and Employment Policies: Denmark 2015: Working Better with Age*, OECD Publishing, Paris, http://dx.doi.org/10.1787/9789264235335-en.

OECD (2014a), *Connecting People with Jobs: Activation Policies in the United Kingdom*, OECD Publishing, Paris, http://dx.doi.org/10.1787/9789264217188-en.

OECD (2014b), *Ageing and Employment Policies: Netherlands 2014: Working Better with Age*, OECD Publishing, Paris, http://dx.doi.org/10.1787/9789264208155-en.

OECD (2013), "Activating jobseekers: Lessons from seven OECD countries", in *OECD Employment Outlook 2013*, OECD Publishing, Paris, http://dx.doi.org/10.1787/empl_outlook-2013-7-en.

OECD (2012), *Activating Jobseekers: How Australia Does It*, OECD Publishing, Paris, http://dx.doi.org/10.1787/9789264185920-en.

Stojak, V. (2014), "Needs of small and medium sized enterprises", PES2PES Dialogue Conference, Brussels, 11 March, http://ec.europa.eu/social/BlobServlet?docId=11557&langId=en.

Zakrajšek, G. and S. Meke (2011), "Efficient Co-operation of Public Employment Services with Employers", International seminar No. 1 in the project on Learning from Experience of PES Practitioners in EU, www.proemployment.eu/index.php?art=254.

ZDR-1 – Employment Relationships Act (2013, unofficial translation), http://www.mddsz.gov.si/en/legislation/.

ZSVarPre – Social Assistance Act (2010), www.uradni-list.si/1/content?id=99232.

ZUTD – Labour Market Regulation Act (2010, unofficial translation), www.mddsz.gov.si/en/legislation/.

Database references

European Commission (2015), Labour Market Policy (http://ec.europa.eu/eurostat/web/labourmarket/labour-market-policy/database).

OECD Employment Database, www.oecd.org/employment/database.

ORGANISATION FOR ECONOMIC CO-OPERATION AND DEVELOPMENT

The OECD is a unique forum where governments work together to address the economic, social and environmental challenges of globalisation. The OECD is also at the forefront of efforts to understand and to help governments respond to new developments and concerns, such as corporate governance, the information economy and the challenges of an ageing population. The Organisation provides a setting where governments can compare policy experiences, seek answers to common problems, identify good practice and work to co-ordinate domestic and international policies.

The OECD member countries are: Australia, Austria, Belgium, Canada, Chile, the Czech Republic, Denmark, Estonia, Finland, France, Germany, Greece, Hungary, Iceland, Ireland, Israel, Italy, Japan, Korea, Latvia, Luxembourg, Mexico, the Netherlands, New Zealand, Norway, Poland, Portugal, the Slovak Republic, Slovenia, Spain, Sweden, Switzerland, Turkey, the United Kingdom and the United States. The European Union takes part in the work of the OECD.

OECD Publishing disseminates widely the results of the Organisation's statistics gathering and research on economic, social and environmental issues, as well as the conventions, guidelines and standards agreed by its members.

OECD PUBLISHING, 2, rue André-Pascal, 75775 PARIS CEDEX 16
(81 2016 20 1 P) ISBN 978-92-64-26533-2 – 2016

www.ingramcontent.com/pod-product-compliance
Lightning Source LLC
Chambersburg PA
CBHW061216240926
51846CB00006B/1242
* 9 7 8 9 2 6 4 2 6 5 3 3 2 *